Satires Against Man

Satires Against Man

The Poems of Rochester

DUSTIN H. GRIFFIN

University of California Press
Berkeley • Los Angeles • London

University of California Press
Berkeley and Los Angeles, California

University of California Press, Ltd.
London, England

ISBN: 0-520-02394-3
Library of Congress Catalog Card Number: 72-95304

Printed in the United States of America
Designed by Jean Peters

For Gale

❧Contents

Preface	ix
Abbreviations	xi
I. *The Mind of a Skeptic*	1
Introduction	1
The Mind of a Skeptic	6
II. *The Uses of Libertinism*	21
The Early Satires: "St. James's Park"	25
The Early Satires: "Timon"	35
The Early Satires: "Tunbridge Wells"	42
"The Maimed Debauchee" (c. 1675) and "To the Postboy" (?1676)	47
The "Heroical Epistle" (c. 1675–1676)	56
The "Epistolary Essay" (c. 1679)	67
III. *The Pains of Sex*	79
Obscenity	81
"The Imperfect Enjoyment"	91
The Songs	100

The Art of Impotence   114

"Artemisia to Chloe"   129

IV. *The Background to Rochester's "Satyr"*   156

   Traditions of Self-Disparagement   158

   The Immediate Background   162

   Le Libertinage   173

   Orthodoxy and Optimism   182

V. *A Reading of the "Satyr Against Mankind"*   197

   The Theme of Paradox   197

   The Flowing Tide   206

   Statement and Qualification   224

   Epilogue   239

   Real and Ideal   243

VI. *Rochester and the Age*   246

   "An Allusion to Horace"   246

   Rochester and Pope   257

   "Upon Nothing"   266

   Rochester and Swift   280

   Rochester and Restoration Drama   287

   Rochester and Dryden   300

   Appendix: Additions to Vieth's "Checklist of Rochester Studies, 1925–1967"   307

   Index   311

•Preface

I have sought in this book to give a full critical account of the poems of Rochester. Such an account, in my view, required careful attention to the poems and to their typical satiric techniques, as well as a sense of the contexts in which we may best understand Rochester's work. Those contexts include comparisons with the satiric masters of the age, Rochester's intellectual heritage, and his own life as a rake. Although I am interested throughout in the qualities of Rochester's mind and in possible relationships between his art and his life, the book is not conceived as a biographical study. No new biographical information is presented; I do, however, reinterpret the data that can be found in the biographical studies of Prinz and Pinto. Nor do I attempt to deal with matters of text or canon, but rely on David Vieth's recent edition.

This book has roots in my Ph.D. dissertation, "Rochester's Poems: A Critical Study" (1969) supervised at Yale University by Professor Maynard Mack. My first debts are to him, especially for his scrupulous attention to style and to the structure of my argument. I wish to thank for their cooperation the staffs of the Sterling and Beinecke Libraries at Yale University, the Henry W. and Albert A. Berg Collection of the New York Public Library, Astor, Lenox, and Tilden Foundations, and the Doe Library of the University of California, Berkeley. I also thank David Vieth, who kindly allowed me to examine the proofs of his edition of Rochester prior to its publication, and George Lord, who made useful comments on the original version of this book. For their readings of and suggestions on later versions, I am grateful to Charles Frey, John Traugott, Mariann McKibben, Peter Manning, Brendan O Hehir, David Vieth, Gardner Stout, and Howard Erskine-Hill. For help with psychoanalytic matters in Chapter III I thank Frederick Crews. For permission to use a reproduction of the Huysmans portrait of Rochester on the dust jacket I thank the National Portrait Gallery, London. I thank the Yale University Press for permission to quote from *The Complete Poems of John Wilmot, Earl of Rochester,* edited by David M. Vieth. Dorset's "I rise at eleven" is reprinted by permission of Princeton University Press from *Rochester's "Poems on Several Occasions,"* edited by James Thorpe.

Finally, I am grateful to my wife Gale, to whom this book is dedicated, for her stern yet gentle editorial eye.

Abbreviations

ARP   Vieth, David M. *Attribution in Restora-*
                tion Poetry (New Haven, 1963).
Burnet   Burnet, Gilbert. *Some Passages of the*
                Life and Death of the Right Honorable
                John Earl of Rochester ([first published
                1680] London, 1787)
Burtt   Burtt, Edwin. *The English Philosophers*
                from Bacon to Mill (New York, 1939).
Complete Poems Vieth, David M., ed., *The Complete*
                Poems of John Wilmot, Earl of Roch-
                ester (New Haven, 1968).
Court Wits   Wilson, J. H. *The Court Wits of the*
                Restoration (Princeton, 1948).
ELH   *ELH: A Journal of English Literary*
                History
Enthusiast in Wit Pinto, Vivian de Sola. *Enthusiast in*
                Wit: A Portrait of John Wilmot, Earl
                of Rochester, 1647–1680 (London, 1962).
Essayes   Montaigne, *Essayes*, tr. John Florio

	(Everyman's Library, London, 1910). 3 vols.
Gyldenstolpe MS	Danielsson, Bror, and Vieth, David M., eds. *The Gyldenstolpe Manuscript Miscellany of Poems by John Wilmot, Earl of Rochester, and Other Restoration Authors* (Stockholm, 1967).
Hayward	Hayward, John, ed. *The Collected Works of John Wilmot, Earl of Rochester* (London, 1926).
Johnson, *Lives*	Johnson, Samuel. *Lives of the Poets* (Everyman's Library, London, 1925). 2 vols.
Letters	Wilson, J. H., ed., *The Rochester-Savile Letters* (Columbus, 1941).
N & Q	*Notes and Queries*
PMLA	*Publications of the Modern Language Association of America*
POAS, 1	*Poems on Affairs of State, 1660–1678*, ed. George Lord (New Haven, 1963).
Poems	Pinto, Vivian de Sola, ed., *Poems by John Wilmot, Earl of Rochester* (Muses' Library, London, 1953, rev. 1964).
PQ	*Philological Quarterly*
Prinz	Prinz, Johannes. *John Wilmot, Earl of Rochester: His Life and Writings* (Leipzig, 1927).
Quaintance	Quaintance, Richard E. "Passion and Reason in Restoration Love Poetry." Unpublished Ph.D. dissertation (Yale, 1962).
RES	*Review of English Studies*
SP	*Studies in Philology*
Spingarn	Spingarn, J. E., ed., *Critical Essays of the Seventeenth Century* (Oxford, 1908–1909). 3 vols.

Thorpe   Thorpe, James, ed., *Rochester's "Poems
                on Several Occasions"* (Princeton, 1950).
Underwood   Underwood, Dale. *Etherege and the
                Seventeenth Century Comedy of Man-
                ners* (New Haven, 1957).

1 The Mind of a Skeptic

Introduction

John Wilmot, the 2nd Earl of Rochester, may justly be considered an excellent poet of the second rank. His works are few (about seventy-five poems, an adaptation of a tragedy, and a scene from an unfinished play), limited in scope, and far less rich in depth and technical virtuosity than those of Dryden or Pope, or even of Marvell. On the other hand, Rochester has always had admirers, from Marvell, who said that he was the "best English satyrist and had the right veine," to Voltaire, who spoke of him as a "Man of Genius" and a "great Poet" of a uniquely "shining imagination," to Tennyson, who used to declaim with "almost terrible force" an admired passage from the "Satyr Against Mankind." [1] Rochester is well known to many twentieth-century readers,

1. John Aubrey, *Brief Lives*, ed. Andrew Clark (Oxford, 1898), 2:304; *Letters Concerning the English Nation*, tr. Lockman, (London, 1733), Letter 21, "On the Earl of Rochester and Mr. Waller," p. 197; Hallam Tennyson, *Alfred Lord Tennyson: A Memoir* (London, 1898), 2:201. All three comments are conviently collected, along with most of the critical notes both long and short for the period 1672–1900, in *Rochester: The Critical Heritage*, ed. D. Farley-Hills (London, 1971).

if only for his "Satyr." Yet he remains an obscure and mis-understood figure on several grounds.

To begin with, our knowledge of his life and thought is limited. The genuine life records are few, though there are enough to plot the major movements of his thirty-three years. He led a turbulent life, quickly passing into the realm of legend, remembered as either the debauched, atheistical aristocrat, or the repentant sinner saved only by a deathbed conversion. Even in his own lifetime, Rochester was a controversial public figure. Of the many references to him by contemporaries which have survived, few are objective: the excesses of friends and favorites, in funeral elegies and dedications, are matched by those of enemies and rivals in satires, letters, or memoirs.

Rochester's numerous twentieth-century biographers, troubled by these and other problems, have not yet produced a biography both readable and scholarly.[2] Too often they have tried to fill out the sketchy portrait of the man by unsupported psychological speculation, accompanied by uncritical identification of Rochester with the speaker of the poems. Some of Rochester's critics have gone on to give unified explanations of the poems according to their understanding of the man, and, conversely, have explained the man from the poems. Disagreement and confusion have resulted.

A second reason for Rochester's present obscurity is the difficulty which literary historians have had in placing Rochester in that strange transitional period between 1640 and 1680 — between the dominance of Jonson and Donne and the dominance of Dryden. In the earlier part of the century, the literary world had been fairly homogeneous; most writers knew each other; they were grouped in London around the Court, the Church, the Inns of Court, and the theaters. But after 1640 both the country and its writers

2. For bibliographies of Rochester biographies, see Prinz, and *Complete Poems.*

seem to fracture and fly apart. Among those active in the sixties and seventies were the older Royalists — Cowley, Cleveland, Waller, Denham, Clarendon, and Davenant. The Cambridge Platonists — Whichcote, More, and Cudworth — were making their literary presence felt perhaps more strongly than earlier university theologians, as were Latitudinarians like Tillotson. Milton was in grand isolation composing his major poems, Bunyan in Bedford jail writing *Grace Abounding* (1666) and *The Pilgrim's Progress* (1678), and Traherne writing quietly in London and Kent. Religious and political satirists — Butler, Marvell, and Oldham — were writing for or against the Puritans, the Jesuits, and the commercial middle classes. Associated with the City of London and at the same time seeking the favor of the Court were professional dramatists, including Dryden and Settle, Crowne, Shadwell, Otway, and Lee. Grouped around the Court were some young aristocratic amateurs, both dramatists and poets — Buckingham, Dorset, Etherege, Sedley, Wycherley, and Rochester, as well as Rochester's close friend, Henry Savile, and his worst literary enemies, Sir Carr Scroope and John Sheffield, Earl of Mulgrave. Though all literary periods are miscellaneous, 1660 to 1680 seems more so than most; it lacks any dominant figure (apart from Milton, who was out of tune with the age, and Dryden, who was not yet the absolutely commanding figure that he became in the eighties) and has no easily discernible connections with earlier periods. In the case of Rochester, the connections forward are clearer, to Pope and Swift, for example; backward, they are more difficult to see. It was claimed by Rochester's contemporaries and by eighteenth-century critics that he admired Cowley and Waller,[3] but to most twentieth-century readers this is not obvious from his works.

Finally, and perhaps most important, Rochester remains obscured because of the inaccessibility of his works and the

3. Burnet, p. 22; Johnson, *Lives*, 1:128. See also *Critical Works of John Dennis*, ed. E. N. Hooker (Baltimore, 1943), 2:248.

uncertainty of his canon and text. Until recently, there has not even been a good critical edition of his works. Thus, he has been comparatively unavailable to the scholar, and has failed to reach the nonspecialist reader. In Vivian de Sola Pinto's Muses' Library edition, available for the last twenty years, his work is inadequately and incompletely presented.[4] In the anthologies, it is commonly confined to the "Satyr" (his best poem) and a few songs.[5] The rest of his songs, his other satires, his translations from Ovid, Seneca, Lucretius, and Horace, and his adaptation of Fletcher's *Valentinian* have gone largely unread. Thus, his few well-known poems stand out in lurid foreshortening, detached from literary, social, and intellectual backgrounds, leaving the rest of his writings in darkness.

This situation has only recently been improved by David Vieth's critical edition of the complete poems.[6] Previously, eight editions of the poems had appeared in this century, none critical, all of them containing poems that Vieth is convinced are not by Rochester.[7] Now that we can be more certain about what Rochester actually wrote, it is possible to set about interpreting and evaluating his achievement as a whole, unhampered by such misconceptions as that he was responsible for all the indecent verse attributed to him by editors and printers shortly after his death, some of which is included in collections of his works published in this century. For it is largely the poems of crude obscenity not by Rochester, read in old editions or heard about, which foster the impression, still current, that Rochester was only a debauched sensualist and sensationalist.

Although such a view of Rochester is no longer seriously

4. *Poems by John Wilmot, Earl of Rochester* (London, 1953, rev. 1964).

5. *The Oxford Book of English Verse* includes only four songs. *The Oxford Book of Seventeenth Century Verse* prints five songs (one not Rochester's) and three satires.

6. *The Complete Poems of John Wilmot, Earl of Rochester* (New Haven, 1968).

7. For a bibliography, see Vieth, *Complete Poems*, pp. lii–liv.

argued, other views, equally inadequate in their exaggeration or simplification, are still offered. Rochester has recently been described as a "spiritual explorer," yearning for transcendence of mere sense,[8] a destructive and unintelligent nihilist,[9] and a traditional "Augustan," sharing a complex of Christian-classical values with Dryden and Pope.[10] My own position is that little is gained by affirming or denying that Rochester is an "Augustan" or an "explorer," terms that have been applied with little critical precision and about which there has been (and, I suspect, can be) little agreement. My view is that Rochester, very much a product of the Restoration, socially, intellectually, literarily, is best understood in such contexts. By no means a mindless sensationalist, a merely sadistic rake, nor a would-be Christian pilgrim lost in doubt's boundless sea, he is a perplexed rather than a dogmatic doubter, delighting in the parody of heroic convention and tradition (as found in Cowley and Waller, for example), attracted to heterodox and paradoxical notions, yet a poet and a man in search of certainties — in love, court life, friendship — which continually elude him. He is shifting, uncertain, undisciplined, able to combine within a single poem widely differing views and tones. His poems are sometimes anxious, sometimes cool and controlled, sometimes "talky," sometimes lyrical, and at the same time savage and gay. They are more memorable and valuable for their intensity and "energy"[11] (a quality con-

8. Pinto, *Enthusiast in Wit*; see also Kenneth Murdock, "A Very Profane Wit," in *The Sun at Noon* (New York, 1939); Charles Williams, *Rochester* (London, 1935). Howard Erskine-Hill defends a modified version of Pinto's view in "Rochester: Augustan or Explorer?", *Renaissance and Modern Essays presented to V. de S. Pinto in Celebration of his Seventieth Birthday*, ed. G. R. Hibbard (London, 1966), pp. 51–64.

9. Underwood, pp. 10–40.

10. Vieth, *ARP*, ch. 4. Paul C. Davies follows Vieth, against Erskine-Hill, in claiming that Rochester defends "traditional standards," "Rochester: Augustan and Explorer," *Durham University Journal*, 30 (1969), 59–64.

11. Vieth's modernization of punctuation smoothes over and to some degree obscures Rochester's roughness and "energy."

temporaries admired), for their vigorous flow, than for their thought or formal perfection. To appreciate these qualities more fully, however, we may first look briefly at the man and his mind.

The Mind of a Skeptic

Biographical details concerning Rochester's activities as soldier, courtier, patron of the drama, and rake are easily available [12] and need not be reviewed here. It is worthwhile, however, to consider one famous incident which sheds some light on Rochester's thinking — the conversations with Gilbert Burnet during the winter of 1679 to 1680, some few months before Rochester's death. Initiated at Rochester's request, these talks between a profligate skeptic and the future Bishop of Salisbury dealt with the competing claims of a morality based on reason and one based on Christian faith.[13]

Rochester's view on religion might be only peripheral to a discussion of his poetry if it were not that at least two of the constant motifs of his work can be illustrated from his conversations with Burnet. One is a rational humanist morality consisting of plain, common-sense rules of conduct: "Reason that distinguishes by sense, / And gives us rules of good and ill from thence" ("Satyr Against Mankind," ll. 100–101). The other is a personal inability to believe in mysteries, coupled with the recognition that those who are able to believe are happy and have found rest and quiet — a divided awareness, in other words, of a world of actuality and of an ideal (not necessarily a transcendent world) which remains, for him, remote and unrealizable.

The Rochester revealed in the conversations, like the

12. In *Enthusiast in Wit* and *Complete Poems*.
13. The conversations were reproduced from memory by Burnet and published in the fall of 1680 as *Some Passages in the Life and Death of John, Earl of Rochester*. I have modernized spelling.

Rochester who wrote the poems, is clearly a moralist, although, as we shall see, he expresses doubts that morals can succeed in governing his own conduct or that of mankind at large. His morals are based on pleasure and pain, and on following "nature" (gratifying the desires of the self) rather than on the laws and restraints of society or religion:

For morality he confessed he saw the necessity of it, both for the government of the world, and for the preservation of health, life, and friendship . . . he told me the two maxims of his morality then were, that he should do nothing to the hurt of any other, or that might prejudice his own health; and he thought that all pleasure, when it did not interfere with these, was to be indulged as the gratification of our natural appetites. It seemed unreasonable to imagine these were put into a man only to be restrained or curbed to such a narrowness: this he applied to the free use of wine and women. [35, 37] [14]

Rochester was aware that he did not follow his own maxim, and particularly that he did not care for his own health. [15] He felt shame, and worried about his reputation. In each case, however, he believed he had transgressed against a human rather than divine order:

He was very much ashamed of his former practices, rather because he had made himself a beast, and had brought pain and sickness on his body, and had suffered much in his reputation, than from any deep sense of a Supreme Being or another state. . . . He confessed he had no remorse for his past action as offences against God, but only as injuries to himself and to mankind [pp. 35–36].

14. In the "Satyr Against Mankind" Rochester apparently took a darker view of "natural appetites." See below, p. 237.

15. Although Burnet said of Rochester's "morality," "though he talked of it as a fine thing, yet this was only because he thought it a decent mode of speaking" (p. 29), Rochester meant, I think, not that he disbelieved his own maxims, but that he failed to follow them. He freely admits to having hurt others and himself (p. 30).

Rochester derived his morality, in Burnet's words, from "philosophy" rather than religion. Rochester, he says, resolved to reform his life, which "he thought he should effect by the study of philosophy" (p. 36). Burnet repeatedly sought to show him "the defects of philosophy for reforming the world" (p. 36) and the necessity of Christianity, but Rochester would have nothing to do with it: "This, he said, sounded to him like enthusiasm, or canting: he had no notion of it, and so could not understand it. He comprehended the dictates of reason and philosophy; in which, as the mind became much conversant, there would soon follow, as he believed, a greater easiness in obeying its precepts" (p. 40). It is unlikely that Rochester had merely imbibed a few catch phrases from a popular "philosophy" of his day, Hobbesian materialism or Epicureanism, along with a glib distrust of Puritan "cant" and "enthusiasm." Though its range was narrow, his mind, as his writings clearly show, was "active and inquisitive."[16] Probably Burnet would not have spent so many sessions with a dilettante. Furthermore, Rochester did not yield to Burnet's elegant and forceful arguments. He held his ground, returning often to the few fixed points of his belief. What he asked of morality was a simple guide to conduct. When Burnet described the "great disorder in our natures, which is not easily rectified," Rochester asked why this could not be "rectified by some plain rules given" (p. 59), rather than dark mysteries and speculations. As he wrote somewhat more savagely in the "Satyr":

> Thoughts are given for action's government;
> Where action ceases, thought's impertinent:
> Our sphere of action is life's happiness,
> And he who thinks beyond, thinks like an ass.
>
> [ll. 94–97]

Morality, for Rochester, was the product of rational thought, not revelation.

16. Johnson, *Lives*, 1:128.

He told Burnet, however, that he believed in a Supreme Being, and in the immortality of the soul. As he reportedly informed his first tutor, who, upon meeting him years later, called him an atheist, "Mr. Giffard, I have been guilty of extravagances, but I will assure you that I am no atheist." [17] Indeed, he told Burnet "he had never known an entire atheist, who fully believed there was no God" (p. 29). Rochester had an idea of God as a creator: "he could not think the world was made by chance, and the regular course of nature seemed to demonstrate the eternal power of its Author" (p. 43). But he had no sense of a good or just Supreme Being: "When he explained his notion of this Being, it amounted no more than a vast power" (p. 39).[18] Burnet was sufficiently struck with this conception (whether the phrase was Rochester's or his own) to repeat it: "he looked on it as a vast power that wrought everything by the necessity of its nature" (p. 43). This sense of a boundless, undifferentiated being, mass, or power recurs in the poems as well, when Rochester tries to envision, to comprehend, doubt, evil, nothing, or death, those metaphysical realities "beyond material sense." [19]

Of the other tenets of orthodox Christianity, Rochester was doubtful. He did not believe in the efficacy of prayer, or in a "Special providence in human affairs" (p. 44). Although he did not believe that the soul dissolved at death, "he doubted much of rewards or punishments" (p. 44).

17. Reported by Giffard to Thomas Hearne, *Remarks and Collections of Thomas Hearne*, ed. P. Bliss (Oxford, 1869), 1:241–243.

18. Rochester may have derived this notion in God at least in part from Montaigne's "Apologie of Raymond Sebond," where God is described as "an incomprehensible power, chiefe beginning and preserver of all things." *Essayes*, 2:216. Compare, too, Rochester's translation from *De Rerum Natura*, 1:44–49, on the remote and uninterested Lucretian gods.

19. "Doubt's boundless sea" ("Satyr Against Mankind", l. 19), "Evil . . . has Co-eternity" (*Valentinian*, 4:3; Hayward, p. 215), "the great united what . . . thy boundless self" ("Upon Nothing," ll. 6, 9), "Dead, we become the lumber of the world, / And to that mass of matter shall be swept" (tr. Seneca, ll. 8–9).

Apparently he had a vague sense of a future state: "He thought it more likely that the soul began anew, and that Her sense of what she had done in this body lying in the figures that are made in the brain, as soon as she dislodged all these perished, and that the soul went into some other state, to begin a new course" (p. 50). With these thoughts, however, we should compare Rochester's powerful translation of Seneca, apparently written during the same months he was speaking to Burnet:

> After Death nothing is, and nothing Death;
> The utmost limits of a gasp of breath.
>
> . . . .
>
> Dead, we become the lumber of the world,
> And to that mass of matter shall be swept,
> Where things destroyed with things unborn are kept;
> Devouring Time swallows us whole,
> Impartial Death confounds body and soul.

The poem also scorns all hope of heaven and fear of hell, in a way inconsistent with what Rochester told Burnet, and probably reflects a turbulent, undecided mind.

Although Burnet urged the reasonableness as well as the joy and truth of Christianity, Rochester remained largely unconvinced. Burnet's talk of "inward strength" seemed to be "the effect of fancy" (p. 43) — a product of the delusive imagination. Rochester similarly stated that "to love God seemed to him a presumptuous thing, and the heat of fanciful men" (p. 44); "all this," he said elsewhere, "might be fancy" (p. 58). Clearly one of his strong prejudices (shared by many in his day) was that religious enthusiasm and inspiration had material causes: "This, he said, must be the effect of a heat in nature" (p. 41). The writers of the scriptures must have had "heats and honesty, and so wrote" (p. 53). Skepticism about such "heats," or vapors — Rochester's version of the mechanical operation of the spirit — is one of the many similarities between him and two other satirists of the Puritans, Butler and Swift.

For himself, Rochester insisted on applying the measure of right reason: "he excepted to the belief of mysteries in the Christian religion, which he thought no man could [assent to], since it is not in a man's power to believe that which he cannot comprehend, and of which he can have no notion" (pp. 66–67). Unable to "believe things against my reason" (p. 67), he said "if a man says he cannot believe, what help is there? for he was not master of his own belief" (p. 55).

On the other hand Rochester recognized clearly that those who are able to believe are happy. Burnet was apparently impressed by this argument, for he returns to it again and again:

He said that he understood nothing of it, but acknowledged that he thought they were happy whose fancies were under the power of such impressions, since they had some what on which their thoughts rested and centered. [p. 43]

He often confessed, that, whether the business of religion was true or not, he thought those who had the persuasions of it, and lived so that they had quiet in their consciences, and believed God governed the world, and acquiesced in his providence, and had the hope of an endless blessedness in another state, the happiest men in the world; and said, he would give all that he was master of, to be under those persuasions, and to have the supports and joys that must needs flow from them. [p. 51] [20]

He did acknowledge, the whole system of religion, if believed, was a greater foundation of quiet than any other thing whatsoever. [p. 52].

He said, that they were happy that believed; for it was not in every man's power. [p. 53]

20. Compare, in the "Satyr," the speaker's distinction between himself and the kind of God-like man "Who, preaching peace, doth practice continence; / Whose pious life's a proof he does believe / Mysterious truths, which no man can conceive" (ll. 213–215).

. . . for he was sure religion was either a mere contrivance, or the most important thing that could be. [p. 76]
Of which I have since a farther assurance from a person of quality who conversed much with him the last year of his life; to whom he would often say, that he was happy if he did believe, and that he would never endeavor to draw him from it. [p. 79]

In the last year of his life, it seems clear Rochester found himself still skeptical of religion but yearning for some kind of faith. How much of this yearning did he feel earlier, while writing his best poems, and what relationship has it to the sense of an unrealizable ideal that characterizes a number of his poems? We should notice the words that he used to describe the happiness of believers: a base on which one's thought "rested and centered"; "quiet in their consciences"; "supports and joys"; "foundation of quiet." Rochester thinks in very traditional fashion of faith as a haven, as a safe and secure foundation, a physical as well as a spiritual stability and certainty. Compare a contemporary expression of the same fear and yearning:

We sail over a vast expanse, ever uncertain, ever adrift, carried to and fro. To whatever point we think to fix and fasten ourselves it shifts and leaves us; and if we pursue it it escapes our grasp, slips away, fleeting in eternal flight. Nothing stays for us. That is our condition; natural, yet most contrary to our inclination; we have a burning desire whereon to build a tower rising to the Infinite; but our whole foundation racks, and the earth yawns to the abyss.[21]

Pascal achieved a sustaining faith. But three months after the last of the conversations with Burnet, Rochester was dead.

About two months before his death in July 1680, his health collapsed. Among those in attendance at his sick bed was Robert Parsons, his mother's chaplain. It was to Parsons

21. Pascal, *Pensées*, tr. H. F. Stewart (New York, 1950), p. 25.

that Rochester made his famous deathbed repentance, confessing abhorrence of his former life, and declaring his firm belief in God and his hope of salvation. Whether Rochester's conversion represents a natural conclusion to a life of unsatisfied skeptical materialism (as Pinto and Murdock have argued), or a conventional end in an age where very few died without formal repentance (a dissolute Charles II died a Papist), or a frightened and momentary capitulation in the face of extinction, we can never finally know, although the first of the three possibilities seems far less likely than the other two. Our ignorance is due partly to our limited evidence about the seriousness of Rochester's intellectual and spiritual interests. The poetry is adequate evidence of the strength and sharpness of his mind, but we have little knowledge of the objects of his intermittent fits of study.

Aside from the plain evidence of the poems themselves, which reveal that he understood enough Latin to translate Seneca, Lucretius, Petronius, Ovid, and Horace — to translate them closely but also to depart from them significantly — and that he was familiar with Hobbesian and Montaignian ideas, the main sources of evidence about Rochester's learning are Burnet and Robert Parsons, the chaplain who attended his deathbed. Unfortunately, their testimony, though firsthand, is not necessarily trustworthy; both may have sought to inflate the brilliance of their noble convert. Burnet wrote that when Rochester was at grammar school,

he was an extraordinary proficient at his book; and those shining parts, which since have appeared with so much lustre, began then to shew themselves. He acquired the Latin to such perfection, that to his dying day he retained a great relish of the fineness and beauty of that tongue, and was exactly versed in the incomparable authors that wrote about Augustus's time, whom he read often with that peculiar delight which the greatest wits have ever found in those studies. [p. 20]

This comment is not necessarily an exaggeration of the classical training of a seventeenth-century English schoolboy. Parsons goes further, commenting on Rochester's education at Wadham:

His natural talent was excellent; but he had hugely improved it by learning and industry, being thoroughly acquainted with all the classic authors, both Greek and Latin; a thing very rare, if not peculiar to him, among those of his quality; which he used not, as other poets have done, to translate or steal from them, but rather to better and improve them by his own natural fancy.[22]

Of Parson's claims for Rochester, some are extreme (that he improved the classics) but others might well be true (that he was more learned than most Court wits).[23]

Rochester told Burnet that after leaving Wadham he had stopped studying, but that his governor on the grand tour, Dr. Balfour, was able to engage him "by many tricks . . . to delight in books and reading." Thereafter, by Burnet's account, he was an avid, if intermittent, reader: "so that ever after he took occasion, in the intervals of those woeful extravagances that consumed most of his time, to read much" (p. 21). What he read is not certain, but it seems to have included various ancient and moderns, histories, and books of physic.[24] Several other contemporary statements about Rochester's learning survive, but they are clearly derivative.[25]

22. In Burnet, pp. 113–114.
23. Burnet makes a similar claim: "He had both as much natural wit, and as much acquired by learning, and both as much improved with thinking and study, as perhaps any libertine of the age" (p. 17).
24. Burnet, pp. 15, 31–32; *Letters*, p. 40. A letter from Savile to Rochester refers to "your Chymical knowledge," perhaps alchemical rather than medical. *Letters*, p. 43.
25. Anthony Wood repeats Parsons verbatim (*Athenae Oxoniensis*, ed. Bliss, 3:229); "Cibber's" *Lives of the Poets* (1753) follows Burnet (2:271); Johnson repeats Wood (*Lives*, 1:128); Frances Giffard, Rochester's first tutor, said he knew very little Greek and but little Latin (*Remarks . . . of Thomas Hearne*, ed. Doble, 3:263).

Some of the modern works that Rochester very likely read, perhaps at Woodstock, were Hobbes's *Leviathan* (1651), Montaigne's *Essais*, either in French or in the 1603 translation by John Florio, and Charron's *Sagesse* ("every reader of any pretensions to cultivation knew Montaigne and Charron intimately").[26] There are a few statements by contemporaries to suggest that he knew Hobbes well. Wood, not a careful witness, says "The Court . . . not only debauched him; but made him a perfect Hobbist."[27] Wood may have been using the term strictly, to mean a disciple of Hobbes in politics, epistemology, and aesthetics, or, more likely, to mean an unorthodox thinker and materialist who had adopted the bold but fashionable view that all knowledge derives from sense.[28] The rest of Rochester's reading is less certain. It is possible that he knew the work of some of the French libertine thinkers and poets — Theophile de Viau, Mathurin Regnier, Jacques Vallée des Barreaux — themselves students of Montaigne[29] and literary forebears of Boileau, whom Rochester is known to have admired. He may have discovered their writings during his several visits to Paris, but could have read them in London as easily. It is possible, too, that he was familiar, as most English freethinkers were, with popularized Epicureanism, either through Walter Charleton's *Epicurus's Morals* (1656) or the second volume of Thomas Stanley's *History of Philosophy* (1656).[30] In Stanley, if he knew him, he could have read Sextus Empiricus's

26. Louis Bredvold, *The Intellectual Milieu of John Dryden* (Ann Arbor, 1934), p. 15.

27. *Athenae Oxoniensis*, 3:229.

28. Compare the reports that Rochester on his deathbed repudiated the philosophy of Hobbes. In Burnet, p. 125, and William Seward, *Biographiana* (London, 1799), 2:509, quoted in Prinz, p. 232. Samuel Mintz reminds us that Rochester was attended in his last illness by noted anti-Hobbists. *The Hunting of Leviathan* (Cambridge, 1962), p. 141. Rochester's exclamations might then have been prompted by his spiritual advisors.

29. Alan Boase, *The Fortunes of Montaigne* (London, 1935).

30. See Thomas F. Mayo, *Epicurus in England, 1650–1725* (Austin, Texas, 1934).

description of Pyrrho's skeptical philosophy. Probably, too, he knew La Rochefoucauld's *Maximes* (1665), translated in 1670. To discover what books Rochester read, however, is less important than to recall the intellectual and social climate, the kinds of ideas and models of conduct available to him. The dominant model in Rochester's maturity can only have been the Court, a world by all accounts delighting in sensual pleasure, and in contempt (despite official pieties) of traditional moral and religious restraints as mere "custom," a licentious world where, as Clarendon wrote, "every one did that which was good in his own eyes." [31]

Rochester partook fully of this libertine heterodoxy [32] both as poet and as notorious rake. But what is particularly striking, liberation from restraint did not seem to bring with it any lasting delight or steady satisfaction with the world or with his own life.

His letters and poems reflect a disgusted sense that life is busy nonsense, at worst an ugly cheat, at best a brittle joy. To Savile, for example, he writes: "The world, ever since I can remember, has been still so unsupportably the same, that 'twere vain to hope there were any alterations; and therefore I can have no curiosity for news." [33] What the world is like he knows too well:

The Lowsiness of Affairs in this place, is such . . . 'tis not fit to entertain a private Gentleman . . . with the Retaile of them, the general Heads, under which this whole Island may be considered, are Spies, Beggars, and Rebels, the Transpositions and Mixtures of these, make an agreeable Variety; busie Fools, and Cautious Knaves are bred out of 'em, and set 'em off wonderfully; tho' of this latter sort, we have fewer now than ever, Hypocrisie being the only Vice in decay amongst us, few Men here dissemble their being Rascals; and no Woman disowns being a Whore.[34]

31. *Life of Edward Hyde, Earl of Clarendon* (Oxford, 1759), 2:29.
32. Well described by Bredvold and Underwood.
33. *Letters*, p. 40.
34. *Ibid.*, p. 73.

Nor, within the smaller sphere of his own life, was Rochester able to attain sensual contentment; his poems, likewise, never reflect a completely satisfying sense experience. Like many of his orthodox Christian contemporaries, he suffered pain from being imprisoned within a body that did not satisfy all his wants. He found, as he wrote to his wife, "soe great a disproportion 'twixt our desires and what is ordained to content them." [35] The "disproportion" of things is a constant theme with Rochester (as with Pascal),[36] a dissatisfaction with all forms of experience, whether as lover, courtier, poet, or reveler. But he never cared to escape from that pain by transcending sense or by scaling down his desires in order to win some lesser happiness. He had only scorn for "those entirely satisfied with theire shares in this world that theire wishes nor theire thoughts have not a farther prospect of felicity and glory." Rochester wittily adapts the religious "prospect" of heavenly glory to the sphere of "life's happiness," as he makes clear in continuing: "were that mans soule plac't in a body fitt for it, hee were a dogg, that could count anything a benefit obtain'd with flattery, feare, and service." [37] Physical dissatisfaction is an instance of a broader anxiety. Rochester seems to have suffered from a radical insecurity about all experience.

As a libertine and skeptic, he rejected convention and orthodoxy, restlessly burning his way through a life of sensation; he was passionate for life, but always disappointed. Yet it is apparent from his letters and throughout his poems that however restless and adventurous he was, he continually longed for some kind of rest and quiet, some assuring certainty. His letters are marked by constant complaints

35. *Hayward*, p. 288.

36. See Fredelle Bruser, "Disproportion: A Study in the Work of John Wilmot, Earl of Rochester," *University of Toronto Quarterly*, 15 (1945–1946), 384–396. Compare Pascal's heading "Disproportion de l'homme," *Pensées*, tr. Stewart, p. 18.

37. Hayward, p. 288.

about his pressing domestic relations, his uncertain life at Court, his battered reputation and frequent illnesses, and with his longing for rest and security. In a letter, for example, to Elizabeth Barry: "You have the Strongest Security our frail and daily-changing Frame can give, that I can live to no End so much, as that of Pleasing and Serving you."[38] In a facetious appeal to Savile: "Dear Savile! as ever thou dost hope to out-do Machiavel, or equal Me, send some good Wine! So may thy wearied Soul at last find Rest, no longer hov'ring 'twixt th'unequal Choice of Politicks and Lewdness!"[39] In a comment on Whitehall: "We are in such a setled Happiness, and such merry Security in this place, that if it were not for sickness, I could pass my time very well,"[40] and in his conversations with Burnet already quoted: "I think those are very happy who are under the power of religious impressions, since they have somewhat on which their thoughts can center and rest" (p. 43).

The weariness and vexation which Rochester describes (and seeks to escape) is for his contemporary Pascal simply the human condition: "Man's condition: inconstancy, ennui, unrest."[41] He recognizes that men seek to escape this condition, but finds the attempt futile: "Let us then cease to look for security and stability. Our reason is ever cheated by misleading appearances; nothing can fix the finite between the two Infinites which enclose it and fly from it."[42] Pascal shares Rochester's sense of man's wretchedness, but for him this sense is the very source of man's greatness (man is a reed, but a "thinking reed"), supported as it is by faith in a hidden God. Though man is puny and his reason impotent, it is "inconceivable that God should exist, and in-

38. Hayward, p. 279. In one letter to Mrs. Barry, Rochester signs himself "Your restless servant."

39. *Letters*, p. 32.

40. *Ibid.*, p. 72.

41. *Pensées*, tr. Stewart, p. 31.

42. *Ibid.*, p. 31.

conceivable that he should not exist." [43] Pascal sought and found his security in a God beyond reason.

Rochester looked not to faith in a transcendent world but to male friendship and the life of a rake as the avenues to security. The letters to Savile are marked by a recurrent concern with the idea of enduring friendship. For a man whose marriage, sex life, life at Court, and life as a wit were all unsatisfying, either in their dullness or mutability, it was no doubt natural to turn to study or male friendship for comfort and support:

if there bee a reall good upon Earth, 'tis in the name of freind without which all others are meerly fantasticall, how few of us are fitt stuff to make that thing, wee have dayly the melancholy experience. However, dear Harry! Let us not give out, nor despair of bringing that about, which as it is the most difficult, and rare Accident of Life, is also the best; nay (perhaps) the only good one.[44]

In his own case, perhaps the hope of enduring friendship was questionable — "If it were the Sign of an honest Man, to be happy in his Friends, sure I were mark'd out for the worst of Men; since no one e'er lost so many as I have done, or knew to make so few." [45] Yet he never gave up the conviction that he had found what he had so long looked for in Savile: "I ever though you an extraordinary Man, and must now think you such a Friend, who, being a Courtier, as you are, can love a man whom it is the great Mode to hate." [46] In his last surviving letter to Savile (April 1680) he expresses once more his deep gratitude: ". . . you have made my heart glad in giving me such a Proof of your friendship, and I am now sensible, that it is natural for you

43. *Ibid*, p. 113.
44. *Ibid.*, p. 34. Compare Stanley's description of the Epicurean view of friendship as a source of "wisdom," "security," and "pleasure." *History of Philosophy* (3rd. ed.; London, 1701), p. 632.
45. *Letters*, p. 37.
46. *Ibid.*, p. 46.

to be kind to me, and can never more despair of it." [47] Savile appears to have been a loyal steady friend for the last ten years of Rochester's life, and to have given him a measure of the security he so desperately sought.

The life of a rake seems to have appeared to Rochester — both in his life and in his art — as another possible means to security. The Restoration rake, on and off stage, through clear self-knowledge and an acute sense of other people's weaknesses, finds a way, through manipulation and exploitation of virgins, fools, cuckolds, and lusting wives, to exert his sexual will. [48] But Rochester's life and poems offer us not images of the rake's mastery, but images of a failure to attain that mastery. He explores the possibilities of the rake only to discover pain and perplexity, insecurity, and enslavement to the vagaries of passion or a time-worn, burnt-out body. The failure to attain mastery in sexual relations stands in turn as an epitome of all of Rochester's failures to attain certainty — in friendship, in court life, in his own mind ("he was not master of his own belief"). Robbed of such support, he is prey to a world like Hobbes's state of nature, "solitary, cruel, nasty, brutish, short." But if Rochester had simply been a suffering rake, he would be of little interest. Through the energy of his wit, Rochester, as poet, made art of that suffering. His clear and unflinching analysis of the rake's painful situation in a base world gave us a handful of masterful poems, and gave himself what may have been the only sense of mastery he enjoyed.

The following two chapters consider the discoveries of baseness, failure, and pain in a series of satires with libertine speakers and in the poems dealing centrally with sexual relations.

47. *Ibid.*, p. 74. See also letters 3–10, 12, 14, 21, 30–31, and 33 (Wilson's numbers).

48. See the description of the rake in John Traugott, "The Rake's Progress from Court to Comedy," *Studies in English Literature*, 6 (1966), 381–407.

2 The Uses of Libertinism

In a general sense, poems are personal, even autobiographical; they inevitably reflect, however directly or obliquely, the varied concerns and self-images of their authors. The rake in Rochester's poems is inevitably a reflection of the historical rake and of the man who, in letters from his country retreat to his friend Savile at court, appears sometimes gaily or thoughtfully detached from the folly and frenzy of London, caring only for word of his few friends, at other times passionately engaged in contempt and bitter reproach. That he delighted in projecting an image of himself is also clear; he presents himself on occasion, quite self-consciously, as bugbear of all orthodoxy, or as ill-natured misanthropist. With boisterous gaiety, for example, he announces his intemperance, asking Savile to send him wine:

Do a Charity becoming one of your pious Principles, in preserving your humble servant Rochester, from the imminent peril of Sobriety. . . . And, if you have a grateful Heart, (Which is a miracle amongst you statesmen) shew it, by directing the Bearer to the best Wine in town; and pray let not this highest Point of sacred friendship be perform'd slightly, but go about it with all due deliberation and care, as holy priests to Sacrifice, or as discreet Thieves to the wary performance of Burglary and Shop-lifting.

 Dear Savile! as ever thou dost hope to out-do Machiavel, or equal Me, send some good Wine.![1]

The combination of flippancy (about drunkenness) and seriousness (about friendship) is characteristic, I think, of Rochester's temperament. Note, too, the element of self-dramatization as a Machiavel, very likely reflecting (and mockingly perpetuating) the image of Rochester in the minds of the Town and the Court.

 When, two years later, he again presents himself as the Court sees him, the gaiety has turned to bitterness. Out of favor with the king and rumored to have died, Rochester writes sardonically to Savile in 1676:

This day I receiv'd the unhappy news of my own Death and Burial. But hearing what Heirs and Successors were decreed me in my place, and chiefly in my Lodgings, it was not small Joy to me that those tidings prove untrue. . . . The King, who knows me to be a very ill-natur'd Man, will not think it an easie matter for me to dye, now I live chiefly out of spight. Dear Mr. Savile, afford me some news from your land of the living.[2]

We can see, perhaps, something of a confession in these words: although there is ample evidence elsewhere in the letters and poems to show that he prized good nature and sought to demonstrate it toward his friends, Rochester confessed to a sense "of what the methods of my Life seem so utterly to contradict" — a sense, that is, of the "kindness" not always evinced in his relations with people.[3] But the letter represents also a willful and self-conscious adoption of the role assigned to him by his enemies: "if the king

1. *Letters*, p. 32.
2. *Ibid.*, p. 39.
3. Letter to his wife, Hayward, p. 291.

says I am ill-natured, that I live only to spite them, then I *will* do so."

A year later, even more melodramatically, calling himself "a man whom it is the great mode to hate," [4] he writes to Savile, "You, who have known me these Ten years the grievance of all prudent Persons, the By-Word of Statesmen, the scorn of ugly Ladies, which are very near all, and the Irreconcilable Aversion of Fine Gentlemen, who are the Ornamental Part of a Nation, and yet found me seldom sad, even under these weighty Oppressions. . . ." [5] Again he combines wit and bitterness, flaunting his disaffection from the social and political worlds around him. The paradigm of this theatricality is the famous portrait of Rochester crowning with laurel the poetic monkey. [6] Holding in his left hand a sheaf of papers, and facing the painter, Rochester very daintily and solemnly (yet possibly with the beginnings of a smile on his lips) settles the wreath with his right hand on the head of the monkey, who hands him in return a crumpled page torn apparently from the small book (of contemporary poems?) in his hand, as if to indicate his low regard for poetry. [7] The formal pose and seeming appeal to the viewer (as if to make sure he is being watched) mock the idea that there is anything lofty or spiritual about poetry, anything of honor in being, like Dryden, Poet Laureate. A monkey, he might be saying, is as good a poet as any of us.

It is in the light of this and similar self-dramatizations, [8]

4. *Letters*, p. 46.
5. *Ibid.*, p. 50.
6. Attributed to Huysmans. Two versions survive, now in Warwick Castle and the National Portrait Gallery in London. The latter is reproduced on the dust jacket. For a color reproduction, see *Gyldenstolpe MS.*
7. H. W. Janson takes the gesture to indicate the ape's lack of regard for reason. *Apes and Ape Lore in the Middle Ages and Renaissance* (London, 1952), pp. 353–354.
8. Compare his theatrical and exaggerated presentation in the letters of his many illnesses, e.g., "Tho' I am almost Blind, utterly Lame, and scarce within the reasonable hopes of ever seeing London again. . . ." *Letters*, p. 46, see also p. 65.

designed to shock, to scandalize, to prompt attention or laughter, rather than of his often-noted fondness for impersonation,[9] that we should view Rochester's satires. The impersonator assumes a mask or "persona," hiding his own identity. But the concept of a persona seems to me to throw no more light on Rochester's work than on the work of Pope or Swift. As an acute critic, who would severely restrict the use of the term "persona" to the "ironical persona", says, "Through his masterpieces, a man defines — not hides — himself. By reading them we are put in touch with him, not with a series of intermediaries."[10] The speakers of Rochester's libertine satires should be seen not as personae, but as exaggerated versions of the poet himself. As self-projector rather than as impersonator, Rochester presents theatrical yet carefully controlled extensions of his own personal libertinism. His purposes are to shock, to scandalize, but finally to win sympathetic attention for his speakers, however knowingly outrageous they may appear to be.

This view of Rochester's relationship with his speakers — a central problem in interpretation of his poems — thus lies midway between the extremes of modern criticism. In some accounts the poems are autobiographical documents, true confessions of a libertine. At the other extreme, it is argued that in two major satires Rochester makes use of an ironical persona, whereby the egotistical speaker himself is unconsciously exposed.[11] In my view the libertine speakers of the

9. Which C. F. Main stresses: "The man who in real life successfully impersonated a woman on one occasion and a mountebank on another must, surely, be permitted to invent a satirical persona." "The Right Vein of Rochester's *Satyr*," in *Essays in Literary History Presented to J. M. French*, ed. R. Kirk and C. F. Main (New Brunswick, N.J., 1960), pp. 98–99.

10. See Irvin Ehrenpreis's "Personae," in *Restoration and 18th Century Literature*, ed. C. Camden (Chicago, 1963), pp. 25–38.

11. By Vieth particularly in his *ARP*. In the edition, Vieth alters his position: "Rochester's poems, to the extent that they are a coherent body of expression, acquire a corporate unity as projections of what we imagine to have been his real-life personality. To a greater or lesser

poems are too much like the historical Rochester to be personae, and too self-consciously, too knowingly, scandalous to be, simply, the man himself. The poems do not simply expose, but make use of, Rochester's libertinism.

The uses of libertinism, as I will attempt to show, are several, they fall generally, like the uses of paradox, into two categories, one playfully impudent, the other more serious. Rochester seems to delight in paradox for its own sake, and for its shock value; yet it also allows him to question orthodox standards without necessarily proposing alternatives. In like manner, Rochester's purposes in the libertine satires seem to be, on the one hand, to shock and scandalize the conventional part of his audience; and on the other, to attack perversity and corruption, to satirize libertinism itself, or to try out, with some detachment, the implications of libertine egoism in making love and writing poems. In each of these satires, furthermore, Rochester wins for his libertine speaker the reader's sympathetic attention, in part because, offensive as he may seem, the libertine points out more offensive behavior around him, and invariably is defeated by life, disgusted, disillusioned, or put to flight. The libertine, we discover, is human too.

The Early Satires: "St. James's Park"

In a group of early satires, written during the period 1672 to 1674, and similar in structure, theme, and speaker, Rochester uses libertinism as the primary attribute of his satiric observer. In each, an openly — even boastfully — libertine speaker, who in several ways resembles the historical Rochester, recounts with varying degrees of amusement and disgust, how, having taken leave of his usual companions, he visited a scene — in park, dining hall, and watering place — of egregious corruption and ridiculousness. In each

degree the 'I' of each poem is always Rochester, even when the speaker is a woman." *Complete Poems*, p. xli.

poem the narrative flow is occasionally halted for the sake of satirical character sketches — of young fops, of decaying beauty, and (in "Tunbridge Wells") of a series of ridiculous "shapes" — and concludes suddenly and violently with a curse, or the speaker's hurried departure from the scene.

In "A Ramble in St. James's Park" the speaker describes how, after dining with fellow rakes, he walked into the Park alone in search of women.[12] In the Park, associated by contemporary stage tradition and by actual circumstances with lechery and with unsuccessful love, he unexpectedly spies his mistress, Corinna, agreeing to an assignation with three "confounded asses." Bitterly denouncing her, not for lust but for passively and indiscriminately submitting to fools, he concludes with a vehement curse.

The poem is designed as the satiric observation of a self-conscious libertine. Rochester takes care to have the speaker present himself as a witty and dissolute rake:

> Much wine had passed, with grave discourse
> Of who fucks who, and who does worse
> (Such as you usually do hear
> From those that diet at the Bear),
> When I, who still take care to see
> Drunkenness relieved by lechery,
> Went out into St. James's Park,
> To cool my head and fire my heart.
>
> [ll. 1–8]

He is a self-confessed drunkard, gossiper, and lecher, but his declaration has something of the theatrical in it; he flaunts his libertinism to the point of caricature. The overstatement suggests, too, that he looks on himself with some sarcasm; but he distinguishes himself subtly from his fellow revelers. The opposition between "those" and "I," each stressed in the metrical pattern, confirmed by the speaker's

12. For the stage tradition, see Chapter VI.

exit, alone, into the Park, indicates that he views himself as both part of and yet apart from his companions. He suggests, half facetiously, that he is morally better than those habitués of the Bear who apparently continue their usual "grave discourse," while he takes care to relieve drunkenness. The wit thrusts in several directions. The speaker takes care (he is thoughtful, sensible, responsible) to achieve a scandalous end; he seeks both to cool his head (like a wise and temperate man) and fire his heart (like a rake) with another sort of intemperance. The poem thus begins with some hint of ironic self-satire (a strategy in which Rochester grew more interested in later satires), but also with a suggestion that the rest of the poem will bear out how, in a curious way, scandalous lechery is defensible.

In the course of his ramble, the libertine attacks a broad range of perverse and unnatural behavior, and through him Rochester also mocks the kind of poetry that prettifies the perversity. The landscape, for example, is monstrously sexual, testifying to the perversity of man in general, and to the mythologizing power of the libertine's sexual imagination:

> But though St. James has th'honor on't,
> 'Tis consecrate to prick and cunt.
> There, by a most incestuous birth,
> Strange woods spring from the teeming earth;
> For they relate how heretofore,
> When ancient Pict began to whore,
> Deluded of his assignation
> (Jilting, it seems, was then in fashion),
> Poor pensive lover,[13] in this place
> Would frig upon his mother's face;
> Whence rows of mandrakes tall did rise
> Whose lewd tops fucked the very skies.
> Each imitative branch does twine

13. The crudeness of the Pict's act is set off by the conventionally elegant description of him as a "pensive lover."

> In some loved fold of Aretine,
> And nightly now beneath their shade
> Are buggeries, rapes, and incests made.
>
> [ll. 9–24]

On one level, Rochester parodies the elegant descriptions of a *locus amoenus*, as in Waller's panegyrical picture of St. James's Park:

> Methinks I see the love that shall be made,
> The lovers walking in that amorous shade;
> The gallants dancing by the river's side;
> They bathe in summer, and in winter glide.
>
> . . . .
>
> The ladies, angling in the crystal lake,
> Feast on the waters with the prey they take;
> At once victorious with their lines, and eyes,
> They make the fishes, and the men, their prize.
>
> . . . .
>
> A living gallery of aged trees;
> Bold sons of earth, that thrust their arms so high,
> As if once more they would invade the sky.[14]

Waller's Watteau-like pastoral, written about 1661 just after Charles had made improvements and opened the Park to the Town, predicts that the park will embody an ideal of graceful elegance. And at first the Park was indeed the scene of elegant sports, such as ice-skating and paille-maille. But a decade later, when Rochester wrote, the Park sports had become erotic. Rochester's anti-pastoral satire, then, measures the distance between Waller's old ideal and present reality [15] by parodying the panegyric, importing its own

14. "On St. James's Park, as Lately Improved by his Majesty," ll. 21–25, 33–36, 68–70.

15. Compare the poems by Rochester and Waller describing the rivalries between the King's several mistresses. In Waller's witty panegyric, "The Triple Combat," suggestions of disparagement yield to the

imagined details and replacing allusions to a golden age with its own mythology, a jumble of sexual lore. The Park is described as a sacred, "all-sin-sheltering grove" (l. 25), sprung up as the result of an incestuous union between "ancient Pict" and mother earth. Aretino, whose obscene sonnets (illustrated by Giulio Romano) were extremely popular during the Restoration, is appropriately invoked as a model for the erotically entwining branches of the monstrous mandrakes. Their forked roots, considered to resemble human legs and thought of as female sexual objects, Rochester transforms into males, perhaps an analogy with Waller's trees, thrusting their arms to invade the skies. Rochester thus reduces Waller's civilized sex to brutal lust: ladies angling on the lake (for both fish and men) become (later in the poem) simply bitches in heat, and elegantly phallic trees now frankly rape the skies and lewdly entwine their branches.

Just as he parodies Waller's pastoral mode, so Rochester subverts a familiar Cavalier love-song convention, the mistress walking queenlike through a garden:[16]

> Along these hallowed walks it was
> That I beheld Corinna pass.
> Whoever had been by to see
> The proud disdain she cast on me
> Through charming eyes, he would have swore
> She dropped from heaven that very hour,
> Forsaking the divine abode

discovery of an ideal: "our golden age / Where Loves gives law, Beauty the sceptre sways" (ll. 44–45). In Rochester's cynical equivalent, "His scepter and his prick are of a length; / And she may sway the one who plays with th'other" ("Satyr on Charles II," ll. 11–12).

16. Compare Robert Heath, "On Clarastella, Walking in her Garden": "See how Flora smiles to see / This approaching deity! / Where each herb looks young and green / In presence of their coming queen." *Seventeenth Century Lyrics*, ed. N. Ault (New York, 1950), p. 245, see also p. 285.

> In scorn of some despairing god.
> But mark what creatures women are:
> How infinitely vile, when fair!
> [ll. 33–42]

He presents Corinna as the conventional, disdainful mistress, a goddess in a sacred grove. Only in the last couplet is there a suggestion that she is not what she seems: for the conventional "How infinitely *cruel*, when fair" Rochester writes "vile." He suggests, too, that the Cavalier mode of writing, like Waller's, presents a false picture of social and sexual behavior.

But it is not lust and lechery (in which he himself engages) or a mistress's disdain that the speaker attacks:

> And nightly now beneath their shade
> Are buggeries, rapes, and incests made.
> Unto this all-sin-sheltering grove
> Whores of the bulk and the alcove,
> Great ladies, chambermaids, and drudges,
> The ragpicker, and heiress trudges.
> Carmen, divines, great lords, and tailors,
> Prentices, poets, pimps, and jailers,
> Footmen, fine fops do here arrive,
> And here promiscuously they swive.
> [ll. 23–32]

The key word here is "promiscuously," which retains its older sense of "consisting of members of different kinds massed together without order" (*OED*, "promiscuous," sense 1). The Park truly comprehends an indiscriminately mixed mass from the great world and behind stairs, a Noah's Ark of Restoration humanity. Rochester's point is, first, the old truism (in the cynic's eye) that, when the clothes are stripped away, the high-born and low-born alike are all propelled by instinctual lust. More serious, however, is the charge, here suggested and later borne out, that the lust displayed in the Park is utterly undiscriminating with respect to its objects, and even perhaps its modes, of gratification ("buggeries, rapes, and incests"). The "ancient Pict" is thus mocked not for whoring (natural, honest, straightforward expression of lust), but for "frig[ging] upon his mother's face" in frustration. The act is viewed ludicrously as a monstrous kind of incest, committed in contempt and insult (perhaps self-contempt).

Corrina, indeed, is the prime offender:

> Had she picked out, to rub her arse on,
> Some stiff-pricked clown or well-hung parson,
> Each job of whose spermatic sluice
> Had filled her cunt with wholesome juice,
> I the proceeding should have praised
> In hope sh'had quenched a fire I raised.
> Such natural freedoms are but just:
> There's something generous in mere lust.[17]
> But to turn damned abandoned jade
> When neither head nor tail persuade;
> To be a whore in understanding,
> A passive pot for fools to spend in!
>   [ll. 91–102]

Lust at least indicates passion, but Corrina indulges in sex unfeelingly.[18] What is equally bad, from the wit's point of view, is that, utterly undiscriminating in her sexual forays, she takes up utter fools, lacking in mental or physical attrac-

17. Rochester may have taken a hint for this seemingly paradoxical line from Juvenal's sixth satire, line 135, translated by Dryden as "Lust is the smallest sin the sex can own." Juvenal later favorably compares the crimes of Medea and Procne, done in passion, with those of contemporary Roman women, done in cool calculation.

18. Compare a poem attributed to Rochester, "Let ancients boast no more": "When she had jaded quite / Her almost boundless appetite / Cloy'd with the choicest Banquets of Delight / She'll still drudge on in tasteless vice, / (As if she sinn'd for Exercise)" (ll. 16–20). Printed in Pinto, *Poems*, p. 135. Vieth says the poem is not Rochester's. *Complete Poems*, p. 229.

tions. As with the promiscuous swivers, Corinna's actions do not correspond to any passion. Honest, generous lust, then, becomes the ideal against which Rochester measures the decadent world of those who feel nothing.[19]

Corinna's behavior, furthermore, is unnatural (against the impulses of nature) and, all the more for that reason, abhorrent to a libertine. Unnatural too, or affected, are her three "knights." In their affectation they fit into the poem's basic satirical pattern. One fool (ll. 46–62) forces nature and, lacking "common sense," displays "universal affection." He imitates the forms without understanding the substance, "looks, and lives, and loves by rote." The second fool, a young wouldwit (ll. 63–68), thinks criticism means disapproval. Like the first, he comes by his opinions secondhand. The third, a prospective heir and future booby squire (ll. 69–74), seeks only to imitate the imitators. In preparation for the proper disposal of his estate, he trains now to become a tearing blade. Like Corinna and the Pict, each of the fools seeks to force nature, to satisfy not instinctual desires, but invented and inappropriate ones.

The libertine speaker clearly sets himself apart from all such unnatural or "forced" behavior. But in a way he is perhaps guilty of the same offense. Rochester, I suggested earlier, is interested not only in using the libertine as a railer, but also in satirizing him. It is possible that the libertine, in defending Corinna's lust, may be forcing his own nature and deceiving himself: his feelings seem to be working against his reason-born ideal. His "head" had "persuade[d]" him that Corinna should be granted "natural freedoms . . . the nice allowances of love," to pursue her pleasure where she pleased, an attitude that forms the basis of a Rochester song.[20]

19. This point is made also by Ronald Berman, "Rochester and the Defeat of the Senses," *Kenyon Review*, 26 (1964), 354–368.

20. "To a Lady in a Letter," *Complete Poems*, p. 82.

Similar agreements, allowing mutual inconstancy,[21] form a convention in many Cavalier and Restoration love songs, but, as another Rochester song makes clear, the male often insisted on a conflicting convention, reserving to himself alone the right to be unfaithful.[22] Furthermore, the defense of (and even exhortation to) female inconstancy, a corollary to the defense of mutual inconstancy, could be used as a witty way of breaking off with a mistress.[23] In such an agreement, although he pretends to tolerance and generosity, the male really gives up nothing. Similarly, in "St. James's Park," Rochester shows another way in which the male does not wholly endorse his own announced policy of allowing sexual freedom:

> Did ever I refuse to bear
> The meanest part your lust could spare?
> When your lewd cunt came spewing home
> Drenched with the seed of half the town,
> My dram of sperm was supped up after
> For the digestive surfeit water
>
> .   .   .   .
>
> Nor ever thought it an abuse
> While you had pleasure for excuse.
>   [ll. 111–116, 123–124]

The speaker's words seem to belie his declared principle: he is clearly displeased at Corinna's mean lust, offended, and even hurt. He presents himself, theatrically, as the wronged and long-suffering lover:

> Ungrateful! Why this treachery
> To humble, fond, believing me.

21. The speaker, too, in "St. James's Park" reserves for himself the right to free pursuit of pleasure. As the poem begins he goes to the Park to "fire my heart," not expecting to find his own Corinna.

22. "Against constancy," *Complete Poems*, p. 82.

23. See the song "Upon Leaving his Mistress," *Complete Poems*, p. 81.

You that could make my heart away
For noise and color,[24] and betray
The secrets of my tender hours
To such knight-errant paramours.
When, leaning on your faithless breast,
Wrapped in security and rest,
Soft kindness all my powers did move,
And reason lay dissolved in love!

[ll. 107–108, 125–132]

Though ostensibly he objects only to having his love secrets revealed to fools, in fact he objects to having secrets betrayed at all.[25] He resents the fact that she is "faithless."

The libertine speaker, who as satirical observer represents a kind of norm for us, is thus subtly qualified. He is qualified, too, by the bitterness into which he is betrayed when the present intrudes on his tender nostalgia:

May stinking vapors choke your womb
Such as the men you dote upon!
May your depraved appetite,
That could in whiffling fools delight,[26]
Beget such frenzies in your mind
You may go mad for the north wind,
And fixing all your hopes upon't
To have him bluster in your cunt,
Turn up your longing arse t' th'air,
And perish in a wild despair!

[ll. 133–142]

24. I.e., "that could dispose of, perhaps destroy, my heart, or reveal my heart's secrets, in return for a speciously attractive lover."

25. The description of Corinna returning after a binge of lust shows some general similarities with passages in Juvenal's sixth and eleventh satires describing the secret return of a faithless wife to her husband after a night of debauchery.

26. From the verb *whiffle*, "to flicker or flutter as if stirred by the wind," hence, *whiffling*, "inconstant, trifling, paltry." Recalling the etymology of whiffling, Rochester makes Corinna's punishment appropriate: for intriguing with such fools she will die of longing for the wind itself.

The curse is vehement, savage, and obscene, and compli-
cates our response to the speaker. It is, I suspect, part of
Rochester's design that the curse seem the exaggerated reaction (like that of a ranting coward, l. 143) of a partly self-
deceived libertine lover dedicated in principle to mutual
inconstancy, but outraged when the principle is put into
practice, especially (but not only, I think) with fools. Yet
the principle, and its corollary, that honestly lustful, passionate action is good, are not rejected. Rather they are qualified
by the concession that, men being what they are, inconstancy
and wayward lust will always enrage a lover. The main
point, however, that unfeeling sex with fools is far worse
than lust, is allowed to stand. From this perspective the
speaker's curse, for all its vehemence and savagery, is at
least a sign of passion, and therefore preferable to Corinna's
passionlessness. There is, furthermore, some appropriateness in the curse. Her punishment for passionless sex will be
to perish from a genuine but unfulfilled longing. And for all
the speaker's obscenity and profanity, the violence he
threatens is less reprehensible than Corinna's violent dese-
cration of herself. Since she insists on acting like a bitch, the
speaker will treat her and all others like her accordingly:
"And may no woman better thrive / That dares prophane
the cunt I swive!" (ll. 165–166).

The Early Satires: "Timon"

The better-known "Timon," written in the late spring of
1674, makes similar use of a libertine speaker. It, too, describes a libertine wit's adventure among fools: Timon, a
young wit and poet, friend of Sedley, Buckhurst, and Savile,
and apparently a customary debauchee and gambler, recounts to a friend how the previous evening he was accosted
in the Mall by a bore, and dragged off to a farcical dinner
party. Timon describes the events of the evening: the *repas
ridicule*, the display by the host and other guests of cor-

rupted taste in food and poetry, and his own disgusted escape into the night.

Unlike "St. James's Park," however, "Timon" shows close ties with classical satire, both French and Roman. Both the *repas ridicule* and the meeting with a bore in a city street had virtually become, even in classical times, satirical topoi. And, as critics have long known, Rochester's poem is a loose imitation of Boileau's *Satire* 3, owing something also to Horace's *Satire* 1:9 for its opening lines.[27] "Timon" appears to have been Rochester's earliest full-scale exercise in imitation, a technique he was later to use with great success in "An Allusion to Horace," and, loosely, in the "Satyr Against Mankind." In "Timon" he is still trying out a new technique, with only moderate success. Boileau's leisurely poem of two hundred and thirty-six lines is condensed to a swifter moving one hundred and seventy-seven lines, of which the most successful, interestingly enough, have no counterpart in Boileau.[28] The speaker, furthermore, is transformed from an urbane Horatian man of good taste and sense into a Rochesterian libertine rake.

Boileau's *Satire* 3 opens with an adversarius who asks why the unnamed poet is pale and troubled. Rochester reduces thirteen lines to four, and has the adversarius compare the poet not to a respectable *rentier* beleaguered by changes in the laws governing *rentes* but to a debauched libertine gambler:

> What, Timon! does old begin t'approach,
> That thus thou droop'st under a night's debauch?
> Hast thou lost deep to needy rogues on tick,
> Who n'er could pay, and must be paid next week?
>
> [ll. 1–4]

27. Like Timon, Horace's poet is accosted in a prominent street, seized by the hand, and addressed familiarly by a man known to him only by name. Boileau's poem, indebted often to the *repas ridicules* of both Horace and Regnier (*Satire* 10), uses none of these four details. For a detail which Rochester borrows from Regnier, see below, p. 174.

28. Lines 13–32, 42–67.

Both Boileau's speaker and Rochester's briefly recount the meeting with the bore and the reluctantly accepted invitation (ll. 5–12). But Rochester goes on to characterize his speaker as a libertine poet with an un-Boileauvian view of poetry. When the fawning bore praises an anonymous and insipid libel — "at last it was so sharp it must be mine" — Timon denies the attribution and claims he writes only to please himself:

> I vowed I was no more a wit than he:
> Unpracticed and unblessed in poetry.
> A song to Phyllis I perhaps might make,
> But never rhymed but for my pintle's sake.
> I envied no man's fortune nor his fame,
> Nor ever thought of a revenge so tame.
>
> [ll. 19–24]

The fool will not be put off, and leaves Timon "choked with his flattery," silenced, and exasperated: "Of a well-meaning fool I'm most afraid, / Who sillily repeats what was well said" (ll. 31–32).[29]

In describing the dinner party itself, Rochester follows Boileau's general plan, making appropriate modifications to suit an English context. The speaker suffers through a crudely prepared, sturdy English meal of hard beef and long carrots, "pig, goose, and capon" covered with sauces and washed down with small beer and claret served in a "wet clout" (Boileau describes an enormous and vulgar display of rich food badly prepared). It remains unclear whether Timon objects to the meal because it is English or because it is crudely prepared. He may be mocking a comic type, the xenophobic solid Englishman, like Hugh

29. The sense is better if we read the final couplet not as a continuation of the previous lines, but as a slightly different idea — he clumsily ("sillily") repeats a *bon mot* — unless we take the line to mean that the fool finds in a bad poem ("sillily repeats" praise) literary excellences ("what was well said" about a good poem).

Clodpate, the country justice in Shadwell's *Epsom Wells* (1672), a "hearty true English coxcomb" and hater of French food: "At my own house [I] spend not scurvy French kickshaws, but much ale, and Beef, and mutton, the Manufactures of the Country [1:1] . . . I hate French Fricassies and Ragousts, and French Dances too; but no more to be said, fill agen. Gud'sooks, here's your true English ale and your true English Hearts" (4:1).[30] Timon's host likewise promises "plain fare," no French "kickshaws, sillery and champagne, Ragouts and fricassees," and, like the Clodpate-type, attributes English victories such as the Armada to solid English beef: "Served up with sauces, all of eighty eight, / When our tough youth wrestled and threw the weight" (ll. 85–86). The sneer at "country bumpkins" (l. 84) and the "sauces . . . of eighty-eight" (boasts which garnish the meal) suggest that Timon finds the English meal crude and the jingoism ridiculous. While Rochester follows (and modifies) Boileau in describing a grotesque meal and foolish literary conversation, he departs from him significantly by providing Timon's host with an aging, eager wife (Boileau's party is an all-male affair). The description of this lady, a familiar figure, like Ladies Cockwood and Wishfort, in Restoration literature, is the highlight of the poem:

> In comes my lady straight. She had been fair,
> Fit to give love, and to prevent despair,
> But age, beauty's incurable disease,
> Had left her more desire than power to please.
> As cocks will strike although their spurs be gone,
> She with her old blear eyes to smite begun.
> Though nothing else, she in despite of time
> Preserved the affectation of her prime:
> However you begun, she brought in love,
> And hardly from that subject would remove.
> We chanced to speak of the French king's success;
> My lady wondered much how heaven could bless

30. Kick-shaws, a corruption of *quelque chose*, means "trifles."

> A man that loved two women at one time,
> But more how he to them excused his crime.
> She asked Huff if love's flame he never felt;
> He answered bluntly, "Do you think I'm gelt?"
> She at his plainness smiled, then turned to me:
> "Love in young minds precedes ev'n poetry:
> You to that passion can no stranger be,
> But wits are given to inconstancy."
> She had run on, I think, till now, but meat
> Came up, and suddenly she took her seat.
>
> [ll. 47–68]

With swift, economical, devastating strokes ("She *had been* fair") the decaying beauty is transfixed. Another portrait, like that of Charles,[31] in Rochester's gallery of impotents, she is the product, too, of skilled wit: the contrast (condensing to a single phrase a lifetime of sex) of desire and power; the vivid aptness of the simile (reinvigorating the dead metaphor of a lady smiting the eyes or heart of an admirer) to show how the veteran of love's wars fights on when the power to smite is gone; the artful syntax ("Though nothing else, she in despite of time / Preserved . . . affectation") to delay the truth (just as the lady refuses to face the truth) that only affectation will outlast time's ravages. So summed up, the lady is then allowed to display herself through her conversation, a fool prattling obsessively of what she can no longer enjoy.

Perhaps the greatest difference between Boileau's and Rochester's poems, however, is not in the alteration of details, the greater speed and density over a shorter length, or in the introduction of the host's wife, but in the character of the speaker. Boileau's poet is a nameless Horatian, Augustan figure, the embodiment of good taste and standards. Rochester's Timon displays, in addition to outraged taste, a seeming obsession with sex; both his name and his obsession are difficult to interpret.

31. See the "Satyr on Charles II," *Complete Poems*, pp. 60–61.

What did Rochester mean to tell his readers by naming his speaker Timon? As Vieth has noted, Timon "resembles Rochester and his character, activities, and social position." [32] The future satirist of man may well at this time (c. 1674) have taken on himself for literary purposes, or been given by others, half in jest, the apt nickname of Timon the misanthrope. But "Timon" was used in Restoration literature for a variety of types, not only a foolish man-hater, but the "one honest man in a corrupt world," and even as the embodiment of ostentatious magnificence.[33] It is unclear which traditional associations, if any, Rochester has in mind.

Unclear too is Rochester's attitude toward Timon's obscenities, for which there is no equivalent in Boileau:

> Up comes a piece of beef, full horseman's weight,
> Hard as the arse of Mosely, under which
> The coachman sweats as ridden by a witch;
> A dish of carrots, each of them as long
> As tool that to fair countess did belong,
> Which her small pillow could not so well hide
> But visitors his flaming head espied
>
> . . . .
>
> Each man had as much room as Porter, Blount,
> Or Harris had in Cullen's bushel cunt.
>   [ll. 76–81, 93–94] [34]

32. *Complete Poems*, p. 65. headnote.

33. See Shadwell's adaptation of Shakespeare's *Timon*; Oldham's translation of Juvenal's third satire, in which Juvenal's speaker Umbricius is called Timon; *The True Character of an Honest Man* (1712), attributed to Thomas Burnet but signed simply "Timon"; a play by Samuel Schelwig, *Timon, oder Missbrauch des Reichtums* (1671). The skeptic philosopher Timon of Phlius is described in Thomas Stanley's *History of Philosophy* (3rd. ed.; London, 1701), as "a lover of wine . . . of acute apprehension and quick in deriding, . . . a great lover of Writing, very skillful in composing . . . Poems, and Verses, and Tragedies, and Satyrs" (pp. 473–475). The poem's traditional title may cast disproportionate importance on the name. Printed first only as "Satyr," it was not called "Timon" until 1704.

34. For identification of the names, see Vieth's notes. Inverting Boileau (ll. 54–56) Rochester makes the table not crowded but too big.

On the one hand, this is perhaps just libertine bawdry, appropriate to the speaker. Yet Timon goes out of his way to satirize obsession of a more refined and pretentious kind in the lady — "However you begun, she brought in love, / And hardly from that subject would remove" (ll. 55–56) — and seems to hold up to scorn Huff's crude answer, "Do you think I'm gelt?" when she asks whether he ever felt "love's flame" (ll. 61–62). Sharing with his companions an obsession with sex, Timon is associated with them in another way whose implications, in Rochester's mind, are hard to judge. Though he clearly dissociates himself from the foolish prattle about the stage, it is curious that Timon occasionally seems to view himself as willing participant in the dinner party. While Boileau's speaker makes it constantly clear that he is present only under protest, and refuses to join in conversations that "they" engage in, Timon more than once uses the first person plural:

> We chanced to speak of the French king's success
>
> .   .   .   .
>
> Left to ourselves, of several things we prate
>
> .   .   .   .
>
> . . . we let them cuff
> Till they, mine host, and I all had enough.
> [ll. 57, 111, 172–173] [35]

While Rochester may simply have inadvertently failed to make Timon dissociate himself sufficiently, it is possible that Timon, by rebuking himself as he hurriedly exits — "I ran downstairs, with a vow nevermore / To drink beer-glass and hear the hectors roar" — sees himself as a fool for assenting to participate at all. Perhaps, once again, Rochester (modifying Boileau) subjects his libertine speaker to slight mockery.

Doubtless, as Wilson, Thorpe, and Vieth agree, Timon

35. See also ll. 89, 96, 102–104.

represents Rochester, or at least embodies "the norm of values by which judgment is passed upon other characters in the poem." [36] Yet none of these critics has faced the problems raised by the poet's unpleasant characterization of the speaker. Perhaps as in "St. James's Park," he sought to create a frank libertine — hence the slightly awkward emphasis at the beginning of the poem on Timon's debauchery and gambling — who exposes corruptions around him far worse than his own. In this case, the decaying lady's obsession with love, her foolish feigning and affectation, are to be taken as more reprehensible (because less frank and natural) than Timon's sexual crudity, the host's false taste in poetry as worse (because it overrates and overspiritualizes poetry) than that of the libertine who openly admits that he writes "but for my pintle's sake," and the quarrelsome hectors, flinging greasy plates, as more truly antisocial than a Timon-like wit — just as Shakespeare's Timon, for all his faults, is in some ways far better than anyone else in the play. The libertine Timon, then, remains as a norm. Though offensive in some ways, he wins our assent to his satirical observations. What makes the poem an unsuccessful whole is an occasional uncertainty — in Timon's attitude toward the meal, his companions, and himself, and in Rochester's attitude toward his speaker.

The Early Satires: "Tunbridge Wells"

"Tunbridge Wells" (1674), the third of these early satires that employs a libertine as satirical observer, is likewise successful only in parts. Structurally resembling both "St. James's Park" and "Timon," the poem describes scenes of foppery at the popular watering-place southeast of London. The speaker, presumably having left his familiar drinking com-

36. Vieth, *ARP*, p. 286. See also Wilson, *Court Wits*, p. 13, where Rochester's attitude is that of the "refined courtier sneering at the crude ways of his social inferiors," and Thorpe, p. 186.

panions, goes to the Wells himself to take the cure, but, overwhelmed by the ridiculous shapes of humanity to be found there, flees in disgust. In this poem, furthermore, Rochester develops the tendency hinted at in the earlier two poems toward satire of the libertine speaker himself.

Disgust is not enough, however, to produce an interesting poem. The satire is both structurally uninteresting and thematically ununified. Consisting simply of a series of brief episodes, the structure might well be called picaresque, in that the hero, a libertine rogue, passes from one group of fools to another. The episodes are linked by the device of his disgusted flight:

> Endeavoring this irksome sight to balk,
> And a more irksome noise, their silly talk,
> I silently slunk down t' th' Lower Walk
>
> . . . .
>
> From hence unto the upper end I ran
>
> . . . .
>
> Amidst the crowd next I myself conveyed
>
> . . . .
>
> Tired with this dismal stuff, away I ran
> [ll. 25–27, 41, 76, 114]

Each episode consists of a satirical attack on one or another kind of folly. Since Rochester has no organizing principle to relate closely each kind of foolishness — as Pope organizes the second *Moral Essay* by stressing first the changeableness of women and next their love of pleasure and sway — the result is inevitably an arbitrarily arranged series of fragments. The speaker satirizes in turn affectation (in the bawling fop who would be a wit and the grave fool), clerical corruption, awkward boobishness, infertility and cuckoldry, boisterous swaggering, and even — what the vic-

tims cannot help — being born ugly or Irish. The most witty
piece of satire is the most effective, a description of the woo-
ing ritual of awkward booby and forward damsel:

> Here waiting for gallant, young damsel stood,
> Leaning on cane, and muffled up in hood.
> The would-be wit, whose business was to woo,
> With hat removed and solemn scrape of shoe
> Advanceth bowing, then genteelly shrugs,
> And ruffled foretop into order tugs,
> And thus accosts her: "Madam, methinks the weather
> Is grown much more serene since you came hither.
> You influence the heavens; but should the sun
> Withdraw himself to see his rays outdone
> By your bright eyes, they would supply the morn,
> And make a day before the day be born."
> [ll. 86–97]

Rochester displays a sure sense of comic concrete detail (the
scrape of shoe, the tug of the forelock) that reveals a dramatic imagination. The movement of the verse seems to imitate the gallant's formal but clumsy preparations, lunging
gracelessness, and breathless delivery of the hoary set compliment. The damsel is equally well realized:

> With mouth screwed up, conceited [37] winking eyes,
> And breasts thrust forward, "Lord, sir!" she replies.
> "It is your goodness, and not my deserts,
> Which makes you show this learning, wit, and parts."
> He, puzzled, bites his nail, both to display
> The sparkling ring, and think what next to say,
> And thus breaks forth afresh: "Madam, egad!
> Your luck at cards last night was very bad:
> At cribbage fifty-nine, and the next show

37. Either "vain" or possibly "seized with a twitch" (*OED*, conceit,
sense 9). The latter is supported by a variant reading recorded in Pinto,
Poems, p. 90: "awkward."

To make the game, and yet to want those two.
God damn me, madam, I'm the son of a whore
If in my life I saw the like before!"
To peddler's stall he drags her, and her breast
With hearts and such-like foolish toys he dressed;
And then, more smartly to expound the riddle
Of all his prattle, gives her a Scotch fiddle.

[ll. 98–113]

Again, the comic detail of gesture makes the scene perfectly visualized. The wooers become the more ludicrous for the way that gestures and language are apparently ill-matched. The thrusting damsel delivers a properly polite (and trite) reply. Nevertheless, the little speech ill conceals her interest in other than mental parts. The gallant, too, lapses back into his native idiom after exhausting his supply of wit: "God damn me, madam, I'm the son of a whore." The movement of the entire scene, from the polite formalities (and pretenses) of courtship to the expression of crude feelings, is repeated in the final lines: the gallant gives his lady first a heap of toys and trinkets, and then a Scotch fiddle, that is, an itch (to be sexually relieved).

In the other episodes, consistently less brilliant than this one, the comedy is darker and more scornful. No single principle, not even affectation or unnaturalness, a central libertine complaint, is invoked. Indeed, nature herself becomes a satirist:

To make him more ridiculous, in spite,
Nature contrived the fool should be a knight.

. . . .

No spleen or malice need on them be thrown:
Nature has done the business of lampoon,
And in their looks their characters has shown.

. . . .

Nature has placed these wretches beneath scorn:
They can't be called so vile as they are born.
[ll. 17–18, 22–24, 74–75]

We are being led to the mood of the "Satyr Against Mankind." Tunbridge Wells, like St. James's Park, is "The rendezvous of fools, buffoons, and praters, / Cuckholds, whores, citizens, their wives and daughters" (ll. 4–5). In one episode the speaker finds himself "amidst the crowd":

But ne'er could conventicle, play, or fair
For a true medley, with this herd compare.
Here lords, knights, squires, ladies and countesses,
Chandlers, mum-bacon women, sempstresses
Were mixed together, nor did they agree
More in their humors than their quality.
[ll. 80–85]

All men are fools; there are no models of rational behavior.

Nor does the libertine speaker offer any norm, as he himself realizes. He gives us no reason not to think him as ridiculous as the rest of humanity. He goes off to Tunbridge Wells, "the rendezvous of fools," for the cure of an illness. Like the "Bear Garden ape, on his steed mounted," and the boisterous cadets, swaggeringly mounted on "cast-off Spavined horse[s]," he too had "mount[ed]" steed that morning to trot to the waters. His own affinity with the ape, while not openly admitted, seems to be the immediate impulse to the speaker's final declaration of man's ridiculousness:

Bless me! thought I, what thing is man, that thus
In all his shapes, he is ridiculous?
Ourselves with noise of reason we do please
In vain: humanity's our worst disease.
Thrice happy beasts are, who, because they be
Of reason void, are so of foppery.
Faith, I was so ashamed that with remorse

I used the insolence to mount my horse;
For he, doing only things fit for his nature,
Did seem to me by much the wiser creature.
[ll. 166–175]

Ironically, the speaker exits from the scene mounted on his horse, apparently fully aware now ("I used the insolence") of his resemblance to the Bear Garden ape. This poem clearly stands as a link between the early satires, "St. James's Park" and "Timon," where a libertine satirizes the world, and the "Satyr Against Mankind." Beginning as an attack by a libertine speaker on the follies of humanity, "Tunbridge Wells" concludes by counting the libertine among the fools. The speaker now quite consciously satirizes himself. Yet, if for nothing else, we appreciate him for the knowledge of his own folly that now distinguishes him from the rest of ridiculous humanity.

"The Maimed Debauchee" (c. 1675) and "To the Postboy" (?1676)

In the three early satires, written between 1672 and 1674, Rochester, as we have seen, directed his satiric attack against the corruptions and perversions of the social world, pointedly presenting a libertine speaker who is dissociated — yet perhaps not completely — from those corruptions. In the third of the satires, "Tunbridge Wells," that speaker himself is clearly included among the foolish and ridiculous shapes of man. Self-satire continued to interest Rochester, both in the "Satyr Against Mankind" (1675), where the attack is universal, and in two slighter, yet very effective, pieces written also during the period 1675 to 1676. In "The Maimed Debauchee" [38] and "To the Postboy," respectively, a dissolute

38. Vieth prints the title "The Disabled Debauchee" as found in five early MSS. The traditional "Maimed Debauchee," found in the 1680 editions and all subsequent printed editions, is more mock-heroic, more concrete, suggesting specifically a damaged limb.

and outrageous libertine speaker wittily exposes his own foolishness and proud viciousness. Other similarities also suggest that the poems be considered together. The speakers of these poems present themselves boastfully as heroically bad, employing, at several points, similar phrasing, and alluding to similar events. On the other hand, the tone and genre of the two satires are markedly different: in the former, gay mock-heroic, in the latter, vehement rogue's confession.

"The Maimed Debauchee" is an address by a dissolute rake to his fellow revelers, in which the speaker imagines his future "days of impotence," when, good for nothing else, he will advise and exhort young rakes to "important mischief." But Rochester is interested in more than satire of libertinism. As one of his earliest critics took for granted, the poem is in part a parody of contemporary heroic poems. Rymer makes the acute observation that Rochester's typical mode is inversion or parody:

No imagination cou'd bound or prescribe whither his Fights would carry him: were the subject light, you find him a Philosopher, grave and profound, to wonder: were the Subject lumpish and heavy, then wou'd his Mercury dissolve all into gaiety and Diversion. You wou'd take his Monkey for a Man of Metaphysicks; and his Gondibert he sends with all that Grimace to demolish Windows, or do some the like Important Mischief.[39]

That Rymer refers to "The Maimed Debauchee" is evidenced by "demolish Windows" and "Important Mischief." [40] He calls the satire by the name of Davenant's unfinished heroic poem, because it is written in a meter which *Gondi-*

39. *Poems* (London, 1691), preface, p. A4. Under the title of "The Maimed Debauchee" Pope wrote in his copy of Rochester's *Poems* (1696), p. 97, "With allusion to Gondibert." I am indebted to the Berg Collection of the New York Public Library (which owns Pope's Rochester) for permission to quote this notation by Pope.
40. See ll. 35–36, 41–42.

bert (1651) had made popular for mid-century works of epic and panegyric,[41] and in a manner which mocks heroic compliment, elevated language, and lofty conceptions of human dignity.[42]

Gondibert was not, of course, Rochester's sole target. In 1655 had appeared Waller's *Panegyric on my Lord Protector*, which, while written in quatrains of two couplets rather than alternating rhyme, purveyed the same kind of epic huffing. Let the Muses, says Waller,

> Tell of towns stormed, of armies overrun,
> And mighty kingdoms by your conduct won;
> How, while you thundered, clouds of dust did choke
> Contending troops, and seas lay hid in smoke.

Rochester, at the other extreme, had satirized his king ("I hate all kings and the thrones they sit on, / From the hector of France to the cully of Britain"),[43] and had parodied, as we have seen, Waller's elegant description of St. James's Park. There is no cause for surprise, then, to find him parodying Waller's *Panegyric:*

> I'll tell of whores attacked, their lords at home;
> Bawds' quarters beaten up, and fortress won;
> Windows demolished, watches overcome;
> And handsome ills by my contrivance done.
>
> [ll. 33–36]

Further provocation to satire was provided by Dryden, whose poetic career began with panegyric. His *Heroic Stanzas* in memory of Cromwell (1659) are written in Waller's

41. See Hobbes's approval of this meter as proper for epic, "Answer to Davenant," Spingarn, 2:57. Hobbes translated Homer into alternate rhyme quatrains in 1675.

42. Rochester was not the first poet to satirize *Gondibert*. See *Certain Verses Written by several of the Authors Friends; to be reprinted with the 2nd edition of Gondibert* (London, 1653).

43. "Satyr upon Charles II," ll. 32–33.

mode and in the *Gondibert* meter.[44] Rochester probably knew the poem, but preferred to spend his wit against a later poem in the same meter, *Annus Mirabilis* (1666). This panegyric describes the extended sea battle in June and July 1666 between Holland and the English forces under the Duke of Albemarle and Prince Rupert, and the heroic behavior of the City of London during the Great Fire. What was, in fact, an indecisive battle, Dryden describes as a heroic struggle between the forces of light and dark.

> In thriving arts long time had Holland grown,
> Crouching at home and cruel when abroad;
> Scarce leaving us the means to claim our own;
> Our king they courted, and our merchants aw'd.
>
> [st. 1]

We can be certain that Rochester laughed at such inflated rhetoric, particularly when we remember that as a younger man he had himself served at sea in both 1665 and 1666, during the Second Dutch War and in the very battle Dryden describes. Although the young Rochester found war fashionable, the same man ten years later considered war and politics a silly sham,[45] and probably looked back contemptuously on his own youthful adventure. The opening stanzas of Rochester's poem parody the heroic idiom of *Annus Mirabilis*. Scattered lines from Dryden's panegyric are echoed in Rochester's satire so as to mock the heroic posturing. The words of the speaker, imagining himself as a retired "brave admiral," may recall the old admiral in Dryden's poem:

44. See Dryden's praise of the heroic dignity of alternate rhyme in the preface to *Annus Mirabilis*. *Of Dramatic Poesy and Other Critical Essays*, 2 vols., ed. G. Watson, (London, 1962).

45. See the epigram on Louis XIV's expansionist policies (*Complete Poems*, p. 21), a drinking song scorning the Dutch War (*Complete Poems*, p. 52), and the scorn of ambitious Louis ("The French Fool, that wanders up and down / Starving his people, hazarding his crown") in the "Satyr upon Charles II."

> Our dreaded admiral from far they threat,
> Whose batter'd riggings their whole war receives,
> All bare, like some old oak which tempests beat,
> He stands, and sees below his scatter'd leaves.
>
> [st. 61]

So, too, Rochester's admiral surveys "the wise and daring conduct of the fight," but from "the top of an adjacent hill," rather than from the deck. Dryden's seamen are so eager that in their sleep they dream of battling the foe: "In fiery dreams the Dutch they still destroy, / And, slumb'ring, smile at the imagin'd flame" (st. 69). Rochester's admiral likewise imagines himself in battle: "Transported, thinks himself amidst the foes, / And absent, yet enjoys the bloody day" (ll. 11–12).[46] In the clichéd and heroic description, wounded sailors, unwilling to leave the battle, are forced to go ashore (st. 74), like Rochester's retired rake, "Forced from the pleasing billows of debauch / On the dull shore of lazy temperance" (ll. 15–16). Dryden's "important quarrel" — "Straight to the Dutch he turns his dreadful prow, / More fierce th'important quarrel to decide" (st. 66) — becomes Rochester's "important mischief": "With tales like these I will such thoughts inspire / As to important mischief shall incline" (ll. 41–42). While no single parallel is convincingly close, they produce a cumulative effect of mockery directed against heroic panegyrical poetry.

Against a background of heroic action and lofty detachment[47] — and in mockery of it — the rake stands. At the

---

46. Compare also "when absent, yet we conquer'd in his sight," *Heroic Stanzas*, st. 24.

47. Rochester may indirectly parody the withdrawn philosopher, like Lucretius, whose detachment is only a cover, so Rochester would say, for his inability to participate in the active life. At the beginning of Bk. 2 of *De Rerum Natura* Lucretius praises (in a famous, much-quoted passage) the serene sanctuaries of philosophy:

> 'Tis pleasant, safely to behold from shore
> The rowling Ship; and hear the Tempest roar;
> Not that another's pain is our delight;
> But pains unfelt produce the pleasing sight.

same time he stands in mockery of himself. The comparison between rake and heroic statesman works, in fact, to discredit both. He is moved to address his fellow debauchees (so suggests the heading in an early manuscript) by a temporary illness and enforced temperance,[48] and so realizes that one day he will be superannuated and forced to retire altogether from the "pleasing billows of debauch." He does not shrink from naming the causes of his future decline — "my days of impotence," "pox, and wine's unlucky chance" — though he dresses them out in elegant phrases. Flaunting its scandalousness, he enjoys already the part he one day will play:

> Nor let the sight of honorable scars,
>> Which my too forward valor did procure,
> Frighten new-listed soldiers from the wars:
>> Past joys have more than paid what I endure.
>>> [ll. 21–24]

The scars of syphilis, in the rake's impudent scheme, are the equivalent of the old warrior's wounds. His tales of past exploits — "whores attacked . . . bawds' quarters beaten up" — will fire the blood of any "cold-complexioned sot."

> . . . .
> But much more sweet thy lab'ring steps to guide,
> To vertues heights, with wisdom well supply'd
>
> . . . .
> From thence to look below on Humane kind,
> Bewilder'd in the Maze of Life, and blind.
>> [Dryden's translation]

Unlike Lucretius, Rochester's admiral does not scorn foolish humanity, and his self-congratulation, unlike Lucretius's, is tinged with self-mockery. See also the scorn of retired philosophers in the "Satyr Against Mankind," ll. 90–93.

48. "Upon his lying in and could not drink," Yale MS. See *ARP*, p. 384. Did Rochester perhaps mean "The Maimed Debauchee" as an answer to Buckhurst's good-natured lampoon against him, "I rise at eleven, I dine about two," entitled in an early manuscript "The Debauch" and in a 1714 edition "The Debauchee"? The lampoon is quoted at the beginning of Chapter III.

Nor shall our love-fits, Chloris, be forgot,
    When each the well-looked linkboy strove t'enjoy,
And the best kiss was the deciding lot
    Whether the boy fucked you, or I the boy.

[ll. 37–40]

One of the least interesting responses to these lines (and indeed to the whole poem) is to condemn the speaker's immorality. While it is true that the additional and more explicit details of debauch stretch the prettifying powers of euphemism, Rochester's purpose is not to have a destructive rake unwittingly expose his own corruption. The speaker is perfectly aware of the impudent immorality of his "handsome ills"; an unconscious violator of traditional norms might have said "handsome deeds." Furthermore, the rake shows clearly, in the poem's last stanza especially, an unillusioned view of his own heroic pretenses:

Thus, statesmanlike, I'll saucily impose,
    And safe from action, valiantly advise;
Sheltered in impotence, urge you to blows,
    And being good for nothing else, be wise.

Each line is a reminder of what the rake will one day be no longer able to accomplish; it becomes clearest in the final line that the role of honored advisor, however much it has been glorified, will be adopted *faute de mieux*.

The conclusion thus exhibits affinities with the cynical tradition which holds — in the manner of La Rochefoucauld — that all human virtue is *faute de mieux*. Chastity is a product of lack of opportunity and railing at vice a sign of the inability to enjoy it.[49] Such libertine cynicism is here directed, however, not against the pious, but against the libertine himself. Yet Rochester shows that the rake's

49. Compare Rochester's use of this tradition in the epilogue to *Circe* (1677), *Complete Poems*, p. 140.

clear-sightedness is at least one thing in his favor. To this end the parodies of the heroic tradition are instrumental. The poem suggests that the retired admiral and the elder statesman are fooling themselves if they do not realize, as the disabled debauchee does, that the alleged honor or serenity of their positions is a polite front, in one sense at least, for their impotence or failure to perform as their younger successors do.

The speaker's lighthearted heroic impudence and self-mockery in "The Maimed Debauchee" can be interestingly compared to the speaker's attitude in "To the Postboy." The heroic tradition works here not as an object of satire but figures, nonetheless, in conveying the picture of a heroically bad rake. The speaker, specified as Rochester himself, turns on his own libertinism with bitter vengeance, and prepares to fling himself to hell: "Son of a whore, God damn you! can you tell / A peerless peer the readiest way to Hell?" (ll. 1–2). Vieth, who notes that Rochester is "working in the tradition propagated by the lampoons written against him," calls the poem "half-boastful, half-penitential."[50] The phrase is apt, though it perhaps exaggerates the penitence:

> I've outswilled Bacchus, sworn of my own make
> Oaths would right Furies, and make Pluto quake;
> I've swived more whores more ways than Sodom's walls
> E'er knew, or the College of Rome's Cardinals.
> Witness *heroic scars* — Look here, ne'er go! —
> Cerecloths and ulcers from the top to toe!
> Frighted at my own mischiefs, I have fled
> And bravely left my life's defender dead;
> *Broke houses* to break chastity, and dyed
> That floor with murder which my lust denied.
> Pox on't, why do I speak of these poor things?
> I have blasphemed my God, and libeled Kings!
> [ll. 3–14, emphasis added]

50. *ARP*, pp. 202–203.

Though Rochester does not deck out his confession in fine-sounding periphrases ("pleasing billows of debauch," "handsome ills)" he boasts nonetheless of epic achievements. "Heroic scars," here displayed as proof of combat, are the debauchee's "honorable scars." This time the cerecloths and ulcers declare more plainly the rake's pox-ravaged body. "Mischief" is viewed in this poem with less gaiety, perhaps because Rochester suffers some remorse for his cowardly part in the brawl that led to the death of Downs, an event apparently referred to in lines 9–10. The attack on the "bawds' quarters" in "The Maimed Debauchee" (ll. 33–35) is matched in this poem by an assault on the home of chaste women, leading not to "watches overcome" but to murder. Unlike the debauchee's convivial address to his fellows, however, this poem is a mighty confession by a peerless peer of the most lurid and Satanic of vices, delivered, with ludicrous appropriateness, to a postboy. The boy's witty and chillingly Mephistophelian answer, furthermore —

R.   The readiest way to Hell — Come, quick!
Boy.   Ne'er Stir:
      The readiest way, my Lord, 's by Rochester.
                              [ll. 15–16]

— prevents us from taking the confession as completely sincere remorse. It is self-punishment but at the same time — as if to outdo Don Juan — the last heroically outrageous act of sending oneself defiantly (not defeated or repentant) to hell.

In the context of Rochester's other satires, this poem stands out as the most theatrical of all. The pose is indeed that of Don Juan — another housebreaker, seducer, drunkard, murderer, and blasphemer — who in Shadwell's exactly contemporaneous play *The Libertine* (1676) remains defiant and unrepentant to the end. "I'll break your marble body in pieces and pull down your Horse," he snorts at the threatening statue. Indeed, Rochester's poem may have been prompted by a remark in Shadwell's play made to Don John, boasting of rapes and murders, by his cowardly servant: "I cannot but admire, since you are resolv'd to go to the Devil, that you cannot be content with the common way of travelling, but must ride post to him" (2:1). It may have been prompted, too, by Rochester's recognition of the striking similarity between his own notorious career (capped by the recent exploit at Epsom) and that of the legendary Don Juan.[51]

The "Heroical Epistle" (c. 1675–1676)

Having moved from satirical observer to self-observer and self-satirist, the libertine becomes basic subject matter in two later poems, "A Very Heroical Epistle in Answer to Ephelia" and "An Epistolary Essay from M.G. to O.B. upon their Mutual Poems," in several ways the most interesting (because most controversial) of Rochester's major satires. In both poems we can see a shifting, ambivalent combination of satire and sympathy toward a libertine speaker who argues a persuasive case for egoism in love and poetry. Critics have, with one exception, largely misjudged the two satires, forcing them into one mold or its antithesis, not content to allow the typically Rochesterian complexities full play.

In the first of the poems the speaker (Bajazet),[52] answering his cast-off mistress, cleverly defends his natural inconstancy. Having dismissed her claims, he imagines the ideal life of the "happy Sultan," never plagued with the reproachful complaints of his harem women.

There have been, roughly, two antithetical views of the "Heroical Epistle," as of the "Epistolary Essay." The first view is the older one, held by the essentially biographical

51. For further similarities between Rochester and Don Juan, see Chapter III.

52. Bajazet is, in fact, not named in the title or the text of Rochester's poem, but it is clear (see below, p. 59) that he is the speaker.

scholars Prinz and Pinto, that Rochester in this poem, speaking in *propria persona*, boldly confesses an egoistic outlook. Thus Prinz says (p. 212) of Rochester the man: "His conception of life was egocentric. 'In my dear self I center ev'rything' he makes his Bajazet write to Ephelia, and we may suppose that these words have the value of a self-confession." Pinto takes a similar line: "He had accepted the materialism of Hobbes and had applied it to the art of living. It led logically to complete egoism, and in one of his poems this egoism is stated frankly and with a boldness that must have shocked many who practiced it in their lives, but who never had the courage to admit such principles openly." [53]

Vieth, on the other hand, drawing on a biographical discovery by J. H. Wilson connecting the Earl of Mulgrave with the poem, and on the notion of the ironic persona, has more recently offered a detailed reading of the poem as a satire on Mulgrave (elaborating, in effect, the reading first proposed by Wilson):[54] "The satire of the Heroical Epistle," Vieth says, "works through Bajazet's unconscious violation of implicit norms, the poem's thematic center being an ironic inversion of that aggregate of traditional ideas well known to literary scholars under the term 'degree.' " [55] Not only does Vieth wish us to read the poem as an expression of views antithetical to Rochester's, but he also wishes us to see in Bajazet an unconscious violator of traditional values, rather than the daring, fully conscious Hobbist-libertine of Prinz and Pinto.[56]

Both the older and the new interpretations seem to me extreme. I would argue that at least two other positions may be staked out between them, which are perhaps closer to Rochester's purposes. It is probable (but not certain)

53. *Enthusiast in Wit*, p. 148.
54. *Court Wits*, pp. 117–118.
55. *ARP*, p. 109.
56. Vieth's reading has been adopted by George Lord: "Rochester employs the oblique device of the candid declaration to satirize the complacency and arrogance of the Earl of Mulgrave." *POAS*, 1:345.

that the poem was written, in part, as Narcissus Luttrell noted, "Ag^t ye E Mulgrave." [57] But viewing the poem as either mere confession or mere ironical satire fails, to take into account details of phrasing and feeling, and the poem's shifting tones and ironies. I suggest that the "Heroical Epistle" can be viewed partly as a playful virtuoso-piece in celebration of inconstancy and an indulgence in sensual fantasy. At the same time, Rochester seems to be testing the logical implications of an egotistic ethic he knows full well to be unorthodox yet universally appealing. Satire on a strutting egotist gives way to sympathetic understanding and, perhaps, identification.

Quite apart from its problematic biographical context, the poem's literary context is simpler to describe. The "Heroical Epistle" belongs, most broadly, to the genre of Ovidian love epistle, a form very popular in the seventeenth

57. Four pieces of evidence connect the poem with Mulgrave: (1) The final lines seem to refer to Mulgrave's affair with Mall Kirke (see Vieth's note), but the context would suggest that some sympathy is being evoked for the speaker. (2) "My blazing star" (l. 21) may pun on Mulgrave's recently granted Star of the Garter (see Vieth's note), but the context is strongly astrological. "Blazing Star" was a current technical term for a comet. (3) The nickname Bajazet was applied to Mulgrave in other poems (*ARP*, pp. 337–338). But Mulgrave was not known by the name before this poem (*Court Wits*, pp. 117, 119). Bajazet may have been chosen as a proud nobleman who later finds himself powerless and humbled in comparison to an eastern ruler. (4) At its first printing, the poem was entitled (on a 1679 broadside) "A Very Heroical Epistle from my Lord All-Pride to Dol-Common." Lord All-Pride was, from about 1679, one of Mulgrave's nicknames. On his copy of the broadside, beneath the argument to the "Heroical Epistle," Luttrell wrote "Ag^t ye E Mulgrave" (the original of this broadside is now in the Newbury Library, Chicago). However, the broadside title is repeated in no other surviving manuscript or printed edition. The printer may possibly have been misinformed, or may have deliberately retitled an old poem in order to capitalize on interest in the renewed Rochester-Mulgrave quarrel. Luttrell may offer no independent evidence. Perhaps he only glosses "All-Pride." On the other hand, he was a reliable and well-informed witness (see J. M. Osborn, "Reflections on Narcissus Luttrell [1657–1732]," *Book Collector* 6 [1957], pp. 15–27) and his testimony should be accepted until stronger evidence appears.

century. The model is Ovid's *Heroides,* a series of fictitious
letters from grieving, guilty, or bitter women forsaken by
or separated from their lovers and husbands. Ovid's epistles,
together with "answers," were often translated and imitated
in the Restoration.[58] The answer poems increased the range
of attitudes toward love: they were used, for example, not
only to declare passion, offer comfort, and promise constancy, but also to extenuate or justify inconstancy.

Within this broad genre of the Ovidian epistle, and the
narrower genre of answers to Ovidian women, Rochester's
poem answers a specific poem, Etherege's "Ephelia to Bajazet" (c. 1675), with which it was often printed. In her
letter, Ephelia complained, in Ovidian style,[59] of Bajazet's
unfaithfulness, the broken vows and cooling passions of the
"great Man" in whom "I center'd all my hopes of bliss."
Rochester's Bajazet wittily responds, claiming he deceived
no one,[60] often echoing Ephelia's phrases, usually with a
clever transformation of her meaning,[61] defending his behavior as appropriate to the "great." [62] When viewed in this

58. In 1680, Tonson published *Ovids Epistles Translated by Several
Hands,* with a preface by Dryden and a list of famous contributors.
Some of the translations may have been made in the early 1670s.

59. The style of an Ovidian heroical epistle, wrote Dryden in the
Preface to the Tonson edition, "is tenderly passionate and courtly, two
properties well agreeing with the Persons, which were Heroines, and
Lovers." (1776 ed., n.p.).

60. Ephelia's opening line, "How far are they deceived who hope
in vain," is answered by "If you're deceived, it is not by my cheat,"
which turns her charge into a case of *self*-deception.

61. When she complains, "Oh! can the coldness that you show me
now /Suit with the gen'rous heat you once did show?" (ll. 48–49), he
answers "You may as justly at the sun repine / Because alike it does not
always shine" (ll. 18–19). Her lament that "our passions were so favored
by Fate, / As if she meant 'em an eternal date" (ll. 7–8) reappears as
his "fatal" star (l. 22), both "fated" (relieving him of responsibility)
and "disastrous" (explaining Ephelia's downfall). "Since when you've
been the star by which I steer'd" (l. 44) Bajazet reinterprets so as to
convert a conventional image of constancy (Shakespeare's "star to every
wandering bark") into an image of glorious *in*constancy, transforming
the fixed star into a comet or "blazing star."

62. Bajazet's "For all disguises are below the great," in one sense

light, as a devilishly cavalier answer to a complaining, cast-off mistress, with the tradition of the Ovidian love epistles in the background, the paired poems of Etherege and Rochester form a self-contained whole, requiring no external reference, to Mulgrave for example, to explain their comic appeal.[63]

The poem needs to be viewed in another way as well, to bring out its literary relations. Bajazet's answer takes the form of a defense of inconstancy, a standard posture in libertine love songs and stage comedy. Bajazet's arguments from change in nature and from fate are anticipated, for example, in Cowley and in one of Rochester's early love songs, "A Dialogue between Strephon and Daphne." Strephon, who later has the tables turned on him, defends his inconstancy:

> Love, like us, must fate obey.
> Since 'tis nature's law to change,
> Constancy alone is strange.
> See the heavens in lightnings break,
> Next in storms of thunder speak,
> Till a kind rain from above
> Makes a calm — so 'tis in love.
>
> [ll. 30–36]

Bajazet argues in similar (and conventional) fashion:

> 'Tis as natural to change, as love.
> You may as justly at the sun repine
> Because alike it does not always shine.
> No glorious thing was ever made to stay.
>
> [ll. 17–20]

impudently vain, in fact adopts Ephelia's words: "So great his passion was. . . . When this great man. . . . Thou greatest, loveliest, falsest man" (ll. 15, 27, 35).

63. In a sense, the Ephelia-Bajazet poems burlesque the Ovidian epistle, but are unrelated to the contemporary "travesties" of Ovid.

He supplements his case with the traditional argument that constant change is a kind of constancy:

> What man or woman upon earth can say
> I ever used 'em well above a day?
> How is it, then, that I inconstant am?
> He changes not who is always the same.
>
> [ll. 3–6]

In the light of libertine conventions, Bajazet does not unconsciously violate standards (as Vieth would have it) or daringly confess egotism (in Pinto's terms), but strikes a traditional pose. Yet the pose is far more than a series of libertine clichés. Bajazet's answers restate the standard arguments with great flair, and pretended plain-dealing. Furthermore, the conventions themselves, as we shall see, are viewed as ironically inadequate to experience.

Bajazet's address to Ephelia falls into four parts, in each of which he offers a different defense of his behavior. He begins with a profession of openness — "Madam, if you're deceived, it is not by my cheat, / For all disguises are below the great" — and, as we have seen, the argument that constant change is a kind of constancy. He then argues from a theory of heroic greatness:

> In my dear self I center everything: [64]
> My servants, friends, my mistress, and my King;
> Nay, heaven and earth to that one point I bring.
> Well mannered, honest, generous, and stout
> (Names by dull fools to plague mankind found out)

64. Perhaps a parody of a love song compliment as well as an "answer" to Ephelia. Compare Sedley's "All that in woman is ador'd / In thy dear self I find" (V. de S. Pinto, *The Poetical and Dramatic Works of Sir Charles Sedley*, 2 vols. [1928] 1:7); Lee's *Princess of Cleve* (*The Works of Nathaniel Lee*, ed. T. B. Stroup and A. L. Cooke, 2 vols. [New Brunswick, 1954–1955], 2:180).

> Should I regard, I must myself constrain,
> And 'Tis my maxim to avoid all pain.
>
> [ll. 7–13]

As has been pointed out, the first lines perhaps echo Dryden's Preface to *Aureng-Zebe* (Feb. 1675/6) addressed to Mulgrave. Dryden compares court life, wrongly called the "great" world, to the private solitude of a garden and the conversation of friends: "True greatness, if it be anywhere on earth, is in a private virtue removed from the notion of pomp and vanity, confined to a contemplation of itself, and centering upon itself." [65] While the line "In my dear self I center everything" may be meant to satirize Mulgrave's acceptance of Dryden's flattering dedicatory preface, it can be read without complete irony as a parody of an ancient ideal. A kind of self-centeredness lies at the basis of the strong seventeenth-century tradition of Epicurean withdrawal from the public life to private pleasures. Rochester's mind, with a taste for paradox, here may be demonstrating the logical extreme of an attitude respectable enough to attract, among others, Cowley and Sir William Temple. Viewed another way, absolute self-centeredness is perhaps the inevitable consequence of a morality based, like Rochester's, on gratification of the senses.[66] The line may indeed be a libertine's honest admission.

It has not been noticed that the libertine Bajazet, in the middle lines of this passage, appears to insult values which would normally be held by libertine and conventional moralist alike. Rochester's purposes, and his irony (if any), are here difficult to measure. Either Bajazet scorns "dull fools"

65. *POAS*, 1:345. See *Works of Dryden*, ed. Sir Walter Scott, rev. George Saintsbury (London, 1892), 1:339. Contrast Whichcote's warning that man should never "center himself in himself." *Select Sermons*, ed. Shaftesbury (1698), p. 213.

66. Burnet, p. 37. "That he should do nothing to the hurt of any other," another maxim of his morality, might be (and was) easily forgotten in the pursuit of sensual gratification.

and the "names" [67] (representing virtues difficult to practice)
they set up, as if deliberately, to "plague mankind" (in this
reading Bajazet is satirized); or, Bajazet sacrifices the principles of honesty and generosity ordinarily endorsed by a
libertine, to more important ones — "follow one's own nature" and "avoid pain." He avoids constraining or forcing
his true nature; constraint is not only unnatural, it is painful, and a good Epicurean instinctively avoids pain. In this
reading, Bajazet's libertine logic compels a kind of sympa
thetic assent.

In the next lines (14–23) he argues for inconstancy, as we
have already seen, by analogy with natural change, and in
a fourth section, punning on "change," argues that love is
merely a financial transaction:

> The boasted favor you so precious hold
> To me's no more than changing of my gold; [68]
> Whate'er you gave, I paid you back in bliss;
> Then where's the obligation, pray, of this?
> If heretofore you found grace in my eyes,
> Be thankful for it, and let that suffice.
> But women, beggar-like, still haunt the door
> Where they've received a charity before.
>
> [ll. 24–31]

By a kind of audacious and perverse logic, Ephelia's "boasted
favor" (her virginity) is fairly exchanged for bliss, both

67. See Hobbes's scorn of "names" that signify nothing, in *Leviathan*, ch. 5, and Lee's *Nero* (1674), 1:2: "Virtue's a Name! Religion's a
thing / Fitter to scare poor priests than daunt a King." Dryden's Preface to *Aureng-Zebe* attacks the pretense of honesty: "Another disguise
[courtiers] have (for fools as well as knaves take other names, and pass
by an alias), and that is, the title of honest fellows."
68. Compare Rochester's early Ovidian poem "The Advice." "Cher-
ish the trade [i.e., love], for as with Indians we / Get gold and jewels
for our trumpery, / So to each other, for their useless toys, / Lovers afford whole magazines of joys. / But if you're fond of baubles, be, and
starve" (ll. 43–47). Where this lover is tartly threatening, Bajazet is
playfully superior.

spiritual and physical. In the next lines, Bajazet invokes the same conception of royal immunity which Dryden finds in Montaigne: "It is a severe reflection which Montaigne has made on princes, that we ought not, in reason, to have any expectations of favour from them: and that it is kindness enough, if they leave us in possession of our own." [69] Having been granted the favor of Bajazet's kind looks,[70] she ought to consider herself lucky. We may deplore Bajazet's heartlessness, yet at the same time smile with delight at his exultant, virtuoso impudence.

Having disposed of Ephelia with a contempt both egotistical and principled, so as to invite a mixture of disapprobation and sympathetic admiration for his witty display, Bajazet suddenly abandons the epistolary form for a reverie-like address to the "happy Sultan":

> O happy Sultan, whom we barbarous call,
> How much refined art thou above us all!
> Who envies not the joys of thy serail?
> Thee like some god the trembling crowd adore;
> Each man's thy slave, and womankind thy whore.
> Methinks I see thee, underneath the shade
> Of golden canopies supinely laid,
> Thy crouching slaves all silent as the night,
> But, at thy nod, all active as the light!
> Secure in solid sloth thou there dost reign,
> And feel'st the joys of love without the pain.
>
> [ll. 32–43]

It is a stunning reversal. The proud Bajazet is gradually revealed as an ordinary mortal beneath the cloak of boastful words, suffering like the woman he has just gaily repulsed, dreaming of a lover's paradise.

Only twice in this reverie does Rochester seem to view

69. *Dryden*, ed. Scott-Saintsbury, 1:335.
70. "Ephelia to Bajazet," ll. 11–12, 29–30, 32.

Bajazet with mocking irony. "Supinely laid" anticipates Fleckno's words to Shadwell in "MacFlecknoe" ("And spread in solemn state, supinely reign" [l. 28]) but the relaxation, both physical and mental, which the phrase implies, remains attractive. "Secure in solid sloth," likewise, anticipates the spirit of "Mature in dullness from thy tender years" ("MacFlecknoe," l. 16), yet the sultan's "secure" joys compare favorably with Bajazet's insecurity and "pains."

Despite a pained awareness of the gap between real and ideal, Bajazet can playfully spin out fantasies of luxuries and prerogatives he cannot enjoy:

> Each female courts thee with a wishing eye,
> Whilst thou with awful pride walk'st careless by,
> Till thy kind pledge at last marks out the dame
> Thou fanciest most to quench thy present flame.
>
> [ll. 43–46]

The offhand precision of "thy present flame" (borrowed from Waller)[71] adds a touch of dry wit, as does the casual terror behind the provisions for the sultan's undisturbed peace:

> No loud reproach nor fond unwelcome sound
> Of women's tongues thy sacred ear dares wound.
> If any do, a nimble mute straight ties
> The true love knot, and stops her foolish cries.
>
> [ll. 49–52]

That quiet is enforced by a mute is a neat stroke of irony. Ironically, too, the woman's cries are stopped with a true

71. "Should some brave Turk, that walks among / His twenty lasses, bright and young, / And beckons to the willing dame / Preferred to quench his present flame . . ." "Of Love," *Poems of Edmund Waller,* ed. G. Thorn-Drury, Muses' Library (1893; 2 vols., 1905), 1:87–88.

love knot,[72] perhaps a witty euphemism for the Turkish
strangler's bowstring.

From playfulness Bajazet turns back, at the poem's conclusion, to the painful memory of his own condition:

> Thou fear'st no injured kinsman's threatening blade,
> Nor midnight ambushes by rivals laid;
> While here with aching hearts our joys we taste,
> Disturbed by swords, like Damocles his feast.
>
> [ll. 53–56]

Whether or not the lines refer to Mulgrave, they undeni-
ably invoke our sympathy. With his defenses down, having
abandoned wit and swagger, Bajazet confesses his kinship
with all lovers ("*our* joys *we* taste"). "Aching hearts" makes
mere bravado of " 'Tis my maxim to avoid all pain." His
words ought to be compared with Rochester's lyric expression of the same feeling in "The Fall," a song that contrasts a state of sensual paradise before the Fall with the
"dull delights" of the speaker's imperfect love:

> But we, poor slaves to hope and fear,
> Are never of our joys secure;
> They lessen still as they draw near,
> And none but dull delights endure.
>
> [ll. 9–12]

The song reveals the same pained consciousness of enslavement and lack of security in love. In both poems the
imagined paradise is lost. Bajazet, in the first half of the
"Epistle," makes love sound like an egoist's paradise, but in
the latter half he reveals that he finds paradise beset with

72. A double-looped bow, or a knot formed by two loops inter-
twined, used as a symbol of true love (*OED*). Partridge gives for "tie the
true lover's knot" "to coit" (19th and 20th centuries). Rochester's line
may represent an unrecorded early usage of this euphemism.

dangers.[73] The poem thus furthers Rochester's exploration of man's painful, anxious state. The "Satyr" and the contemporary "Artemisia to Chloe" suggest that only exploiters escape pain. The "Heroical Epistle" suggests that even exploitive and tyrannical lovers suffer.

In sum, whether or not Mulgrave is involved, the "Heroical Epistle" is more than a simple confession or piece of ironic inversion. It displays many conventional characteristics — of the Ovidian heroical epistle, or the libertine defense of inconstancy — and some affinities with Rochester's love songs. It invites us both to deplore and to appreciate the impudent logic, the zany sweet reasonableness of libertinism, and then to recognize, wryly and ruefully, that even for the libertine egotist, love proves to be a Feast of Damocles.

The "Epistolary Essay" (c. 1679)

The "Epistolary Essay from M.G. to O.B. upon their Mutual Poems" has been rightly read as a companion piece to the "Heroical Epistle" and, like the earlier satire, has generated antithetical interpretations whose main lines will be familiar. Both poems purport to be letters from an outspoken libertine whose views about love and poetry seem boldly heterodox and egotistic. The speaker of the "Epistolary Essay" writes to a friend in praise of the latter's poems and in defense of his own writing. The older critics viewed the poem as an "intimate personal confession" and a declaration of literary principles:

73. The final line may conceal an irony. The sword that hung over Damocles' head presumably hung over the king, too, when *he* sat on the throne. Perhaps then the sultan himself (the equivalent now of Damocles' king) is less happy than Bajazet thinks. A popular tradition held that Eastern monarchs, proverbially omnipotent, enjoyed utter content. But one of Montaigne's themes is that kings are, in one sense, less happy than citizens. The "Grand Turke in his Seraille," for example, is deprived, through plenty, of the "sowre-sweet tickling" of love. *Essayes*, 1:300–301.

Rochester laid down the two main planks of his literary platform: 1) he would write to please himself and pay no heed to the "saucy censurers" of the Town, and 2) he would criticize the writings of others on the arrogant assumption that only his judgment was sound. Perhaps none of his friends would have stated the matter so bluntly, but they surely had the same independent spirits and highly developed egos.[74]

In this interpretation, Rochester, in his own voice, addresses Mulgrave just prior to their quarrel in 1669. More recent critics argue that the poem, written about 1679, is purportedly an address from Mulgrave to Dryden (another critic suggests Martin Clifford to Buckingham) and is intended as an ironical satire: "the self-centered speaker renders himself ridiculous by unconsciously violating traditional conceptions of good writing."[75]

In my view, the poem is neither unconscious self-exposure nor direct personal confession. "An Epistolary Essay" can be read as a knowing and playful celebration of an egoistic theory of writing,[76] a theory consisting of a number of principles, most of them reasonable in themselves, but here pushed to and beyond their usual logical limits. Such an interpretation shifts our attention, as in the reading of the "Heroical Epistle," from the identity of the speaker and his correspondent to the poem's ideas, allowing us to judge more disinterestedly their reasonableness. M.G. and O.B. may represent Mulgrave and Dryden, or perhaps Rochester and Buckingham, or another pair; the evidence for

74. Prinz, p. 118. See also pp. 176, 211; Wilson, *Court Wits*, p. 174; Thorpe, pp. 172–173; Hayward, p. 356; Pinto, *Poems*, pp. 191–92, stated more extensively in "John Wilmot, Earl of Rochester, and the Right Veine of Satire," in *Essays and Studies* (The English Association), new ser., 6 (1953), 56–70, and reaffirmed in *PQ*, 53 (1964), 381–384.

75. Vieth, *Complete Poems*, p. 144. See also *ARP*, pp. 104–136; Lord, *POAS*, 1:348; M. D. Palmer, "The Identity of 'M.G.' and 'O.B.,'" in *Modern Languages Notes*, 75 (1960), 644–647.

76. Egoistic, "regarding self-interest as the foundation of morality," usually entails egotistic, "conceited," but there is no agreed distinction in general use.

any given pair is not conclusive.[77] In any case, the poem is not simply an ironical satire on its speaker, whoever he is.[78]

Appropriately, the "Epistolary Essay" is personal, informal, and rambling. M.G., who has apparently failed to win the poetic "bays" he claims to have deserved, opens his letter by scorning the envious "saucy censurers" of the "dull age," and complimenting the poems of his friend, O.B., whom he seems to have served either as collaborator, patron, or host ("through me / They are partakers of your poetry"). He then turns casually to a description of himself and his principles of writing.

> I'm none of those who think themselves inspired,
> Nor write with the vain hopes to be admired,
> But from a rule I have upon long trial:
> T'avoid with care all sort of self-denial.
> Which way soe'er desire and fancy lead,
> Contemning fame, that path I boldly tread.
> And if, exposing what I take for wit,
> To my dear self a pleasure I beget,
> No matter though the censuring critic fret.
> Those whom my muse displeases are at strife
> With equal spleen against my course of life,

77. Against the theory that M.G. is Mulgrave, and the true author of "An Essay on Satyr," falsely attributed to O.B. — Dryden (who probably helped in revising the "Essay") — I offer these objections: (1) "Mutual Poems" may mean "respective" rather than "common," and thus refer to two separate but similar bodies of writing, possibly Rochester's and Buckingham's, not a single joint effort. (2) "Through me / They are partakers of your poetry" need not refer to Mulgrave's patronage of Dryden. It may simply suggest informal encouragement or hospitality, such as Rochester provided fellow poets at Woodstock Lodge (*Letters*, p. 49). (3) In November 1679 (Vieth's date for the "Epistolary Essay") Rochester thought the "Essay on Satyr" Dryden's, not Mulgrave's (*Letters*, p. 73).

78. Howard Erskine-Hill ("Rochester: Augustan or Explorer?", *Renaissance and Modern Essays presented to V. de S. Pinto*, ed. G. R. Hibbard [London, 1966], p. 63), who likewise challenges Vieth's view of the poem as consistent ironic inversion, finds the speaker "ambiguous," but he accepts the theory that M.G. and O.B. represent Mulgrave and Dryden.

The least delight of which I'd not forgo
For all the flattering praise man can bestow.
If I designed to please, the way were then
To mend my manners rather than my pen.
The first's unnatural, therefore unfit,
And for the second, I despair of it,
Since grace is not so hard to get as wit.

[ll. 12–29]

Vieth sees in these lines "a doctrine of unlimited self-indulgence in opposition to self-discipline or external restraint," arguing further that "the first half of the passage satirizes M.G.'s methods of writing by presenting them as ironic inversions of traditional standards which almost any Augustan would have considered essential to good poetry." [79] Setting aside the very doubtful assumption that Rochester is a doctrinaire Augustan, a reader need not conclude that even an Augustan like Pope could never have said as much. The principles of composition set forth here (that even fools can think themselves inspired, that writing for admiration and fame is contemptible, that a poet ought to reverence his own genius, that critics are splenetic and their judgments worthless) might well be held, in suitably moderated and qualified form, by any Augustan. What M.G. does is to present them without qualification, as part of a calmly considered and self-consciously egoistic theory that might well appeal to aristocratic, amateur, libertine poets such as Rochester and his friends.

Having scorned, in the "Satyr Against Mankind," the idea that man partakes of the divine, either as its image or through the gift of reason, Rochester here scorns, through M.G., the idea, used too often as an excuse for writing ill,[80] that poetry has a divine source. M.G. may here comically contra-

79. *ARP*, pp. 121, 122.
80. Compare Wolseley, *Preface to Valentinian*: "every Ass that's Romantick believes he's inspir'd." Spingarn, 3:12.

dict his earlier claim of writing "in poetic rage" (l. 3), unless that term, which can mean poetic inspiration, is taken
as satiric fury. Denying the divine, M.G. denies also the
social aspect of poetry: he writes not to be admired, but to
please himself, an attitude not so far from Horace's "Quis-
quis erit vitae scribam color" (*Satires* 2:1, l. 60).

Perhaps most egoistic — and seemingly ego*tistic* — are the
lines on "my dear self" (a pointed echo of the "Heroical Epistle") and the avoidance of "self-denial." Our first impulse is
to read the lines as satire,[81] an impulse seconded by Butler's
character of a "Small Poet": "When he writes he never proposes any Scope of Purpose to himself, but gives his Genius
all Freedom. For as he, that rides abroad for his Pleasure,
can hardly be out of his way; so he that writes for his Pleasure, can seldom be beside his Subject. It is an ungrateful
thing to a noble Wit to be confined to any Thing."[82] But
"dear self" seems to have been a cliché in the Restoration,
so that it would probably be used self-consciously by any
speaker.[83] Indeed, I think Rochester self-consciously and
seriously considers — at least for the moment — an idea
about genius which Butler mocks. To avoid self-denial implies on the one hand self-indulgence, but on the other, a
principled egoism. M.G.'s boldness courts our disapproval,
but invites us also to recall the libertine precept of following one's own "nature." "Avoid self-restraint," says the
libertin Pierre Forget: "never say or do anything that is
repugnant to your own genius." "Find out what is natural to
you, and never depart from it," advises La Rochefoucauld.[84]

81. Compare the attack on Scroope in the "Epistle to Julian," "To
his dear selfe of Poetry he talks." *Gyldenstolpe MS*, p. 206.

82. *Characters and Passages from Notebooks*, ed. A. R. Waller (Cambridge, 1908), p. 51.

83. Shadwell argues that poets can make people hate vice and folly
"not only in others, but (if it be possible) in their dear selves." Quoted
in James Sutherland, *English Literature of the Late Seventeenth Century* (Oxford, 1969), p. 125.

84. Pierre Forget, *Sentiments Universels* (1630, 1636, 1646), p. 35.
Boase describes Forget as a liberal Catholic and fideist for whom, ex-

Probably drawing on the general climate of libertine thought rather than on any particular source, Rochester argues cogently for a conception of the poet's role that is both daringly self-centered and based on soundly considered principles. The overarching principle (implied in the observation that what is "unnatural" is "unfit") of "follow nature," here comically invoked to excuse any alteration of one's course of life, seems both egoistic and, in its way, reasonable.

The following lines take the impudent application of reasonable principles to seemingly ridiculous lengths:

> Perhaps ill verses ought to be confined
> In mere good breeding, like unsavory wind.
> Were reading forced, I should be apt to think
> Men might no more write scurvily than stink.
> But 'tis your choice whether you'll read or no;
> If likewise of your smelling it were so,
> I'd fart, just as I write, for my own ease,
> Nor should you be concerned unless you please.
>
> [ll. 30–37]

M.G. reminds us of what we easily forget: no one is forced to read. In the case of a poet like M.G., who presumably, like Rochester, did not bother to publish his work, no one, apart from a few friends, is even encouraged to read his work. Within his own logic, M.G. is unassailable.

> I'll own that you write better than I do,
> But I have as much need to write as you.
> What though the excrement of my dull brain
> Runs in a costive and insipid strain,

cept in matters of religion, "there is no real evil except constraint." He derives much from Charron. See *Fortunes of Montaigne* (London, 1935), pp. 155–157. La Rochefoucauld, *Reflexions*, 3, "De L'Air et des Manières," not published until the eighteenth century. For other expressions of the "follow nature" principle, see Théophile de Viau, *Satire* 1; Regnier, "Le Gout particulier decide de tout," Charron, *De la Sagesse* (1621 ed.), 2:3, 4.

Whilst your rich head eases itself of wit:
Must none but civet cats have leave to shit?
[ll. 38–43]

Punning on "ease," he moves from the claim that he writes for his own "enjoyment," to the claim that he writes for "relief" from poetic pressure within him; he is naturally led to the metaphor of excrement.[85] It goes without saying that "M.G.'s notion of poetry as mere physical excrement contrasts ironically with the traditional belief that poetry was a product of those higher faculties, such as speech, reason, and a moral sense which differentiated man from beasts."[86] To say as much ought to suggest that debasing poetry from such an exalted conception is just the sort of thing the poet of the "Satyr Against Mankind" (and of the Huysmans portrait) would do.

Our sympathy with M.G. is reduced, perhaps, by his insistence on the excremental metaphor, but we ought to grant that the comparison is in some sense just. Rochester is playing, I suspect, with ideas of poetic afflatus, by recalling the original materiality (i.e., wind or divine vapor) implied by the word "inspiration." Vieth rightly adduces Pope's *Peri Bathous,* which, like the "Epistolary Essay," probably parodies the old idea (as found in the *Ion* and *Phaedrus* as well as Longinus's treatise *On the Sublime*) that the poet is bursting with what he has to express. Pope's speaker affirms "What seems to me an undoubted Physical Maxim, That Poetry is a natural or morbid Secretion from the Brain. . . . I have known a Man thoughtful, melancholy, and raving for divers days, but forthwith grow wonderfully easy, lightsome

85. To "ease oneself" meant to relieve the bowels. One might also "ease" the stomach or even the soul by relieving pressure or pain. See also the song "Fair Chloris," ll. 36–37 (*Complete Poems,* pp. 27–28). "Excrement" could still be used in 1680 to mean "outgrowth" in a figurative or literal sense, e.g., hair, fingernails, or figuratively, any "product."

86. *ARP,* p. 123.

and cheerful, upon a Discharge of the peccant humour, in exceeding purulent Metre." [87] But while Pope mocks his speaker, Rochester underscores, by means of his disgusting comparison, the idea of the natural as opposed to the spiritual or supernatural origin of poetry.[88]

After this point the poem seems to change direction.[89] Having scorned the world's judgment, M.G. now writes with an ironic eye on the world:

> In all I write, should sense and wit and rhyme
> Fail me at once, yet something so sublime
> Shall stamp my poem, that the world may see
> It could have been produced by none but me.
> And that's my end, for man can wish no more
> Than so to write, as none e'er writ before.
>
> [ll. 44–49]

The purpose and tone of these lines are difficult to judge. In part tongue-in-cheek self-depreciation by M.G., they also boast uniqueness and independence of the world's standards, as ironically masked under a bathetically expressed wish to write with originality.

After naively and patiently arguing (ll. 50–68) that the distribution of wit, alone among all other blessings in the world, is equal, that he has as much wit as any poet, M.G. then thumbs his nose at the rest of the literary world: "Yet

87. *ARP*, p. 124, citing *The Art of Sinking in Poetry*, ed. E. L. Steeves (New York, 1952), pp. 12–13, 98–99. Rochester, who uses the word "sublime" in line 45, may have known *Peri Hypsous* in Boileau's 1674 translation. On the necessity for the poet to speak out, see the end of ch. 6; on the materiality of inspiration, see ch. 11. Boileau, *Oeuvres Completes*, ed. C.-H. Boudhors (Paris, 1942), 4:60, 74.

88. M.G.'s theory is not, as Pinto and others have implied, a Romantic theory of self-expression. The Romantics, even more than the Neoclassicists, thought poetry came from the soul. M.G.'s poetry is conceived in the wits and the body.

89. A feature, either stylistic or thematic, of many Rochester poems, the "Satyr," "St. James's Park" (the introduction of Corinna), the "Heroical Epistle" (Bajazet's reverie), and "Upon Nothing."

most men show, or find great want of wit, / Writing themselves, or judging what is writ" (ll. 69–70). In subsequent
lines his arrogance returns:

> But I, who am of sprightly vigor full,
> Look on mankind as envious and dull.
> Born to myself, myself I like alone
> And must conclude my judgment good, or none.
> For should my sense be nought, how could I know
> Whether another man's be good or no?
> [ll. 71–76]

Beneath the witty circular logic lies a legitimate argument
that in some sense a poet is his own best critic and must rely,
in the end, on his own self-judgment.

For the remainder of the poem, however, M.G. largely
repeats and expands upon what he has already said. He is
satisfied with self-praise, freely admitting that he may be
arrogant: "If then I'm happy, what does it advance /
Whether to merit due, or arrogance?" He refuses to prostitute his sense to censurers and musty customs, perhaps
partly out of offensive arrogance, but from a righteous and
reasonable indignation too.

> There's not a thing on earth that I can name
> So foolish and so false as common fame.
> It calls the courtier knave, the plain man rude,
> Haughty the grave, and the delightful lewd,
> Impertinent the brick, morose the sad,
> Mean the familiar, the reserved one mad.
> Poor helpless woman is not favored more:
> She's a sly hypocrite, or public whore.
> Then who the devil would give this to be free
> From th'innocent reproach of infamy?
> [ll. 89–99]

The concluding couplet, in one sense an anticlimax, offers
another change in tone: "These things considered make me,

in despite / Of idle rumor, keep at home and write" (ll. 99–100).

The modest conclusion makes M.G. seem attractive; he assumes the classic stance of the rational, sensitive, urbane gentlemen (like Horace, Wyatt, or Pope) who has retired to the country to contemplate the corruption of the town. It is a tone which Rochester himself assumed: "this thought has soe intirely possesst mee since I came into the Country (where only one can think, for you att Court thinke not att all or att least as if you were shutt up in a Drumme, you can thinke of nothing but the noise y^t is made about you." [90] Like M.G., Rochester (according to Burnet) "would often go into the country, and be for some months wholly employed in study, or the sallies of his wit, which he came to direct chiefly to satire" (p. 30). And like M.G., Rochester was at least twice plagued by "idle rumour," complaining of the "false idle Story" that put him in the ill graces of the Duchess of Portsmouth, and of the "unhappy News of my own Death and Burial." [91] Rochester, again like M.G., in "To the Postboy" and in several letters to Mrs. Barry, wittily and theatrically declared his egoism.[92] And finally, M.G.'s scorn of critics and of popular taste is consistent with Rochester's declarations of literary principles in "An Allusion to Horace." The conclusion is inescapable, I think, that Rochester could have endorsed many of the ideas and attitudes in the "Epistolary Essay."

We may read the poem as another of Rochester's paradoxes. What it proposes is on the face of it absurd — writing is like defecating, egotism is the major principle in writing well — yet proves not so absurd after all. Rochester shocks the orthodox, yet, more seriously, subjects their ideas to provocative criticism. Ultimately, M.G.'s theory of compo-

90. *Letters*, p. 34. In a number of letters Rochester declares he has no interest in coming to town.
91. *Letters*, pp. 34, 39.
92. See below, p. 122.

sition interests us less for its positive proposals than for the comic discomfiture it causes among the conventional, and the complex response it evokes in an open-minded reader. We find M.G. deliberately offensive, impudent, and arrogant. Yet at the same time we find his wit audacious, his case against critics and common fame sufficient to win sympathy, and his argument for egotism, in its way, logically consistent and attractive.

The uses of libertinism, then, are various. To think of the poems we have considered as the utterances of libertine speakers is to see both the unity and the complexity of Rochester's satire. His use of his speakers — all of them projections of himself — varies from poem to poem, and within each poem, but in no case is it consistently or solely ironical. Most often, in fact, his attitude toward them is one of sympathy, edged, from time to time, with irony. In the early satires, "St. James's Park," "Timon," and "Tunbridge Wells," a libertine speaker finds forms of behavior which, even in the eyes of an orthodox moralist, are more despicable than libertinism, and begins to find even libertinism foolish. "The Maimed Debauchee" and "To the Postboy" satirize libertinism, but not without boasting of it too, or mocking the self-deceptive postures of the retired hero. Finally, in the "Heroical Epistle" and "Epistolary Essay," a libertine speaker evokes from us a complex and shifting — often sympathetic — attitude toward his egoism. In short, the poems are far less Augustan than has been claimed, and far less confessional as well. Never wholly serious, yet never wholly facetious, they mock and strike, inviting us to deplore and admire and sympathize.

Viewed another way, what Rochester has done in these poems is essentially to analyze the possibilities of the figure of the libertine rake. What he discovers is somewhat surprising — that the rake is not the unlimited master of pleasure and pain, but a prey to fools, or impending old age, to jealousy, or to other sexual discomforts, or to the disease of humanity. Only in the "Epistolary Essay" does the rake attain mastery over his situation. In "St. James's Park" he is betrayed by a lustless nymphomaniac and by his own feelings; in "Timon" he is trapped into an evening of bad food and worse talk, and can only flee in disgust; he must ashamedly flee, too, from the ridiculous "shapes" of man in "Tunbridge Wells." As an aging roué in "The Maimed Debauchee," he exposes his own poxed, wine-weakened, impotent body, and, above all, in the "Heroical Epistle," he reveals the painful uncertainty and sexual fantasy (the longing for utter sovereignty) beneath the haughty heartless banter. From this perspective, the "Epistolary Essay" assumes a prominent place in the libertine satires. In this poem, the rake (like the poet of the *Letters*) keeps at home, solacing himself with friendship, writing, and doctrinaire self-centeredness, the one set of fantasies that Rochester (both here and in the "Allusion to Horace") refuses to puncture.

❧3 The Pains of Sex

One of the prominent features of Rochester's poetry — including the libertine satires we have just examined — is its preoccupation with sexual relations, especially in some of their extreme forms, impotence, reckless promiscuity, homosexuality, "rapes, buggeries, and incests." In an age notorious for both its erotic poetry and its satire on women, Rochester produced a remarkable body of poems about sex, including a variety of tender, comic, or harshly threatening love songs, obscene and violent poems of loathing or cursing, a fine Ovidian elegy, and a sweeping satire on sexual relations in the beau monde. These poems need to be discussed as a whole in any thorough account of Rochester and his work. No single approach, however, can adequately describe them. They clearly stand in close relation to literary conventions (love-song conventions, for example), to Rochester's other satires, and to his own life as a rake.

Like the libertine speaker of the satires, the libertine lover of the songs is a projection of the poet himself. The erotic activities and concerns of the lover are recognizably those of the historical Rochester, notorious in his own licentious age for whoring and sexual profligacy. Married at nineteen, with the King's approval, to a beauty and heiress he had pursued for nearly two years, Rochester soon established his wife in the country and continued his own sexual career in town. He kept a mistress (two have been identified) but casual encounters with maids of honor, demi-mondaines, and common whores are unnumbered.

A contemporary (c. 1672) song, "The Debauchee," gives a popular and not unfriendly view of a typical day in his sexual life:

> I rise at eleven, I dine about two,
> I get drunk before seven, and the next thing I do:
> I send for my whore, when for fear of a clap,
> I spend in her hand, and I spew in her lap:
> There we quarrel, and scold, till I fall asleep,
> When the bitch, growing bold, to my pocket does creep;
> Then slyly she leaves me, and to revenge th'affront,
> At once she bereaves me of money, and cunt.
> If by chance then I wake, hot-headed and drunk,
> What a coil do I make for the loss of my punk?
> I storm, and I roar, and I fall in a rage,
> And missing my whore, I bugger my page:
> Then crop-sick all morning, I rail at my men,
> And in bed I lie yawning, till eleven again.

The song, probably by Dorset,[1] may be a reasonably accurate picture, as we shall see, of Rochester's chronic drunkenness, whoring, homosexuality, violent temper, and vehement ambivalence about women — contempt for the very sexual object he continually craves. For yet more accurate and interesting pictures, we can go to Rochester's own poems, a remarkable collection of songs and satires in which he appears to look on himself, his excesses and failures, with a clear-sightedness and guiltless candor rare in literature.

1. *ARP*, pp. 168-172. The text of the poem is from Thorpe, pp. 59-60 (spelling and capitalization have been modernized).

Obscenity

We may begin with Rochester's obscenity, a matter that has attracted (or repelled) his readers, and plagued his critics since the beginning. It is worth trying to establish the extent and the purposes, literary and psychological, of that obscenity.

Until now it has been impossible to do this, due to the sensationalists on the one hand and to the censors on the other among Rochester's printers and editors. Vieth prints nineteen poems, indecent in whole or in part — the Rochester canon now stands at seventy-five poems — which, in Pinto's edition, had been either omitted or completely expurgated of any offensive words.[2] Expurgation has long been Rochester's fate. The 1691 Tonson edition omitted some poems and censored others;[3] a hundred years later Johnson gave a copy of the poems to the bookseller Steevens "to castrate for the edition of the poets."[4] On the other extreme, unreliable printers and editors, from the original *Poems on Affairs of State* to Hayward's *Collected Works* published in this century, have printed as Rochester's a great many indecent poems he did not write. To remedy the situation, in 1950 Thorpe's facsimile edition of the 1680 *Poems* printed eleven of the nineteen indecent poems in their original uncensored form, and now Vieth has printed all nineteen in full.

The conscious purposes of obscenity are difficult to establish. A poet might well wish to stimulate the appetite for

2. Pinto censors by omitting lines from four, by altering or omitting single words from four more, and by relegating one to his Appendix; he is not permitted by the publishers to print two ("St. James's Park," "The Imperfect Enjoyment"), and omits eight altogether.

3. Tonson censored several bawdy poems by omitting an offending stanza, e.g., stanzas referring to homosexuality in "The Maimed Debauchee" and the song "Love a woman/ You're an ass," and the final stanzas in "How happy Chloris, were they free" and "Fair Chloris in a pigsty lay."

4. *Life of Johnson*, ed. G. B. Hill, rev. L. F. Powell, 3:191.

sex. Rochester seems to recognize this purpose in his description of Sedley's songs:

> For songs and verses mannerly obscene,
> That can stir nature up by springs unseen,
> And without forcing blushes, warm the Queen —
> Sedley has that prevailing gentle art,
> That can with a resistless charm impart
> The loosest wishes to the chastest heart;
> Raise such a conflict, kindle such a fire,
> Betwixt declining virtue and desire,
> Till the poor vanquished maid dissolves away
> In dreams all night, in sighs and tears all day.
>
> ["An Allusion to Horace," ll. 61–70]

Despite the (perhaps partly facetious) praise of Sedley's kindling power, I think Rochester's own purposes are never to stimulate.[5] Herein he may be distinguished from many of the writers of bawdry in the Restoration. Some, like Sedley, titillate chiefly by coy hints and double entendres. Others stimulate openly; two common fantasies are the catalogue of naked delights and the voyeuristic description of a disrobing (and unsuspecting) girl, followed sometimes by a weakly resisted rape.[6]

A second purpose, perhaps part of the first, is pure sensationalism. The poet might seek to attract attention to his writing by appealing to his reader's interest in sex, especially violent or unusual sex. Or he may simply want to

5. I disagree with a recent editor of Rochester, Ronald Duncan, who says: "I can find nothing offensive in him. His most bawdy poems do not shock me, his pornography delights me. . . . Pornography is the art which attracts you towards sex." *Selected Lyrics and Satires of Rochester* (London, 1948), p. 11. Duncan's discussion of Rochester's pornography is vitiated by his belief that Rochester did not write "St. James's Park" or "Signior Dildo."

6. A selection from Restoration "drolleries" is available in *The Anthology of Restoration Erotic Poetry*, ed. E. Gray (North Hollywood, 1965). Cf. also *The Cabinet of Love*, available in *The Works of . . . Rochester, Roscomon, and Dorset* (London, 1735).

shock and scandalize by his plain speaking. Indeed, Rochester habitually shows an interest in the scandalous, the outrageous, in whatever will shock the imagined audience. In the "Satyr Against Mankind" he audaciously claims he would rather be an animal than a man; libertine speakers in other poems shock readers with their bold disregard for convention, and their egoism; impudent lovers defend their inconstancy. Obscenity, too, can be a way of shocking an audience, and I suspect Rochester's obscenity can always be set down in part to this motive. But delight in shocking accounts for less in Rochester than it does in much of the more rollicking hudibrastic bawdry of the period. The Buckhurst-Etherege epistles, for example [7] —

> Dreaming last night on Mrs. Farley,
> My prick was up this morning early
>
> . . . .
>
> So soft and amorously you write
> Of cunt and prick, the cunt's delight

— seem little more than high-spirited but rather sophomoric effusions of wits who take delight in crying out "cunt" and "prick."

Obscenity may also have an aesthetic or moral purpose. Among Rochester's purposes in writing indecently are, I think, the wish to describe "nature," to describe what happens in sexual relations and what various feelings are generated. Juvenal chose for his subject *quidquid agunt homines*, whatever men do; comic writers since Aristophanes have claimed the body and its excretory and generative functions as part of their province. Rochester may justifiably claim to be writing about a central part of human experience, and may claim the right to use the necessary language. As he wrote in another context, "Expressions must descend

7. Printed in *The Poems of Etherege*, ed. J. Thorpe (Princeton, 1963), pp. 35–45, and discussed in *ARP*, ch. 9.

to the Nature of Things express'd."[8] To avoid four-letter
words in writing openly about sex is already to falsify experience. In addition, Rochester at times describes the obscene
or indecent in order to attack both what he thinks is corrupted sexuality in women, and the vehement outrage
(perhaps partly ironical) this corruption arouses in a libertine. "St. James's Park" is again the best example, but there
are other similar poems.

That his obscenity is in part aesthetic and moral may
seem more likely when we read a contemporary defense of
it on those grounds in Robert Wolseley's preface to Rochester's *Valentinian*, written just five years after the poet's
death. Wolseley was answering an attack by Mulgrave, who
had objected that Rochester's "nauseous songs" were only
"bawdry bare-fac'd," and "pall'd the appetite" they "meant
to raise," because their "obscene words" were "too gross to
move desire."[9]

In defense of Rochester, Wolseley first justifies the poet's
right to choose any subject, however low or ugly, and the
right to be judged on "the manner of treating his Subject."[10]
He goes on to defend "the wit of my Lord Rochester's obscene Writings," by which he means bawdry that is "a
true and lively expression of Nature," rather than "bawdry
alone, that is, obscene words thrown out at random like
Bullies Oaths, without Design, Order, or Application" (pp.
21, 24). This defense, on aesthetic grounds, corresponds to
the aesthetic defense I outlined above — the poet's right to
describe nature in the necessary language.

8. *Letters*, p. 73.
9. "Essay on Poetry" (1682), in Spingarn, 2:288. Macaulay and
Taine, like Mulgrave, assume that Rochester sought to titillate but
could only nauseate. *History of England*, vol. 1, ch. 3; *History of English Literature*, tr. H. Van Laun (New York, 1871), 1:469–70. An
anonymous eighteenth-century critic, on the other hand, thought
Rochester's "looser songs" dangerously obscene precisely because they
were *not* "nauseous." The inauthentic "St. Evremond memoir," repr.
in Q. Johns, *Poetical Works of Rochester* (Halifax, 1933), p. xxx.
10. "Preface to *Valentinian*," in Spingarn, 3:15–16.

Wolseley hesitates to defend obscenity on moral grounds. Since Mulgrave had not attacked Rochester for immorality, he defends Rochester's wit, not his manners. He admits, however, that wit can be "libertine" and "immoral" and that the obscene poems must be "reckon'd among the Extravagancies of his Youth, and the carelesse gayeties of his Pen" (pp. 24–25). But after forswearing the moral defense, Wolseley gingerly takes it up, arguing indirectly in generalities, without specific reference to Rochester. He seems motivated more by animosity toward Mulgrave than concern for Rochester's reputation. Bawdry, he argues, is usually considered a dangerous stimulant of lawless lust. But if "barefaced bawdry" in fact stifles such desire (as Mulgrave claimed Rochester's did) then it is more pardonable than any other bawdry. Having discovered something in Mulgrave's argument which can be used against him, Wolseley pushes even further:

Does he think that all kind of obscene Poetry is design'd to raise Appetite? Does he not know that obscene Satyr (of which nature are most of my Lord Rochester's obscene Writings, and particularly several of his Songs) has quite a different end; and is so far from being intended to raise, that the whole force of it is generally turn'd to restrain Appetite, and to keep it within due Bounds, to reprove the unjust Designs and check the Excesses of that lawlesse Tyrant? If, therefore, some of my Lord Rochester's Songs should miss a Mark which they neither did nor ought to aim at, I believe no body but the Essayer will think it a Fault.

[pp. 27–28]

Wolseley still refrains from explicitly defending Rochester as a deliberate moralist in his obscenity; he prefers to say what Rochester did not do.[11] Other critics, however, were

11. Later (p. 31), in fact, he says the obscene poems are "of such an unhappy Kind as few will examine." Earlier (p. 25) Wolseley offered to excuse Rochester's indecency by considering that the poet's audience was private and restricted.

willing to say more. The author of the second of the two prologues to *Valentinian*, though he says nothing of indecency, reminds the audience of Rochester's continual reproof of the social and sexual follies of women:

> Our author lov'd the youthful and the fair,
> But even in those their Follies could not spare;
> Bid them discreetly use their present store,
> Be friends to Pleasure, when they please no more;
> Desir'd the Ladies of Maturer Ages
> If some remaining Spark their Hearts enrages,
> At home to quench their embers with their pages,
> Pert, patch't, and painted, there to spend their days;
> Not croud the fronts of Boxes at new Plays.[12]

Some thirty years later he was still being praised for his refining effect on his society by a critic who must have known of Rochester's obscenity:

> Sackville and Wilmot then sat Censors here,
> Kind to the Sex, but to its Faults severe;
> Such Satire flow'd from their abounding Store,
> Tho' France did much, their Pens refin'd us more.[13]

These conclusions, I think, may be accepted [14] and expanded. Several early obscene satires, "Signior Dildo," "St. James's Park," and "Quoth the Duchess of Cleveland to counselor Knight," however much they display a relish in bawdry and a desire to shock, are probably secondarily moral. Rochester palls and disgusts the reader with descriptions of corrupt and unnatural sex. While veiled descrip-

12. Printed in Tonson's 1691 edition, n.p.
13. John Durant Breval, *The Art of Dress, A Poem* (London, 1717), p. 15.
14. Clearly a devoted and at times uncritical admirer of Rochester, Wolseley has been accused of "special pleading" (James Sutherland, *English Literature of the Late Seventeenth Century*, [Oxford, 1969] p. 168). But Wolseley by no mean whitewashes Rochester.

tions of forbidden delights might incite heat and lust, his direct naming of parts and actions, like "the free and full survay" of the body's generative organs in Montaigne, is anti-erotic, and even, as for Ovid, a *remedia amoris*.[15] Sexual feeling is crudely exposed as a matter of organ size and friction.

In these three poems Rochester's target is not the lustful, cosmetic-using, vain, and treacherous woman of traditional misogynist satire. There is something generous, as Rochester says in "St. James's Park," in mere lust. He attacks rather the debased means by which women satisfy their lust. In the slightest of these satires, "Quoth the Duchess of Cleveland to counselor Knight," the speaker rails at women who seek out as sexual partners not the aristocratic wits but strapping, brawny servants, porters, and laborers. The Duchess of Cleveland, notorious for her nymphomaniac lust, is represented as asking Mary Knight, another of the King's mistresses, where she can find some good men. Advised to retire to a cellar in Sodom (the name of a seedy part of London), "Where porters with black-pots sit round a coalfire," and where all she need do is buy the men ale, she replies, at the poem's end: "For I'd rather be fucked by porters and carmen / Than thus be abus'd by Churchill and Jermyn." [16] The poem is obscene, but not without reason; it seeks to attack a fashion and to arouse disgust toward such women as Cleveland, who in following it rob sex of all thought and all but the crudest feelings.

Morophilia — the love of fools, especially if they are brawny [17] — is the secondary target in another poem from

15. "Apologie for Raymond Sebond," quoting *Remedia Amoris* 2:33, in *Essayes* 2:181–182.

16. Two courtiers with whom Cleveland had had affairs.

17. The relationship of the old belief that the ignorant and low-born make up for their lack of wit and intelligence with sexual potency — and are thus desirable lovers — to seventeenth-century antirationalism in love is thoroughly discussed by Quaintance, "Passion and

the same period (1672–1673), "Signior Dildo," a rollicking satirical lyric on the popularity among the English duchesses of the modest young man "in a plain leather coat." In this poem Rochester, while exceeding him in obscenity, comes closest to the tone of Dorset. The satire describes how Signior Dildo has proved so popular and serviceable that he threatens to replace the robust fools that women now prefer:

> Our dainty fine duchesses have got a trick
> To dote on a fool for the sake of his prick:
> The fops were undone, did Their Graces but know
> The discretion and vigor of Signior Dildo.
>
> [st. 9]

The Countess of Falmouth, says the speaker, might give up her footman (st. 7), and the citizens' wives the "foremen of shops." The point of the poem, made playfully rather than bitterly, is that if women want only size and vigor they may as well use artificial means. As Artemisia was to say in a later and much better satire, "To an exact perfection they have wrought / The action, love; the passion is forgot." In "Signior Dildo," the duchesses satisfy their lust by a means even more unnatural and mechanical than morophilia. The poem's crudity is largely redeemed by its humor. Punctuated by the names of seventeen courtiers, the poem was probably intended as scandalous amusement for the Court.

In the third and by far the best of Rochester's obscene satires, "St. James's Park," female lust is yet more perverse and passionless. Indiscriminate and passive nymphomania becomes the worst offense against sex and stimulates in the speaker not playful mockery but sardonic outrage. These three early obscene satires are not, in Wolseley's terms, "bawdry alone." The obscenity seems purposive; it seems

Reason in Restoration Love Poetry" (unpub. Yale Ph.D. dissertation), ch. 2.

motivated, at least in part, by a prejudice against the debasement of sex.[18]

Obscenity seems morally purposive, too, in the famous "Satyr on Charles II," a slighter but funnier poem than "St. James's Park." Rochester combines intimate compliment ("the easiest King and best-bred man alive") with daring bawdry ("His sceptre and his prick are of a length"). Though Charles is declining in years, he will not give up women: "Restless he rolls about from whore to whore, /A merry monarch, scandalous and poor." It is not wenching itself that Rochester satirizes, but the compulsiveness, the lack of self-control. "Poor Prince! thy prick, like thy buffoons at Court, / Will govern thee, because it makes thee sport." [19] The King debases not sex but himself. Women in this poem do not figure as objects of satire. While the rest of Rochester's obscene poems are contemptuous of women, here Carwell, Charles's mistress, escapes censure, and "poor, laborious" Nell Gwyn gets a flash of rueful sympathy for her painful struggle with "hands, fingers, mouth, and thighs" to please the King — a solicitous concern Rochester seems really to have felt.[20]

Not all of Rochester's obscene poems are informed by

18. The same prejudice is at work, I think, in the obscene play, *Sodom*, which, though long attributed to him, was very probably not written by Rochester (see R. M. Baine, "Rochester or Fishbourne: A Question of Authorship," *RES*, 22[1946], 201–206). Although it is a foolish exaggeration to call the play "a great and essentially moral work" (Albert Ellis, ed., *Sodom*, North Hollywood, Calif., 1966, p. viii), it is true that the play is moral: it endorses natural sex and explicitly condemns both artificial sex and sodomy. I think the play is probably not Rochester's — on internal evidence. Its doggerel couplets are far less interesting than those in Rochester's couplet satires. Furthermore, the play offers itself, in the first prologue, as a stimulant to the audience, actors, and author alike. Rochester's genuine work, as I have suggested, is almost never erotic.

19. Perhaps recalling Cowley's "Poor Prince, whom Madmen, Priests, and Boys invade! / By thine own Flesh, thy ingrateful Son, betray'd," in *Davideis*, 1, *Works* (1710), 1:300. Saul's betrayal by his "own Flesh" is heroic, Charles's ludicrous.

20. See the letter to Savile containing Rochester's advice to Nell Gwyn, *Letters*, p. 57.

moral purpose. Some four songs — most of them, significantly, written against specific women — seem to derive from a scurrilous misogyny and hatred of sex, together with an impulse to scandalize. I do not include among these the conventional anacreontic:

> Love a woman? You're an ass!
> 'Tis a most insipid passion
> To choose out for your happiness
> The silliest part of God's creation.[21]

But when this kind of light banter begins to fester, it produces poems whose obscenity is not redeemed by wit or moral outrage. Nor can these poems be excused as youthful extravagances.[22] Vieth dates them all in Rochester's final period, 1676–1680. These songs may well reflect Rochester's utter disillusionment with sex and with women.[23] One poem, "When to the King I bid good morrow," gives a crude and contemptuous picture of the King and his rival mistresses. Another, "The Mock Song," parodies a tender lyric of Scroope's by describing a nymphomaniac monster. A third is a virulent curse against a court prostitute. A fourth urges Phyllis not to wear foul linen, revealing not Crazy Jane's clear knowledge, but rather a contemptuous mockery that love has pitched his mansion in the place of excrement.[24]

Such poems of contempt and disgust are in themselves of only minor interest. But they deserve some comment as an extreme version of a constant theme in Rochester: sensual experience (though it is all man has) is essentially a failure. Poems with wider appeal (the "Heroical Epistle," for example) also expose the pains of sexual love. Many of

21. Or the satirical squib "On Cary Frazier."

22. The attack on poxed court ladies in "On the Women About Town" (c. 1673) is still wittily mock-serious.

23. Rochester's most virulent invectives against men date also from this period. See *Complete Poems*, pp. 132, and esp. 141, 142.

24. *Complete Poems*, pp. 137, 139.

them, indeed, hint more specifically at what those "pains" include.

"The Imperfect Enjoyment"

A central example, in which sexual failure provides an occasion for both laughter and disgust, is "The Imperfect Enjoyment," an indecent poem about premature ejaculation. The indecency is in part conventional. The poem is a loose imitation of Ovid's *Amores* 3:7, and needs to be seen first in relation to a minor tradition of poems about "imperfect enjoyment." We should also see the poem in relation to Rochester's other work and (very likely) to his own personal experience as a rake. Out of that experience, mediated through Ovidian convention,[25] Rochester constructed a serio-comic dramatization of a kind of sexual failure which every male lover risks.

The tradition to which this poem belongs has been thoroughly discussed by Quaintance, but since his work is not readily accessible,[26] it deserves summary here. Ovid's *Amores* 3:7 is the ultimate source of the "imperfect enjoyment" poems. Ovid's speaker, alone with a lovely and willing young lady, finds himself unable to perform:

> I lay without Life's animating Spring,
> A dull, enervate, worthless, lumpish thing.

25. Rochester has a handful of Ovidian elegies, six poems of moderate length, all dealing wittily and gaily with love, and written in pentameter couplets: "The Discovery," "The Advice," "The Submission," the untitled "Could I but make my wishes insolent" (technically perhaps an epistle, but similar to the elegies in subject, tone, and versification), "To Love" (a close translation of Ovid's *Amores* 2:9), and "The Imperfect Enjoyment." All were probably written early in Rochester's career. Except for "The Advice" (a wittily conceited poem in which compliment yields finally to open threat) and "The Imperfect Enjoyment," these poems are of little interest beyond demonstrating Rochester's roots in literary conventions.

26. Quaintance's "French Sources of the Restoration 'Imperfect Enjoyment Poem,'" *PQ*, 42 (1963), 190–199, gives only the bare bones of his dissertation research.

> My neck she folded with a soft embrace,
> Now kiss'd my Eyes, now wanton'd o'er my face,
> Now lov'd to dart her humid tongue to mine,
> Now would her pliant limbs around me twine
>
> . . . .
>
> In vain, alas! the Nerves were slacken'd still,
> And I prov'd only potent in my Will.[27]

Cursing his fate, Ovid's speaker speculates on the cause of his impotence, and is at last interrupted by the lady, who gaily calls for water to wash herself.

The comic possibilities of inopportune inadequacy were also exploited by Petronius, whose *Satyricon*, especially chapters 128–140, helped develop the tradition. Encolpius twice proves unable to satisfy the magnificent courtesan, Circe, who stingingly rebukes him and has him flogged. Encolpius, overcome with shame, in his turn, undertakes to punish the offending member with a razor:

> Three times with razor raised I tried to lop;
> three times my trembling fingers let it drop,
> while he, as limp as cabbage when it's boiled,
> with prickish fright my purpose foiled . . .[28]

Baffled, he gives "the laggard" a piece of his mind: " 'What do you have to say for yourself,' I cried, 'you shame of gods and man? Obscenity, unspeakable sullen pendant, is this what I deserved? To be snatched from the doors of heaven and spindled down to hell? To have this scandal of decrepit, limp old age fixed upon my youth, my green and swelling years.' " The offender is unmoved, and Encolpius suddenly is overcome with shame a second time:

27. Translated by "an unknown hand" in the Tonson-Dryden edition of *Ovid's Epistles: with his Amours* (London, 1776), p. 322. Quaintance does not use this translation.

28. Petronius's prose is interspersed with passages of verse. I quote (here and below) from the translation by William Arrowsmith, *The Satyricon of Petronius* (Ann Arbor, 1959), pp. 162–163.

The blood rushed to my head, and I blushed all over to think how far I had forgotten my self-respect by stooping to argue with that part of me which no serious man thinks worthy of his thoughts. For some time I lay there, ruefully rubbing my forehead. Then the absurdity of my shame struck me. After all, I thought, why not? What's so unnatural or wrong about working off one's feelings with a little plain-spoken abuse? Don't we curse our guts, our teeth, our heads, when they give us trouble? Didn't Ulysses himself have a parley with his heart?

To Ovid's comedy derived from the irony of impotence, Petronius adds the grotesque comedy of the lover's vehement curse against his own member. Ovid's curse, in comparison, is brief and mild: "Begone, untimely Nerves! I trust no more. . . . Go for a silly, unperforming thing." [29]

Neoclassical imitations of Ovid and Petronius began with Remy Belleau's "Impuissance," written about 1577 and published in 1618, and continued to appear in France and England during the seventeenth century.[30] Rochester's "Imperfect Enjoyment" (c. 1672–1673) is a more or less original variation of what had developed into a traditional theme. The chief innovation of the later imitations is to make the lover's failure not impotence but premature ejaculation. Quaintance adduces evidence (the use of a standard dramatic situation and plot, stock diction, isolated echoes of earlier poems) to suggest that the Restoration "imperfect enjoyment" poets were conscious of writing in a tradition. Rochester may have known Etherege's poem, or Aphra Behn's poem (perhaps written much earlier than 1680). While not deliberately imitating any previous poem, he very probably went back to Belleau for a few details, and to Aphra Behn, Ovid, or Petronius for another.[31] More gen-

29. Tonson-Dryden tr., p. 325.

30. By Régnier (1613), Beys (1651), de Morangle (1652), de Cantenac (1660), Etherege (c. 1672), Aphra Behn (1680), and two anonymous poems (1674, 1682). For a bibliography, see Quaintance, "French Sources," *PQ* (1963), p. 190.

31. Quaintance, p. 210.

erally, he probably derived from Belleau or from Petronius the idea of ending his poem with a thundering curse.

Anyone writing on Rochester's poem, or on the Restoration "imperfect enjoyment" poem as a minor genre, is indebted to Quaintance's discernment of a tradition and compilations of the texts, illuminated as they are by a vast amount of classical and Renaissance lore on impotence. I disagree with him, however, in his discussion of the "meaning" or "argument" of Rochester's poem. Drawing on seventeenth-century antirationalism, and in particular on Montaigne's essay, "Of the force of imagination," [32] Quaintance reads the Restoration "imperfect enjoyment" poems as antirationalist texts. Montaigne, he notes, spoke of the power of the imagination to affect the body's functions, offering as illustrations both nocturnal emissions and impotence due to a mental rather than physical condition. The libertine poets seem to him to adopt Montaigne's analysis of the mind as a cause of impotence. Morangle's speaker says "nous pensâmes trop," Etherege's says "My zeal does my devotion quite destroy" ("zeal" here is assumed to involve some mental activity). Quaintance is then led to conclude,

Surely the major "argument" of the Restoration "Imperfect Enjoyment" poems is that fancy, idealization, speculation on the fair one's charms, all such immaterial considerations merely impede the performance of an act at best spontaneous, instinctive, irrational. . . . [The poems present] an attitude of suspicion or scorn toward faculties not sensual which are allowed to meddle in a sensual act, and a vivid dramatic demonstration of the damage they can do. [pp. 214, 198]

I find Quaintance's argument [33] persuasive when applied to the poems by Morangle, Beys, and Etherege, but not when

32. *Essayes*, 1:xxi.

33. In his *PQ* article, Quaintance modifies the stress on antirationalism. The poems, he there says, suggest "that there should be a common-sense limitation of the emotion" built up prior to consummation (p. 199).

applied to Rochester's. In his "Imperfect Enjoyment," the mind, the nonsensual faculties, have nothing to do with the lover's failure; indeed, the culprit is the unruly member which is imagined to have a will of its own. It is the offending organ, not the meddling mind, that is cursed.

The poem begins with eighteen lines of spirited description of the act of love, one of the rare erotic passages in all of Rochester's works: [34]

> Naked she lay, clasped in my longing arms,
> I filled with love, and she all over charms;
> Both equally inspired with eager fire,
> Melting through kindness, flaming in desire.
> With arms, legs, lips close clinging to embrace,
> She clips me to her breast, and sucks me to her face.
> Her nimble tongue, Love's lesser lightning, played
> Within my mouth, and to my thoughts conveyed
> Swift orders that I should prepare to throw
> The all-dissolving thunderbolt below.
> My fluttering soul, sprung with the pointed kiss,
> Hangs hovering o'er her balmy brinks of bliss.
> But whilst her busy hand would guide that part
> Which should convey my soul up to her heart,
> In liquid raptures I dissolve all o'er,
> Melt into sperm, and spend at every pore.
> A touch from any part of her had done't:
> Her hand, her foot, her very look's a cunt.
> [ll. 1–18]

Belleau, by contrast, gives over twelve of his eighteen precatastrope lines to a traditional erotic *blazon*, describing what he sees of his luscious lady. Quaintance finds Rochester's lines laughably exaggerated, a "breezy," comic contrast to the "hothouse atmosphere" of Belleau's "voyeuristic brooding on erotic charms" (pp. 211–212). The com-

34. There is nothing in Rochester to equal the eroticism of Ovid's *Amores* 1:5, a "perfect enjoyment" poem similar to Donne's *Elegy* 19, "To his Mistris Going to Bed."

parison is unfair to Belleau, and misrepresents the genuine erotic appeal of Rochester's lines. Belleau merely describes what he sees, Rochester primarily what he and his lady do.

The imagery skillfully and exuberantly conveys both the bodily joys and the seemingly bodiless ecstasy of sexual intercourse. The submerged metaphor of the hovering bird, "sprung" from his hiding place by the "point"[ing] dog (her kiss), suggests the floating-fluttering before the explosion, death, and fall, and makes love a communion of souls. On the other hand, the metaphor of the lesser and greater lightning insists on the material communion that is the means, literally, of any spiritual communion. The "soul" (descending now into matter) is "convey"[ed] (a neo-Platonic term wittily adopted for a physical transaction)[35] by the thunderbolt-part, just as the "orders" to love are conveyed to his "thoughts" by the "lesser lightning." Indeed, the imagery (in both cases original with Rochester) makes the point that "thoughts" are a natural part of love-making: far from meddling, they make it possible. The immediate cause of disaster, it appears, is not the speaker's mind but the lady's touch, "her busy hand," though the speaker in his exuberance and exaggeration says that "a touch from any part of her had done't."

In the opening lines the playful hyperbole is never so strong as to destroy the erotic appeal. The lines that follow introduce a new point of view, the lady's, by which we find the rapt and hyperbolic speaker gently mocked:

> Smiling, she chides in a kind murmuring noise,
> And from her body wipes the clammy joys,
> When, with a thousand kisses wandering o'er
> My panting bosom, "Is there then no more?"

35. Neo-Platonic language about "conveying" souls into souls had already been satirized. See poems by Jaspar Mayne (in N. Ault, ed., *Seventeenth Century Lyrics* [New York, 1950], p. 230) and Cartwright (*Comedies, Tragi-Comedies, and Other Poems* [London, 1651], p. 246).

> She cries. "All this to love and rapture's due;
> Must we not pay a debt to pleasure too?"
>
> [ll. 19–24]

"Clammy joys" — an elegant periphrasis, here both apt and mock-formal — shows that the speaker begins to poke fun at himself. The lady's wit and her recapitulation of "love" (from l. 7) and "rapture" (from l. 15) serve to undercut the speaker's rapturous language in the opening passage. As Quaintance rightly suggests (p. 205), she is also the more practical, down-to-earth of the two, trying to repair the damage and saying, in effect, "rapture is well and good, but let us not forget our primary purpose."

In the third section of the poem, the lover describes, in mountingly exaggerated, even melodramatic, language his inability to satisfy her desire for pleasure. He presents himself as "the most forlorn, lost man alive," a "cold hermit," and a "wishing, weak, unmoving lump," his organ once a "dart of love," now a "withered flower." A skillful triplet summarizes his plight:

> Eager desires confound my first intent,
> Succeeding shame does more success prevent,
> And rage at last confirms me impotent.
>
> [ll. 28–30]

Quaintance comments that the lines demonstrate "how the mind has obscured spontaneous physical drives" (p. 205). While the lines seem to lend themselves to his interpretation, I think rather that the "eager desires" have been shown (in ll. 1–18) to be shared by body and mind alike; shame and rage may prevent the lover's "recovery" but have nothing to do with the initial problem, caused as it is by an over-active body.

Perhaps more charcteristic of Rochester than even the theatrical self-presentation is the vehement twenty-seven line curse that concludes the poem. Its violence, obscenity, and obsession with disease look forward to "St. James's Park," to parts of "Tunbridge Wells," to the address "To the Postboy," and to some of the shorter obscene satires on women. Like those poems, it is strongly anti-erotic, creating an overwhelming sense of disgust. At the same time, however, the disgust is both grotesquely comic and traditional, in the manner of Petronius and Belleau:

> Thou treacherous, base deserter of my flame,
> False to my passion, fatal to my fame,
> Through what mistaken magic [36] dost thou prove
> So true to lewdness, so untrue to love?
> What oyster-cinder-beggar-common whore
> Didst thou e'er fail in all thy life before?
> When vice, disease, and scandal lead the way,
> With what officious haste dost thou obey!
> Like a rude, roaring hector in the streets
> Who scuffles, cuffs, and justles all he meets,
> But if his King or country claim his aid,
> The rakehell villain shrinks and hides his head;
> Ev'n so thy brutal valor is displayed,
> Breaks every stew, does each small whore invade,
> But when great Love the onset does command,
> Base recreant to thy prince, thou dar'st not stand.
> Worst part of me, and henceforth hated most,
> Through all the town a common fucking post,
> On whom each whore relieves her tingling cunt
> As hogs on gates do rub themselves and grunt.
>
> [ll. 46–65]

The lines in part recall the boastful confessional of "To the Postboy." There, the speaker has "swived more whores more ways than Sodom's walls e'er knew," has broken houses, libeled kings, and fled like a coward when courage was needed. Here, the denunciation is turned not against the

36. A vestige of classical beliefs (as expressed in Ovid, for example) that impotence was due to sorcery. For the background, see Quaintance, pp. 168 ff.

speaker himself, but against a piece of him, a treacherous whoremongering pintle that fails to perform with a witty and no doubt high-born woman (clearly not a whore) whom the speaker claims to desire and "love."

In passion and energy, the lines far outdo Ovid's address to his "pars pessima" or Petronius's "plain-spoken abuse." Rochester shares with his classical predecessors an impulse to grotesque hyperbole. His model may be Belleau, who condemns the offending organ to an old and toothless woman, decaying and worm-eaten, stinking like an old marsh. Rochester's barnyard image conveys, I think, a sense of loathing not completely dissolved by laughter.

In the final lines the speaker wishes diseases on his "worst part":

> Mayst thou to ravenous chancres be a prey,
> Or in consuming weepings waste away;
> May strangury and stone thy days attend;
> May'st thou ne'er piss, who didst refuse to spend.
> And may ten thousand abler pricks agree
> To do the wronged Corinna right for thee.

Here the tone lightens. The catalogue of urinary diseases suggests that Rochester may be echoing, in a ludicrously low context, the formal curse of excommunication, and in particular the terrible curse of Ernulphus, an eleventh-century Bishop of Rochester [!] whose Latin imprecation is later quoted in Sterne's *Tristram Shandy* (3:11) by Dr. Slop against the hapless Obadiah: "May he be cursed . . . in pissing, in his groin, . . . in his genitals." On the other hand it is possible that Rochester is echoing Belleau's conclusion: "Adieu, contente toy, et, ne pouvant dresser, / Que ce boyau ridé te serve de pisser." Six of the 1680 editions read "ne'er piss," four omit "ne'er." Quaintance thinks (p. 210 n) it more likely that the correct reading is "May'st thou piss," to imply that "if you can't perform your other function, then stick to this one." But if Rochester remembered Ernulphus, he may have written "ne'er piss," as if to say "may you be damned in this too."

The Songs

Although they do not overtly specify a particular problem, Rochester's songs extend this exploration of man's painful sexual condition. These poems have been given very little detailed scrutiny, but have been widely admired for three centuries, even when his satires were denounced as loathsome and obscene. Critics have found it difficult to talk about neoclassic love songs, but almost all who have commented on Rochester's have felt that he surpassed his fellow songwriters, forging from an impersonal and conventional medium an instrument for the expression of intense, original, and highly personal feelings.[37] The problem for the critic now is to characterize, with as much precision as possible, Rochester's distinctive lyric voice.

Some six or ten of Rochester's songs, it is true, seem indistinguishable from those of any other Restoration lyricist. Almost wholly impersonal and toneless exercises about a cruel, fair mistress — including the popular "My dear mistress has a heart" — they are the product of a community spirit rather than of an individual sensibility. They are written usually in four, five, or six-line stanzas, in ballad measures or tetrameter couplets, and filled with the stock furniture — master and slave, the lover's chains, Cupid's dart, pleasurable pains, love's war — and the stock vocabulary — heaven, glory, bliss, charms; pride, disdain, scorn, despair; eyes, heart, breast; fire, fate, flames, cruelty, die, kill, wound, languish — of the conventional love lyric. Rochester's individual voice is heard in the songs where he dis-

37. On the conventional qualities of the Restoration song, see Mulgrave's *Essay on Poetry* (1682), ll. 63–79; J. H. Wilson, *Court Wits*, p. 87; C. W. Peltz, "The Neo-Classic Lyric, 1660–1725," *ELH*, 10 (1944), 112.

turbs the smooth, polished surface by means of a sudden witty turn, a gradual or sudden descent from compliment to harshness and threats, or an intensity of tender painful feeling that strikes the reader as an anxious lover's authentic cry.

The sudden witty turn enables Rochester to parody song convention, to work a surprise variation on an old theme, or to uncover an unexpected level of erotic gratification. The erotic pastoral, for example, is a delicate, frilly, rococo form well suited for parody. The coy refusals and submissions, the sweet, reluctant, amorous delay of shepherdesses, had long provided good material for elegantly playful poems. Rochester himself wrote a song of this type, concluding,

> She faintly spoke, and trembling lay,
>   For fear he should comply [i.e., desist],
> But virgins' eyes their hearts betray
>   And give their tongues the lie.
>
> Thus she, who princes had denied
>   With all their pompous train,
> Was in the lucky minute tried
>   And yielded to the swain.
>   [*Complete Poems*, p. 27, ll. 17–24]

The prettiness of the pastoral fiction is easily parodied by replacing the conventional dreaming shepherd [38] with a swineherdess:

> Fair Chloris in a pigsty lay;
>   Her tender herd lay by her.
> She slept; in murmuring gruntlings they,
> Complaining of the scorching day,
>   Her slumbers thus inspire.
>   [*Complete Poems*, p. 27, ll. 1–5]

38. See poems #50 and #61 in *England's Helicon*, ed. Hyder E. Rollins (Cambridge, Mass., 1935), pp. 76–77, 90. In #61 Corin dreams he saves Chloris from a satyr, is offered a reward — but wakes to find all vanished.

Chloris, surrounded by the tender murmurs of her pigs (as if they were her moaning lovers), in fact cheaply dreams that she is a pastoral maiden in a literary Arcadia:

> She dreamt whilst she with careful pains
>   Her snowy arms employed
> In ivory pails to fill out grains,
> One of her love-convicted swains
>   Thus hasting to her cried.
>   [ll. 6–10]

The "snowy arms" and "ivory pails," and "love-convicted swains" are the stuff of pastoral romance and not of her own barnyard experience. She dreams that a swain leads her to a cave where one of her pigs is caught in a gate, only to throw himself lustfully upon her at their arrival. The penultimate stanza in the original 1680 version — the final stanza in Tonson's censored version of 1691 — parodies the pretty conclusion of Rochester's other pastoral:

> Now pierced is her virgin zone;
>   She feels the foe within it.
> She hears a broken amorous groan,
> The panting lover's fainting moan,
>   Just in the happy minute.
>   [ll. 31–35]

Gentle seduction is replaced, in the pointed climax, by a crude rape. Yet the poem is bawdier, and better, when the original concluding stanza is retained:

> Frighted she wakes, and waking frigs.
>   Nature thus kindly eased
> In dreams raised by her murmuring pigs
> And her own thumb between her legs,
>   She's innocent and pleased.
>   [ll. 36–40]

This final stanza restores the frame of the dream, implies that Chloris desired what she dreamed and pretended to resist, and makes comic use of a physical detail (the murmuring pigs) introduced in the opening lines. "Innocent and pleased" neatly describes this only partly self-deceived nymph: on the one hand she is "innocent" (naive) — not fully aware of what has happened — and "pleased" that it was only a dream; on the other, she has had the "pleasure" of orgasm but technically has retained the "innocence" of virginity.

It is true that neither indecency of this kind nor parody of pastoral artifice is unique to Rochester. The conventional fiction that all shepherdesses are pure and disdainful was often undercut by the cynical fiction (equally conventional) that they are secretly lustful. Rochester goes farther, to suggest that Chloris, in matters of sex, is on a level with her pigs, or with the hogs in "The Imperfect Enjoyment," who "on gates do rub themselves and grunt." Rarely if ever was a pastoral artifice so deftly yet so crudely parodied. The parody is extended to include the "disappointed dreamer" of a popular Restoration erotic song beginning "She lay all naked on her bed, / And I myself lay by."[39] Priming himself with a delicious description of her charms, the rake throws himself upon the girl, only to wake: "But pox upon't! 'Twas but a dream, / And so I lay without her" [i.e., masturbated]. Rochester's parody, by substituting swineherdess for aristocratic rake, discovers crudity not only in pastoral but in erotic fantasies (even punctured fantasies) as well.

Likewise in the "Pastoral Dialogue between Strephon and Daphne," Rochester parodies the conventional defense of male inconstancy. Instead of the expected love lament or persuasion to enjoy — Rochester's own "Pastoral Dialogue

39. In *Wit and Drollery* (1656), and frequently reprinted. See *Anthology of Restoration Erotic Poetry*, (n. 6 above), pp. 62–63, which also prints a variation on the theme (pp. 64–65).

between Alexis and Strephon" is typical of numerous
seventeenth-century examples — we hear Strephon taking
leave of his mistress, Daphne, arguing in fashion orthodox
for libertines but unusual for shepherds, that "Since 'tis nature's law to change, / Constancy alone is strange" (ll. 31–
32), and boasting of his honesty in declaring his inconstancy.
Daphne at length resigns herself, and Strephon urges her
to follow his example and "faith to pleasure sacrifice." Then
comes the witty reversal:

> Daphne. Silly swain, I'll have you know
> 'Twas my practice long ago.
> Whilst you vainly thought me true,
> I was false in scorn of you.
>
> By my tears, my heart's disguise,
> I thy love and thee despise,
> Womankind more joy discovers
> Making fools, than keeping lovers.
> [ll. 65–72]

As in the "Heroical Epistle," the libertine's mastery is exposed as a sham.

Such parodic reversals, exposing unexpected lower depths,
distinguish Rochester from the songwriters of his age. So,
too, do the songs in which a self-abasing lover becomes a
threatening cynic. Within a seeming compliment or complaint Rochester will plant tauntingly facetious praise, or
a hint of menacing savageness toward the woman he pretends to adore. While it is true that most of the sentiment in
Restoration love songs is tinged with irony, Rochester's use
of the ironic or sarcastic hint or thrust can be contrasted
with Sedley's and Dorset's, the former almost always grace-
fully polite and almost never intense or passionate with
love or hate, the latter gruffly and openly ironic, given less
to the indirect thrust concealed within praise than to open

raillery and witty scorn. Rochester's poems of threat recover the spirit of Carew.

In several slight songs [40] Rochester adopts the gallant pose of obeisant lover. At the same time, he reveals the masterful smile of the rake who only pretends to be powerless:

> But if this murder you'd forgo,
>   Your slave from death removing,
> Let me your art of charming know,
>   Or learn you mine of loving.
>   ["Whilst on those lovely looks I gaze"]

By the song's end, however, the mask slips, and the rake delivers hints at revenge, or a sarcastic rebuke to the "victor" who "lives with empty pride." In other songs the threat is even clearer. "Phyllis, be gentler" begins as a "persuasion to enjoy" but ends by flaunting the dull horrors of old age:

> Phyllis, be gentler, I advise;
>   Make up for time misspent:
> When beauty on its deathbed lies,
>   'Tis high time to repent.
>
> Such is the malice of your fate:
>   That makes you old so soon,
> Your pleasure ever comes too late,
>   How early e'er begun.
>
> Think what a wretched thing is she
>   Whose stars contrive, in spite,
> The morning of her love should be
>   Her fading beauty's night.

40. "Give me leave to rail at you," "While on those lovely looks I gaze." See also the rebuke of a lady in two Ovidian elegies: "I fall a sacrifice to Love, / She lives a wretch for Honor's sake" (*Complete Poems*, p. 14), "Live upon modesty and empty fame, / Forgoing sense for a fantastic name" (p. 19).

> Then, if to make your ruin more,
>   You'll peevishly be coy,
> Die with the scandal of a whore
>   And never know the joy.

We are left not with a mixed sense of beauty's transience and the urge to enjoy — the sweet sad tone of Herrick's "Gather ye Rose-buds," or the lusty urgency of Marvell's "Coy Mistress" — but with the bitter, soured tone of Carew's "Ingratefull Beauty Threatened":

> Know Celia, (since thou art so proud,)
> 'Twas I that gave thee thy renowne.
>
> Tempt me with such affrights no more,
> Lest what I made, I uncreate.
> [ll. 1–2, 13–14]

Both Carew and Rochester begin with imperative coldness — "I advise," "know" — and close with explicit threats of a kind of destruction.

Closer in theme to Carew's poem is another early lyric, in which Rochester strategically sustains two points of view on his disdainful mistress, his own slavish loyalty, and the indifference of other men:

> Insulting beauty, you misspend
>   Those frowns upon your slave:
> Your scorn against such rebels bend
> Who dare with confidence pretend
> That other eyes their hearts defend
>   From all the charms you have.
>
> . . . while I languish in despair,
> Many proud, senseless hearts declare
> They find you not so killing fair
>   To wish you merciful.

The speaker at once scorns other men as "dull," and reminds the lady that her appeal is limited. The point becomes clear in the last stanza:

> Nor am I unrevenged, though lost,
> Nor you unpunished, though unjust,
> When I alone, who love you most,
>   Am killed with your disdain.

The threat need not be uttered. The point is made that the mistress's power depends on her slave, not simply (as in "Phyllis, be gentler") on time's indulgence.[41]

More important than parody or threat, however, as the distinctive mark of Rochester as lyricist, is a handful of songs in which wit is suffused with tenderness or with pain, in which the lover is not triumphant (in his "servile chain," his wit, or his threat) but a prey to the uncertainties of love. "The Mistress," for example, presents a pair of lovers who suffer whether they are together or apart. Absence causes lovesick fancies, reunion leads to quarreling. But their complaints and jealousies, says the speaker, are "sacred," the "only proof . . . we love, and do not dream":

> Fantastic fancies fondly move
>   And in frail joys believe,
> Taking false pleasure for true love;
>   But pain can ne'er deceive.
>
> Kind jealous doubts, tormenting fears,
>   And anxious cares, when past,
> Prove our hearts' treasure fixed and dear,
>   And make us blest at last.

It is almost as if pain has been so habitually associated with true sexual pleasure that it becomes desired as a sign of

41. For a discussion of this theme as first developed by the Stuart love poets, see Hugh Richmond, *The School of Love* (Princeton, 1964).

authentic passion and even as a prerequisite for sexual bliss ("make us blest" is probably a gravely playful euphemism for a union both physical and spiritual).[42]

Love's pains are endemic too in "The Fall," which, as we have seen, develops feelings similar to those in the "Heroical Epistle":

> How blest was the created state
>   Of man and woman, ere they fell,
> Compared to our unhappy fate:
>   We need not fear another hell.
>
> Naked beneath cool shades they lay;
>   Enjoyment waited on desire;
> Each member did their wills obey,
>   Nor could a wish set pleasure higher.
>
> But we, poor slaves to hope and fear,
>   Are never of our joys secure;
> They lessen still as they draw near,
>   And none but dull delights endure.

The Fall is not offered as an explanation of flawed pleasure, only as a convenient indication of the differences between ideal and actual eroticism.[43] Nor, I think, is post-lapsarian fallibility associated with post-coital detumescence. The dull delights and insecure joys refer to more than the dullness of fruition. The poem expresses a general disillusion, felt by both man and woman, with all sensual pleasure.

42. Compare Butler: "Our pains are real things, and all / Our pleasures but fantastical." *Satires and Miscellaneous Poetry and Prose*, ed. R. Lamar (Cambridge, 1928), p. 36. Compare Etherege's "To ease my passion and to make me blest / The obliging smock falls from her whiter breast" ("The Imperfect Enjoyment," *Poems of Etherege*, [n. 7 above] p. 7), and Nemours' engaging "Be blest!" in Lee's *Princess of Cleve* (*The Works of Nathaniel Lee*, 2 vols., ed. T. B. Stroup and A. L. Cooke, 1954–1955, 2:203).

43. I disagree with Ronald Berman who finds nothing erotic "in this picture of two machines copulating eternally." "Rochester and the Defeat of the Senses," *Kenyon Review*, 26 (1964), 351.

The fourth stanza hints, however, that there may be a specific pain:

> Then, Chloris, while I duly pay
>   The nobler tribute of my heart,
> Be not you so severe to say
>   You love me for the frailer part.

The flesh is traditionally frail morally (easily tempted), but here frailty appears to be some physical disability. "Frailer part," in combination with "Each member did their wills obey" (the Edenic condition), suggests that this lover's frail member does not obey his will (cf. "The Imperfect Enjoyment"), that in effect he suffers from some form of impotence. Since the frailer part is unable to satisfy the lady, the speaker can only offer "the nobler tribute of my heart" (verbal professions of devotion). But he anticipates that, like the woman in "The Imperfect Enjoyment," she prefers "pleasure" to "love and rapture."

In "Absent from thee" the torments of love are not focused on the problem of temporary impotence, but on a compulsive "wandering." The lover, about to leave his mistress,[44] addresses her passionately:

> Absent from thee, I languish still;
>   Then ask me not, when I return?
> The straying fool 'twill plainly kill
>   To wish all day, all night to mourn.
>
> Dear! from thine arms then let me fly,
>   That my fantastic mind may prove
> The torments it deserves to try
>   That tears my fixed heart from my love.

44. A favorite theme with Rochester. Compare "Strephon and Daphne," "Heroical Epistle," "Tell me no more of constancy," "How happy, Chloris, were they free," "All my past life," " 'Tis not that I am weary grown."

When, wearied with a world of woe,
  To thy safe bosom I retire
Where love and peace and truth does flow,
  May I contented there expire,

Lest, once more wandering from that heaven,
  I fall on some base heart unblest,
Faithless to thee, false, unforgiven,
  And lose my everlasting rest.

Pinto has found in this song "the expression of a complex mood in which the poet at once regrets his infidelities and at the same time finds in them a contrast that increases his appreciation of the only love that can bring him happiness."[45] This comment is fine as far as it goes, but it only isolates two of the elements in the speaker's "complex mood." It suggests too much, furthermore, that the address and the plan are calculated efforts by a libertine lover to heighten pleasure. The song should be seen against a background of libertine defenses of inconstancy, but also as a comment on them. Although a hint remains of the strategic departure, the overwhelming sense in this song is that the speaker feels compelled to fling himself from woman to woman, like Charles II, restlessly rolling about from whore to whore.

The second striking characteristic of this song (besides the sense of irrational compulsion) is its proleptic quality. As in "The Maimed Debauchee," "Phyllis be gentler," and the "Song of a Young Lady," this song is filled with an imagination of future catastrophe so vivid that what is to come seems represented as already happening. Although he has not yet left his mistress, the speaker already languishes; already he suffers from her anticipated incessant wishing and mourning. His mind experiences even before leaving, "The torments it deserves to try / That tears my fixed heart from my love." He anticipates both his return to her safe bosom

45. *Enthusiast in Wit*, p. 54.

from weary wandering, and (in the very act of wishing the contrary) the inevitable urge to wander again. The nature of the final catastrophe is left vague. A "base heart unblest" may perhaps mean a miserable, or a wicked whore. Having envisioned a haven of security and a "fixed heart" the speaker declares finally his inability to rest.

The two women in the song are remarkably opposed to one another. The mistress is hardly sexualized at all. She is a protector (encircling arms, a safe bosom), associated not with desire but with "love and peace and truth," and represents to the speaker a kind of secularized salvation (she is a "heaven," the traveler's haven after a "world of woe," the promise of forgiveness and "everlasting rest"). In contrast, the other woman is "base" and "unblest," degraded and unsanctified, and the cause of deserved torments. The speaker seeks eternal union with the former, a figure who can only be described as maternal. That union cannot come about through his will. Only if he "expires" [46] in her bosom will he be able to avoid wandering to the deserved torments of an unending series of whores. Not only must this lover guiltily fly from safety to deserved torments, but he feels himself already hurried along. The same sense of helplessness in the face of "flying time" appears in a related song, "All my past life," another address by an inconstant lover:

> All my past life is mine no more;
>   The flying hours are gone,
> Like transitory dreams given o'er
>   Whose images are kept in store
>   By memory alone.
>
> Whatever is to come is not:
>   How can it then be mine?
> The present moment's all my lot,

46. Emits his last breath, with suggestions of sexual "dying," and perhaps the emission of semen, a kind of breath or spirit.

And that, as fast as it is got,
Phyllis, is wholly thine.

Then talk not of inconstancy,
    False hearts, and broken vows;
If I, by miracle, can be
    This livelong minute true to thee,
    'Tis all that heaven allows.

This lover disclaims all sense of guilt (reproach comes now from the lady), but shares with the lover in "Absent from thee" a sense that external and irrational forces (heaven, miracles) control his actions, and let him live his life one moment at a time [47] ("livelong minute" suggests that each moment, though brief, is a life).

It is true, of course, that the defense of inconstancy is is a traditional libertine departure strategy, and one that Rochester often employed.[48] In such a context, we can see something sophistical and impudent in the claim that heaven itself sanctions inconstancy. But impudent wit (if we sense it at all) is fused with a plaintive sense of powerlessness and transience that is lacking, for example, in Etherege's conventional "To a Lady, asking him how long he would love her":

Chloris, it is not in our power
To say how long our love will last,
It may be we within this hour
May lose those joys we now may taste;

47. Anne Righter acutely compares Kierkegaard's analysis of Don Giovanni: "'he does not have existence at all, but he hurries in a perpetual vanishing, precisely like music, about which it is true that it is over as soon as it has ceased to sound, and only comes into being again, when it sounds again' (*Either / Or*, Part 1)." "John Wilmot, Earl of Rochester," *Proc. Brit. Acad.*, 53 (1967), p. 60.

48. "A Pastoral Dialogue between Strephon and Chloe," "An Heroical Epistle," "'Tis not that I am weary grown," "Absent from thee."

The blessed that immortal be
From change in love are only free. (st. 1)

. . . .

Then since we mortal lovers are,
Let's question not how long 'twill last,
But while we love let us take care
Each minute be with pleasure past;
  It were a madness to deny
  To love because we're sure to die. (st. 3) [49]

Both Rochester's and Etherege's are "ask me not" songs, arguing the inevitability of change in love, and urging attention to the present moment. Etherege's witty melody, essentially a *carpe diem* lyric, illuminates by contrast Rochester's plaintive cry, and suggests that we need to look beyond literary convention for the source of power in this song and in "Absent from thee."

With such poems and with the obscene songs and "The Imperfect Enjoyment," we must move from literary traditions to psychological needs. The scurrilously obscene songs, for example, seem clearly a vehicle for Rochester to vent hostility and loathing for women and for sex. Obscene humor, in Freud's view, expresses a kind of hostility (arising from inhibition of the libidinal impulse), issuing in sexual aggression designed to "expose" the person at whom it is directed.[50] The appearance of such hostility and disgust in the poems of a notorious libertine invites speculation. Can it be traced to anxiety and self-disgust at sexual excesses or sexual failures? Freud argues also that obscene jokes make possible the satisfaction of a lustful instinct in the face of an obstacle.[51] They can thus serve, in the words of a recent Freudian analyst of sexual humor, to "absorb and control,

49. *Poems of Etherege*, (n. 7 above), p. 2.
50. "Jokes and their Relation to the Unconscious," *Standard Edition of the Complete Psychological Works*, ed. J. Strachey, et al., (London, 1953–1966), 8: 97–100.
51. *Ibid.*, p. 101.

even to slough off, by means of jocular presentation and laughter [a] great anxiety," to make "endurable, if only as a 'joke' " a "highly-charged neurotic situation." [52]

There is abundant evidence in Rochester's life of a highly charged neurotic situation, of constant sexual excess, and perhaps of failure (he writes to Savile of being an "Errant Fumbler" with women).[53] Impotence, in fact, is a common subject in the poems. In response to the suggestion that "The Imperfect Enjoyment" is properly seen as (in large part) a product of Rochester's painful sexual experience, it might be objected that the poem is after all conventional, even in specifying the problem as premature ejaculation. One can then counter by recalling the numerous other instances of impotence in his poems; or by asking why Rochester should choose this particular convention; or by noting how the vehemence of the curse exceeds convention. Some kind of psychological speculation is clearly invited by this poem, as it is by the love songs describing compulsive sexual wandering.

The Art of Impotence

A psychological and even a psychoanalytical approach to Rochester, while it is not the mode of analysis I have generally chosen to follow, seems to reach deeply into the meaning of a number of Rochester's poems about sex. Psychological material — fantasies, compulsions, aggressions, anxieties — is often remarkably overt or near the surface of his poems and should not be ignored. His life, as we know independently from biographical sources, was rich in neurotic activity — notorious philandering, chronic alcoholism, a violent combativeness — and it would hardly be surprising if his neuroses helped shape his poems, particularly since it

52. G. Legman, *Rationale of the Dirty Joke: An Analysis of Sexual Humor* (First Series, New York, 1968), pp. 13, 17.
53. *Letters*, p. 33.

has been almost universally felt that Rochester's songs are intensely personal. In the songs, where there is little opportunity for conventional analysis of speaker, theme, or style, psychological analysis can perhaps shed light. Rochester, however, is an unusual case. Freudian analysis is usually brought to bear upon literary materials in order to uncover hidden or disguised fears, anxieties, or obsessions, something the poet himself is not conscious of. This is not the case with Rochester. In his poems everything — or virtually everything — is manifest. Freudian analysis can tell us little that Rochester does not plainly tell us himself.

Consider first the many poems that are obsessed with compulsive sexual promiscuity and with several forms of sexual inadequacy — premature ejaculation, mechanical joyless copulation, or the debilities brought on by age or drink. In "To the Postboy," for example, Rochester boasts of having "swived more whores more ways than Sodom's walls / E'er knew, or the College of Rome's Cardinals." "St. James's Park," as we saw earlier, presents a series of promiscuous swivers, each more compulsive than the last — the speaker himself; the "ancient Pict" jilted by his whore and frustratedly frigging; the "Carmen, divines, great lords, and tailors" who come to the Park for "buggeries, rapes, and incests"; and finally Corinna, once the courtesan of half the town, and now a "whore in understanding," drawn compulsively into mechanical, joyless sex (indeed, a kind of psychical impotence),[54] "where neither head nor tail persuade." The lover in "Against Constancy" declares he will change mistresses every night until he is dead and fate changes him to worms. A self-avowed excellent lover, he longs "to be often tried." Constancy is a mere "pretense," a cover for the jealous and the dull, or for those "Old men

54. Freud includes psychanaesthetic patients — those who "never fail in the act but who carry it out without getting any particular pleasure from it" — among the psychically impotent. *Standard Edition,* 11:184.

and weak, whose idle flame / Their own defects discovers."
Inconstancy, in effect, becomes a proof (to himself and to
others) that the lover is neither dull nor defective. Impotence is the unspoken fear.

In several other poems compulsive sexual activity is explicitly associated with forms of impotence. The premature
lover in "The Imperfect Enjoyment" contrasts his presently
withered flower with its past performances:

> This dart of love, whose piercing point, oft tried,
> With virgin blood ten thousand maids have dyed;
> Which nature still directed with such art
> That it through every cunt reached every heart —
> Stiffly resolved, 'twould carelessly invade
> Woman or man, nor ought its fury stayed:
> Where'er it pierced, a cunt it found or made —
> Now languid lies in this unhappy hour.
> [ll. 37–44]

Charles II, in the satire upon him, is a man of high desires
but faulty execution: he is made helpless by his vast appetite — his prick "governs" this "poor Prince." [55]

> 'Tis sure the sauciest prick that e'er did swive,
> The proudest, peremptoriest prick alive.
> Though safety, law, religion, life lay on't,
> 'Twould break through all to make its way to cunt.
> Restless he rolls about from whore to whore,
> A merry monarch, scandalous and poor.
> ["A Satyr on Charles II," ll. 16–21]

"Poor" suggests that the King not only has exhausted the
royal treasury, but is sexually exhausted as well (without
sexual riches, unable to "spend"). This poverty is made
clear in the following lines, where "declining years" leave

---

55. In "The Imperfect Enjoyment" the speaker calls himself
"prince" and his penis a "base recreant," another link between the
two poems.

him "dull" and "graceless" in bed, and "cost" Nell Gwyn
(the spending metaphor again) endless pains "Ere she can
raise the member she enjoys." "The Maimed Debauchee"
works another variation on the impotent rake. Ostensibly
this philanderer imagines his future "days of impotence,"
when, "good for nothing else," he will advise from the side-
lines, and tell tales of his bold sexual exploits. The poem
hints, however, that the speaker is already impotent; concern with future impotence suggests a present problem.[56]

In a related poem about future decay, anxiety about impotence is also suggested.

> Ancient person, for whom I
> All the flattering youth defy,
> Long be it ere thou grow old,
> Aching, shaking, crazy, cold;
> But still continue as thou art,
> Ancient person of my heart.
> ["A Song of a Young Lady to her Ancient
> Lover," ll. 1–6]

The lover's age is no doubt exaggerated; he is apparently
not yet "old." But it is unclear to what condition "continue
as thou art" refers, and whether the lady goes on to speak
of what she will do in his old age, or what in fact she does
now:

> Thy nobler part, which but to name
> In our sex would be counted shame,
> By age's frozen grasp possessed,
> From [his] ice shall be released,
> And soothed by my reviving hand,
> In former warmth and vigor stand.
> [ll. 15–20]

As in "Absent from thee", the lover is in effect hurried into
his own future.

56. "Past joys have more than paid what I endure" (l. 24) is
grammatically a statement about the speaker's present, not his future.

The poems we have looked at make clear that Rochester was deeply concerned — indeed obsessed — with compulsive sexual promiscuity and with impotence. Although we may find the association paradoxical, Rochester often sees the promiscuous all-swiving rake as a figure plagued by sexual failure, or by doubts and fears of impotence. Psychoanalytic theory bears out the connection that Rochester establishes. The Don Juan in modern clinical descriptions (and in the legends that gave the pattern its name) is a compulsive philanderer. Though a sexual boaster, he spends his life trying to prove to himself that he can excite and conquer women and thereby prove his masculinity.[57] He is often a poor lover — psychically impotent — and his flight from woman to woman may be in effect a flight from each instance of his inadequacy.[58] Even when successful, "his doubts arise concerning other women whom he has not yet tried." Would he be potent with them?[59]

More deeply, according to Freudians, the Don Juan is fleeing from incest, from a strong emotional attachment to the mother, established in early infancy and never outgrown, the classical Oedipus complex: "The many women whom Don Juan has to replace again and again represent to him the irreplaceable mother."[60] Yet he must also flee from any mother-figure because of the ingrained prohibition against

57. Otto Fenichel, *The Psychoanalytic Theory of Neurosis* (New York, 1945), p. 243.

58. Gregorio Marañón, "Notas para la biologia de Don Juan," *Revista de Occidente* 3 (1924), 15–53. Marañón's argument that the Don Juan's promiscuity is a cover for impotence and homosexuality, at first controversial, has now received wide acceptance. He took up the subject again in *Don Juan y Donjuanism* (Madrid, 1940).

59. Fenichel, *The Psychoanalytic Theory*, pp. 243–244; G. H. Graber, "Die impotenten Don Juans," *Psychotherapy and Psychosomatics* 4 (1956), 140.

60. Otto Rank, "Die Don Juan Gestalt," *Imago* 8 (1922), 145; Freud, "A Special Type of Choice of Object Made by Men," *Standard Edition*, 11:109; Fenichel, *The Psychoanalytic Theory*, p. 243: "Don Juan's behavior is no doubt due to his Oedipus complex. He seeks his mother in all women and cannot find her."

incest. Associated with this pattern is the tendency to divide women into virginal mothers and lusty whores, those for whom one feels love (respect and affection) and those for whom one feels desire (but no respect). Where a man loves, says Freud, he cannot desire, and where he desires he cannot love.[61] The mother is at once sought and avoided. For she cannot be admissibly desired (only respected). In response to this dilemma, the subject seeks out an object he cannot respect, in order that his "sensual current" may be freed. To enjoy a women he must debase and despise her.

It would appear that "Absent from thee" is a particularly clear example of what Freud calls the failure of the "affectionate" and "sensual" currents to combine, a union he believes necessary (but rare) "to ensure a completely normal attitude in love." [62] The lover seeks union with a protective maternal figure, yet he must leave her. The "torments" he must experience would appear to be sexual, a "base heart unblest" very likely a common whore who will give him pleasure but cost him "forgiveness." The tendency may also lie behind "The Imperfect Enjoyment," where the pattern is somewhat clearer. Though the lady bears little apparent resemblance to a mother,[63] the speaker contrasts her — whom he is unable to satisfy — with the whores he has had. His member has been "true to lewdness" but "untrue to love" (l. 49):

> What oyster-cinder-beggar-common whore
> Didst thou e'er fail in all thy life before?
> When vice, disease, and scandal led the way,
> With what officious haste dost thou obey!

61. "On the Universal Tendency to Debasement in the Sphere of Love," *Standard Edition*, 11:183.

62. *Ibid.*, p. 180.

63. "Clips me to her breast" (l. 6) and "chides in a kind murmuring noise" (l. 19) might suggest a nursing mother, though they equally suggest a lover both vigorously passionate and affectionately ironic.

Like a rude, roaring hector in the streets
Who scuffles, cuffs, and justles all he meets

. . . .

Ev'n so thy brutal valor is displayed,
Breaks every stew, does each small whore invade,
But when great Love the onset does command,
Base recreant to thy prince, thou dar'st not stand.

[ll. 50–61]

The emphasis on disease and vice of the common street, and especially on the fact that his whores are "small" and "common," not high class courtesans, but "oyster-cinder-beggar-common whores," suggests the pattern of necessary debasement that Freud noticed.

The pattern appears too, though less distinctly, in the "Satyr on Charles II." Although Louise de Kéroualle (the Duchess of Portsmouth) and Nell Gwyn are whores, they are royal whores and great ladies, in contrast (presumably) to the series of unnamed sexual targets of the king's rambling invasive prick that restlessly rolls "from whore to whore." The poem implies that if Charles displays any virility at all, it is with the unnamed common whores, and that he especially has difficulty satisfying Carwell and Nelly, who exist for him (and for the reader) as individualized human beings (with names, feelings, and an imagined life).[64]

Psychoanalysts associate Don Juanism and psychical impotence — especially premature ejaculation — by tracing them to the same cause, a fixation of erotic attachment on the mother, an event likely to happen in cases where the child is either spoiled (smothered with love) or rejected (pushed

64. Morophilia (which figures, as I have already noted, in a number of poems) may also be a projection of the male need for debasement of the sexual object onto woman (Freud believed that women did not have this need [*Standard Edition*, 11:186–187]). Chloris cares not how dull her admirers are "so that their cods be full" (*Complete Poems*, p. 83). Corinna in "St. James's Park" picks up not wits but brainless fops, wouldwits, and boobies. The Duchess of Cleveland would "rather be fucked by porters and carmen" than by courtiers.

into manhood) by a strong mother.[65] The Don Juan and the premature ejaculator, furthermore, are both intensely narcissistic, the former striving for "narcissistic supplies in order to maintain self-esteem," the latter invariably in love only with himself.[66]

Biographical evidence would appear to bear out the possibility that Rochester himself suffered from the Don Juanism and psychical impotence he so often described. He was an only child, brought up by his strong-willed Puritan mother (he may never have even seen his father)[67] at the family home of her first husband.[68] Educated first at home, he was sent to university at twelve. There appear to have been ample opportunities for Rochester to have developed a strong and ambivalent bondage to such a mother.[69] Relations between them in Rochester's maturity must have been strained. She had to endure his notoriety, quarreled with her daughter-in-law, but triumphed in the end. She lived long enough to bury her "poor child," and fiercely defended the authenticity of his return to the bosom of the church.[70]

65. Freud, "Tendency to Debasement," *Standard Edition*, 11:180–181; Sandor Ferenczi, "The Analytic Interpretation and Treatment of Psychosexual Impotence," *First Contributions to Psycho-Analysis* (London, 1925), ch. 1; Karl Abraham, "Ejaculatio Praecox," in *Selected Papers*, tr. D. Bryan, A. Strachey (London, 1949), pp. 290–293.

66. Fenichel, *The Psychoanalytic Theory*, p. 243; "the psychoanalysis of every case of ejaculatio praecox reveals an abundance of other manifestations of narcissism as well." Abraham, *Selected Papers*, p. 291.

67. Henry Wilmot, a Royalist general, was with the Stuart kings, in battle or in exile, from 1647 until his death in 1658. There is no evidence that he ever saw his son.

68. Ditchley, the family seat of Sir Francis Henry Lee (d. 1640).

69. If the King (seventeen years Rochester's senior and a companion of his father) served as a kind of father-figure (he helped arrange Rochester's marriage, enjoyed his wit at court, and usually indulged his pranks), then Rochester's ambivalent attitude toward Charles — an indulgent master, a carousing partner, a fool to be lampooned, a withholder of favor — may be a kind of father-hatred linked (in the Oedipus complex) with love-hatred for his mother.

70. Five letters to her sister, describing the deathbed scene, are printed in Hayward, pp. 321–326.

He himself seems to have been intensely narcissistic. Extreme self-centeredness is perhaps the inevitable consequence of a morality based on gratification of the senses. In letters to one of his mistresses he claims — perhaps only half in jest — that "nothing is so agreeable to my Nature, as seeking my own satisfaction" and reminds her of its being "notorious that I mind nothing but my own Satisfaction." [71] In the "Heroical Epistle" and the "Epistolary Essay," as we have seen, a libertine openly professes that "in my dear self I center everything: / My servants, friends, my mistress, and my King; / Nay, heaven and earth to that one point I bring" — an almost schematic statement of narcissistic incorporation of external objects into the self — and that he writes poetry only to beget pleasure to his "dear self." Even if we discount some of these instances as playful exaggerations, Rochester's extreme concern for his "dear self" is at least a serious probability.

The hypothesis that Rochester lived and wrote as an impotent Don Juan would make coherent sense of (or at least not be contradicted by) a number of prominent psychological features associated by psychoanalysts with this problem, and characteristic of Rochester's life and poems. To take first the often-noted poems about homosexuality: the Don Juan, in some cases, flees from fears of latent homosexuality.[72] Freud has traced homosexuality to an early intense erotic attachment to the mother, especially when the father was weak or absent. This love is repressed; "he puts himself in her place, identifies with her, and takes his own person as a model in whose likeness he chooses the new objects of his love." [73] In many cultures homosexuality must be suppressed, and the suppression produces anxiety. This would not appear to be the case with Rochester. His age tolerated

71. Hayward, pp. 279, 277.
72. Marañón, "Notas para la biologia de Don Juan," (n. 58 above).
73. "Leonardo da Vinci and a Memory of his Childhood," *Standard Edition*, 11:99–100.

a certain degree of bisexuality, especially among libertine aristocrats. In a few poems ("The Platonic Lady," "Love a woman? You're an Ass!", "Upon His Drinking a Bowl," and "The Maimed Debauchee") the delights of young boys are openly admitted or even preferred to those of women. But in each case, as in these lines from "Love a woman?" the tone is light and witty —

> Then give me health, wealth, mirth, and wine,
> And, if busy love entrenches,
> There's a sweet, soft page of mine
> Does the trick worth forty wenches.

— suggesting that whatever homosexual tendencies Rochester may have had were easily expressed and satisfied.

A second feature of Rochester's poems which may plausibly be related to psychic impotence is the extraordinary imagery used in describing the vagina. Modern studies of *ejaculatio praecox* have discovered in many patients a "marked dread of the female genital," ultimately a castration anxiety, often a fear of losing the penis through the sexual act itself.[74] Rochester nowhere expresses overt dread of the vagina, but frequently describes it as a vast and hungry devourer. In an apparently gratuitous bit of obscenity associating sex and eating, the huge dining table in "Timon" is compared to the "bushel cunt" of a notorious court beauty. The Duchess of Cleveland, in "Signior Dildo," has "swallowed more pricks than the ocean has sand." One song urges Celia to imitate the "willing womb" of the "kind seed-receiving earth," and be "the mistress of mankind."[75] In another, also encouraging female promiscuity, the lover urges Chloris to let him drink (take in the "lusty juice of grapes") while she whores (takes in "the juice of lusty

74. Abraham, "Ejaculatio Praecox," pp. 288–289; J. Frois-Wittman, "Analyse d'un cas de troubles sexuels avec anxieté et symptomes hypochondriaques," *Revue Française de Psychanalyse* 5 (1932), 535–539.
75. *Complete Poems*, p. 81.

men") .[76] Most notable for this pattern of imagery, of course, is "St. James's Park," where Corinna's voracious and aggressive lust [77] is imagined in terms of eating:

> When your lewd cunt came spewing home
> Drenched with the seed of half the town,
> My dram of sperm was supped up after
> For the digestive surfeit water.
> Full-gorged at another time
> With a vast meal of nasty slime
> Which your devouring cunt had drawn
> From porters' backs and footmen's brawn,
> I was content to serve you up
> My ballock-full for your grace cup.
>   [ll. 113–122]

While the earlier cited examples are only brief eating metaphors, which bear little apparent loathing or fear, this is an extended and vehement denunciation. Note further that the vagina is a prodigious consumer, while the speaker sees himself as diminuitive: he can provide only a "dram" or a "ballock-full," a "grace-cup" as opposed to a "vast meal." The passage reflects back on the "grave discourse / Of who fucks who, and who does worse" at the beginning of the poem (where eating and sex are already associated). It is clear that woman "fucks" man — and ("worse") eats him up. This is perhaps not overt dread (indeed the speaker claims he was "content"), nor overt fear of castration. This *vagina* is not explicitly *dentata*. On the other hand, the dread of being eaten, according to psychoanalysis, is "indissolubly connected with the idea of being castrated." [78] Furthermore,

76. *Ibid.*, p. 85.

77. It is made clear that she is the sexual aggressor: "Had she *picked out, to rub her arse on,* / Some stiff-pricked clown or well-hung parson, / Each job of whose spermatic sluice / Had filled her cunt with wholesome juice" (ll. 91–94).

78. O. Fenichel, "The Dread of Being Eaten," *Collected Papers: First Series* (New York, 1953), p. 159.

fixated emotional attachment to a strong mother, in Freud's classical account, often brings with it a fear of being castrated or being absorbed into her dominating self. To a child, or to someone who still thought as a child, a vagina would no doubt seem huge and threatening.

Hostility toward the mother may also lie behind two apparently unrelated features of "The Imperfect Enjoyment" and "St. James's Park." In the latter poem incest figures twice, as a common form of swiving in the Park, and as a magical explanation of the landscape. The frustrated Pict, jilted by his whore, "frig[s] upon his mother's face" (the "teeming earth"), whence phallic mandrakes grow, "Whose lewd tops fucked the very skies." One element of this complex fantasy would appear to be a hostile contempt of the mother through a desire to soil her (as if she had been the one who caused his sexual frustration). A hostile desire to soil the woman (mother) has also been recognized in *ejaculatio praecox*. Instead of gratifying a woman, a man ejaculates (as it were) in her face.[79] "The Imperfect Enjoyment," on an unconscious level, may in fact represent a hatred not of the penis but of the woman. If she, like other women in the poems, is thought of as an omnivorous mouth, then he denies her the demanded meal.

Not only does the psychoanalytic hypothesis offer a fairly coherent account of some essential elements of Rochester's poems about sex and women, but it may set in relation several often noted characteristics of his behavior. While the poems are, of course, our central concern, it is interesting to note what psychoanalysis might suggest about Rochester's notorious quarrelsomeness, cowardice, and alcoholism, as well, perhaps, as his hypochondria. The first three characteristics are well known from the Epsom incident where, drunk and in a whoring mood, Rochester quite without provoca-

79. Abraham, "Ejaculatio Praecox," pp. 295–296. Such exhibitionism is, in fact, ambivalent, a sign of both hostility and of love (through the offering of a "gift").

tion "drew on the constable" and then fled when a companion was mortally wounded. The incident was not an isolated one: he told Burnet that "for five years together he was continually Drunk." His quarrelsome — not to say homicidal — temper got him into three duels, all of them averted, one (it seems likely) when Rochester refused to fight.[80] The attack on the phallic garden "dial" at Whitehall is an interesting example of drunken violence perhaps combined with castration anxieties. Hypochondria is suggested by the numerous (often theatrical) complaints about his illnesses throughout his letters, and by a riposte from Savile on one of those occasions ("If your Lordship was as ill as you told mee in your letter, either you are a greater philosopher in bearing of pain or a greater hypocrite in making it more then it is then we can ordinarily meet with in these parts").[81]

Such a combination of psychological characteristics is perhaps not unusual in a Restoration rake. Psychoanalysis suggests they might all be related to impotence. In men suffering from premature ejaculation, "the tendency to be quarrelsome, to have fits of anger, and to commit violent acts, is extraordinarily marked . . . in so far as it is not paralyzed by another character trait which distinguishes them, namely, cowardice."[82] Hypochondria has been traced to castration anxieties and intense fixation on the mother.[83] It has been

80. Evidence of Rochester's cowardice on this occasion is not conclusive.

81. *Letters*, p. 48. Rochester's interest in "books of physic" (Burnet, p. 31) may be another suggestion of hypochondria. He complained several times of "stone" (a concretion in the kidney or bladder). *Letters*, p. 65; Hayward, pp. 292, 295. Cf. "The Imperfect Enjoyment," l. 68.

82. Abraham, "Ejaculatio Praecox," p. 287.

83. "As a rule, [hypochondria] represents, in a distorted manner, castration anxiety. . . . The typical hypochondriac is a conspicuously narcissistic, seclusive, and monomaniacal creature." Fenichel, *The Psychoanalytic Theory*, (n. 57 above), pp. 262–263. Cf. A. Hesnard, "Le mécanisme psychanalytique de la psychonévrose hypochondriaque," *Revue Française de Psychanalyse* 3 (1929), 110–121, and 4 (1930), 549–550.

linked, furthermore, with both premature ejaculation [84] and with philandering.[85] Alcoholism, too, is often intimately-associated with impotence. Men whose sexual powers become weakened often turn to alcohol, imagining it "increases their virility, because it gives them a feeling of sexual power." [86] Excessive use of alcohol, in fact, is more likely to take men off than set them on. It can aggravate impotence and lead to further frustration and drinking (Rochester was drunk "five years together"). But alcoholics often fail to recognize that drink has not helped their potency. "They will not give up alcohol, and they continue to identify it with their sexuality and to use it as a surrogate of the latter." [87] Some such identification may lie behind several poems where drinking is preferred to sex:

> Farewell woman! I intend
> Henceforth every night to sit
> With my lewd, well-natured friend,
> Drinking to engender wit.[88]

Drinking is quite explicitly a surrogate "engendering." Another poem, already quoted, makes an extensive comparison

84. Frois-Wittman, *"Analyse d'un cas de troubles sexuels,"* (n. 74 above), 513–517.

85. "There are innumerable examples of [married] philanderers who become neurotic health complainers because of their need for self-punishment following some transgression." F. S. Caprio, *The Sexually Adequate Male* (New York, 1952, p. 115).

86. K. Abraham, "Sexuality and Alcoholism," in *Selected Papers*, (n. 65 above), pp. 86–87. Cf. Rochester's letter to Savile: "send some good Wine! So may thy wearied Soul at last find Rest, no longer hov'ring 'twixt th'unequal Choice of Politicks and Lewdness!" *Letters*, p. 32; "of the three businesses of this Age, Woemen, Polliticks, and drinking, the last is the only exercise att wch. you and I have nott prouv'd our selves Errant Fumblers," *ibid.*, p. 33. Cf. also his remark about "The strange decay of Manly Parts," *ibid.*, p. 46.

87. Abraham, "Sexuality and Alcoholism," p. 87.

88. *Complete Poems*, p. 51. The poem goes on to profess a delight in boys. The associations, in psychoanalysis, between alcoholism and homosexuality, are numerous. Abraham, "Sexuality and Alcoholism," p. 83; Fenichel, *The Psychoanalytic Theory*, p. 379.

between Chloris's drinking "the juice of lusty men" and the speaker's drinking "the lusty juice of grapes." The "rival bottle" (l. 7) is clearly a surrogate woman.

It ought not to be concluded from such psychoanalytic speculation that Rochester's poems are of interest only because they appear to reveal his neuroses. That the poems have indeed appealed to a wide range of readers is an established fact. Psychoanalysis might suggest why the poems have been so appealing. Rochester's psychological concerns are not merely his own. Modern theorists have argued, indeed, that castration anxiety, the tendency to degradation in love, and especially psychical impotence, are to a certain degree characteristic of the love life of civilized man.[89] The poems, furthermore, are not the confessions of a libertine on the couch, but works of art. Whatever private impulses they contain have been mediated by the shaping forces of Rochester's vigorous wit and energy. The appeal of the poems does not depend on our intimate acquaintance with his psyche. On the other hand, their particular power and intensity — Rochester clearly excels all his song-writing and woman-satirizing contemporaries — may derive from the richness of the fantasy material, manifest or unusually close to the surface, from his apparently deep personal stake in them, and from his remarkable ability to confront such material directly and openly, to reflect upon it and become, as it were, a spectator of himself.

The importance of Rochester's self-consciousness, his unillusioned self-regard (both regard *of* — self-knowledge — and regard *for* — egotism) cannot be overemphasized. He regards himself without pretense, without guilt. It is as if he pulls back his own stage curtain, and invites us to look on with him. We see nothing in Rochester that he does not see himself. For a reader, the psychological and aesthetic effect is curious. Just as Rochester seems to display in these poems

89. Freud, "On the Universal Tendency to Debasement in the Sphere of Love," *Standard Edition*, 11:184–187.

neither guilt, nor shame, nor perverse pleasure in his wickedness (he is neither confessing sinner nor exhibitionist), so we feel no embarrassment or guilt. We are an invited audience, struck here (as always in his poems) with Rochester's candor — he bluntly says what is on his mind — and with his clarity of observation. But because he hides nothing from himself or from us, Rochester's invitation carries with it something of a discomforting challenge. What discomfort we feel is not the secret shame of a voyeur; we are more clearly and openly thrown on the defensive. In the poems about sex the author of the "Satyr Against Mankind" may speak of private experience, but by implication he claims that if men were honest about their feelings and fears, they might recognize themselves in him. Our self-esteem and comfortable notions of human dignity and decency are challenged by a conception of the naked human animal that we are asked to accept or refute.

For Rochester himself the effect was no doubt rather different. For him, perhaps, neurotic fantasy was turned into art. The anxiety is clearly observed, understood, in part controlled, and in a sense mastered. It is perhaps only through artful expression of anxiety that Rochester attained that mastery of his situation he always sought. With artistic potency, perhaps, he both explored and compensated for sexual impotence. The rake may have lacked control over his unruly penis, but the poet displays a witty control of his objects, central among them that very inadequacy.

"Artemisia to Chloe"

Clearly not all of Rochester's poems are so intensely personal, or so closely bound up with private anxieties. In much of his work he presents himself fiercely engaged — some of the songs, the "Satyr Against Mankind," "Timon," "Tunbridge Wells," "St. James's Park," "The Imperfect Enjoyment," the "Heroical Epistle" — but elsewhere he chooses a kind of amused detachment. Always a controlling artist and to some degree a "spectator" (even in intimate poems where, as libertine lover, he is beset with anxieties), on one major occasion he observes not himself but the world. The libertine is neither speaker nor subject, nor is he even present (except in a minor off-stage role) in "A Letter from Artemisia in the Town to Chloe in the Country" (c. 1675), his longest satire, and a performance which may come to be considered his best. This poem displays the same concerns treated in the songs and other satires — sex and love are bound up with pain, hostility, and exploitation — but here those concerns are even more distanced from the poet, projected onto a wide social panorama. "Artemisia to Chloe," a dramatic poem whose speakers are all women, presents with satire and sympathy the attitudes toward love of three quite different kinds of women: Artemisia herself; the "fine lady" whose antics she describes in her letter; and poor Corinna, whose triumphs, falls, and recoveries in love are recounted by the "fine lady." For this satire Rochester drew not on the traditions of literary misogyny, but, as with "St. James's Park" and "Tunbridge Wells," on contemporary English stage comedy, a fact which may help to account for the poem's vivid scenic quality, its dramatization of conflicting points of view, and the acutely conversational, "talky" quality of its couplets.

"Artemisia to Chloe" draws also on Rochester's earlier poems spoken by women. He had experimented with a female speaker as early as 1673, in the "Letter from Miss Price to Lord Chesterfield," a poem interesting only for its use of this technique, and in the much better "Song of a Young Lady to her Ancient Lover" (c. 1674–1676). But we can most clearly observe Rochester preparing for "Artemisia to Chloe" in an untitled fragment of fifty-five lines beginning "What vain, unnecessary things are men!" Not published until the twentieth century, these lines represent one of the few clues we have about Rochester's process of composition and revision.[90] And although the precise relationship between this fragment and the completed "Artemisia to Chloe" remains unclear, it seems likely that this revised poem was itself drawn on, radically revised perhaps, for the more ambitious satire.

The female speaker of the fragment rails against her fellow women, who meanly submit to the beastly men of the age. She is far more vehement and contemptuous of men than Artemisia, but her attack on the female sex anticipates Artemisia's angry complaint that the corruption of love by "ill-bred customs" is due chiefly to women:

> But what yet more a woman's heart would vex,
> 'Tis chiefly carried on by our own sex;
> Our silly sex! who, born like monarchs free,
> Turn gypsies for a meaner liberty,
> And hate restraint, though but from infamy.
> [ll. 54–58]

The following lines, the best in the fragment, present from the woman's point of view a vivid picture of the "women-fairs," where men come to pick out women as if they were horses. One cries:

> . . . "Look! de God, that wench is well enough:
> Fair and well-shaped, good lips and teeth, 'twill do;
> She shall be tawdry for a month or two
> At my expense, be rude and take upon her,
> Show her contempt of quality and honor,
> And, with the general fate of errant woman,
> Be very proud awhile, then very common."
> [ll. 14–20]

This contempt for women is, in effect, protested by presenting the scene from a woman's point of view. The passage, as

90. For a discussion of Rochester's revisions of this poem and of others in the Portland MS, see *ARP*, ch. 7.

we shall see, was perhaps transmuted into the story of
Corinna, who, deserted by her lovers, endures want and
dirt "that for one month she tawdry may appear."

Like Artemisia after her, the woman speaker of the fragment looks back to an older ideal of love:

> Ere bear this scorn, I'd be shut up at home,
> Content with humoring myself alone;
> Force back the humble love of former days
> In pensive madrigals and ends of plays,
> When, if my lady frowned, th' unhappy knight
> Was fain to fast and lie alone that night.
> But whilst th'insulting wife the breeches wore,
> The husband took her clothes to g[i]ve his ————,
> Who now maintains it with a gentler art:
> Thus tyrannies to commonwealths convert.
>
> [ll. 21–30]

No sooner does she imagine herself on the pedestal of a
former day than she realizes how that pedestal, and the husband, must be shared with a whore. Having begun by
scorning men, she now realizes the way of the world —

> Then, after all, you find, whate'er we say,
> Things must go on in their lewd natural way,
> Besides, the beastly men, we daily see,
> Can please themselves alone as well as we.
>
> [ll. 31–34]

— and asks the "kind ladies of the town" to return the husbands they have ravished. The reversal is skillfully managed,
and the speaker's acquired wisdom — a somewhat dispassionate, skeptical assessment of love — contributed something,
I suspect, to the even-handed, finally quite dispassionate
survey of the ways of love and lovers in "Artemisia to Chloe."

In the latter poem, the speaker relates to her country correspondent what has happened in town "since you and I

met last." She begins ironically by reminding Chloe (and herself) of the dangers in writing poetry and then resolves to plunge ahead anyway. Lamenting that love has been debauched, she blames chiefly women, and offers as an example a "fine lady" whom she had met while visiting "the other night." The remainder of the poem is spent describing the lady and in quoting her rambling monologue in defense of fools as "true women's men." The fine lady offers as an example the story of Corinna, whose misfortunes in love were repaired when she conquered and lived off a fool. Artemisia concludes the letter with a few final comments, and promises to write more of such stories by the next post.

Thematically, the poem is quintessential Rochester. Just as the "Satyr Against Mankind" is his broadest view of man as a reasoning animal whose pride in reason causes him to overextend himself and ultimately to suffer, escaping pain (if at all) only when he cheats other men, so the letter from "Artemisia to Chloe" is his most comprehensive view of man as a social animal whose endeavors in writing poetry, in courtship, and in marriage, except when he resolves to exploit other men, are self-destructive. Just as in the "Satyr," all men are dishonest, the only difference being "who's a knave of the first rate," so in "Artemisia to Chloe" all men and women prey on each other, seeking to discover who can better "undo" the others.

Rochester's world is like the Hobbesian state of nature: war of all on all. Victory goes not to the wits, but to the cheats, crafty and self-interested, and to women. Victory does not necessarily draw forth our approval, but neither does it elicit condemnation. "Artemisia to Chloe" is curiously reluctant to make judgments without going on to qualify them. The poem, unlike wit comedy, has no hero. Artemisia, who at times seems to represent some sort of norm, is herself qualified and satirized by herself and by the reader. The poem ends not with marriage but with the death of a foolish husband, and Artemisia's own attitudes toward and relations with men are left unstated.

The poem begins curiously. Apparently Chloe, her correspondent, has asked Artemisia to write a poetical epistle:

> Chloe,
> In verse by your command I write.
> Shortly you'll bid me ride astride, and fight:
> These talents better with our sex agree
> Than lofty flights of dangerous poetry.
> Amongst the men, I mean the men of wit
> (At least they passed for such before they writ),
> How many bold adventurers for the bays,
> Proudly designing large returns of praise,
> Who durst that stormy, pathless world explore,[91]
> Were soon dashed back, and wrecked on the dull shore,[92]
> Broke of that little stock they had before!
> How would a woman's tottering bark be tossed
> Where stoutest ships, the men of wit, are lost?
>
> [ll. 1–13]

Like other major satires by Rochester — the "Satyr Against Mankind," "An Allusion to Horace," the "Epistolary Essay" — this one is in part about poetry. Artemisia, commanded to write in verse, self-consciously sets about her task in the very process of urging its dangers. She ironically exaggerates what was probably Chloe's request to the status of a command. Ironically, too, she inflates the dangers of poetry's lofty flights: the voyaging metaphor she employs

91. Possibly parodying the exaggerations in humble prefaces, e.g., Alexander Brome's dedicatory epistle to the *Poems of Horace* (1666). Brome delayed writing, he said, until "I had broken through all the difficulties which my imbecility contended with; and thrown myself on this audacious adventure" (Sigs. A_4–Av_4 1). Compare also Oldham, "A Satire dissuading from Poetry," in which the voice of Spenser warns him "To shun the dangerous rocks of Poetry," *The Works of Mr. John Oldham*, (final rev. ed. 1722), 2:149.

92. Compare "The Maimed Debauchee," l. 16, "The dull shore of lazy temperance."

to describe the danger is itself a lofty flight sustained through seven lines.

These opening lines introduce three features which find their analogues in the larger design of the poem: ironic, self-conscious self-mockery in the speaker, whose actions seem to contradict her own advice; self-destruction, in which men (in this case the men of wit) are shown to work their own woe;[93] and qualification (as in the "Satyr") in which a statement, observation, or judgment is made and then adjusted: "Amongst the men, I mean the men of wit / (At least they passed for such before they writ)." Artemisia twice qualifies "men" — first to "men of wit," and then (skipping the stage of "one-time men of wit") to men who once could pass successfully for men of wit.

Self-consciousness is a marked feature of the following lines:

> When I reflect on this, I straight grow wise,
> And my own self thus gravely I advise:
>   Dear Artemisia, poetry's a snare;
> Bedlam has many mansions; have a care.
> Your muse diverts you, makes the reader sad:
> You fancy you're inspired; he thinks you mad.
> Consider, too, 'twill be discreetly done
> To make yourself the fiddle of the town,
> To find th'ill-humored pleasure at their need,
> Cursed if you fail, and scorned though you succeed!
> Thus, like an arrant woman as I am,
> No sooner well convinced writing's a shame,
> That whore is scarce a more reproachful name
> Than poetess —[94]

93. Compare "Satyr Against Mankind," l. 32, "Pride . . . made him venture to be made a wretch," and the early song, "While on those lovely looks I gaze / To see a wretch pursuing, / In raptures of a blest amaze, / His pleasing, happy ruin."

94. Compare Oldham, "A Satire dissuading from Poetry," claiming that even the poetess Sappho, if revived, would have to be a whore to make a living (*Works*, 2:155), and Gould, "The Poetess, a

Like men that marry, or like maids that woo,
'Cause 'tis the very worst thing they can do,
Pleased with the contradiction and the sin,
Methinks I stand on thorns till I begin.

[ll. 14–31]

The main thrust of Artemisia's meaning is clear: "I realize
the dangers in writing poetry, but I will write anyway."
Clear, too, is the kind of irony and self-mockery in "gravely,"
"I . . . grow wise," "discreetly," and "like an arrant woman
as I am." But some of the sallies of her wit are oblique. She
combines a light, almost frivolous, tone — the parody of
heaven's many mansions, and the colloquial "fiddle of the
town" — with a bitter jibe: "To find th'ill-humored pleasure at their need, / Cursed if you fail, and scorned though
you succeed." The sense of the first line is unclear: if "ill-
humored" is a noun standing for the people of the town,
then the poet becomes a court-jester for an ill-natured
king;[95] if, as is less likely, "ill-humored" is an adjective
modifying "pleasure," then poetry itself, paradoxically, becomes an "ill-humored pleasure." These lines serve the
added purpose of developing the pattern of willful self-
destruction: men marry and maids woo *just because* it is the
worst thing they can do. So Artemisia writes in verse with
full knowledge of its pitfalls, perhaps even because of its
pitfalls — what she seems to call "the contradiction and the
sin." As poetry, the lines are uneven. The half-line is used
well, putting scornful stress on "poetess," and leaving a
pause for still greater emphasis. But the couplet rhetoric —
"Pleased with the contradiction and the sin" — is not well
managed. It is not clear whether "contradiction" belongs
with "men," and "sin" with "maids," or vice versa, or

Satyr," attacking a hostile poetess as a whore (Gould's *Works* [Lon-
don, 1709], 2:15–25).

95. Cf. "Satyr Against Mankind," l. 36, "pleasing others at his own
expense," and the translation of Ovid, *Amores* 2:9, 1:21, "The har-
assed whore, who lived a wretch to please."

whether "contradiction" and "sin" refer only to writing poetry. "Contradiction" probably means, in general, the contradiction between one's own best interests and the actions one takes, either between what men know they ought to do and what they end up doing, or what they approve and what they in fact follow, as in Ovid's "I see the better, I approve it too: / The worse I follow." [96] "Sin," along with "shame" and "reproachful name," seems to reflect no more than Artemisia's habit of ironic exaggeration. There is no clear reason why she should exaggerate in this particular way; the question of the ethics of writing is not really significantly raised; "pleased with the sin" parodies (by exaggeration) the guilty pleasure of willfully disobeying prohibitions. The passage concludes with a neat irony: Artemisia stands on thorns until she begins her letter.[97] Not only does a practicing poet suffer anxieties; even the would-be poet suffers privation. Poets, it appears, are damned when they write, and damned when they don't. Her poetical letter, we soon discover, promises to be little more than social gossip:

> Y'expect at least to hear what loves have passed
> In this lewd town, since you and I met last;
> What change has happened of intrigues, and whether
> The old ones last, and who and who's together.
> But how, my dearest Chloe, shall I set
> My pen to write what I would fain forget?
> Or name that lost thing, love, without a tear,
> Since so debauched by ill-bred customs here?[98]

Artemisia would relay news of the latest intrigues, but (with characteristic exaggeration) says she cannot begin to

96. *Metamorphoses* 7:20–21 (tr. Sandys).

97. Artemisia may allude to the traditional claim that it is difficult *not* to write. See Juvenal, *Satire* 1, Horace, *Satire* 2:1.

98. Cf. "What vain, unnecessary things are men," ll. 3–4: "Whence comes that mean submissiveness we find / This ill-bred age has wrought on womankind."

speak of love's corruptions or even mention the word "love."
She goes on, of course, to speak of "Love" in the next
breath ("Love, the most generous passion of the mind," l. 40)
and to describe at great length, although indirectly, the
intrigues of Corinna. The lines are marked by a mock-
gravity, and by a continuing facetiousness which prevent us
from taking them seriously. What is perhaps most remarkable, however, is the fidelity to the rhythms of casual correspondence, or even to clichés of conversation — "What
change has happened of intrigues, and whether / The old
ones last, and who and who's together." [99] No other poet in
the Restoration wrote couplets with as fine an ear for informal speech.

After declaring her inability to set pen to paper, Artemisia
launches into the poem's loftiest passage, in praise of the
ideal of love now lost:

> Love, the most generous passion of the mind,
> The softest refuge innocence can find,
> The safe director of unguided youth,
> Fraught with kind wishes, and secured by truth;
> That cordial drop heaven in our cup has thrown
> To make the nauseous draught of life go down;
> On which one only blessing, God might raise
> In lands of atheists, subsidies of praise,
> For none did e'er so dull and stupid prove
> But felt a god, and blessed his power in love —
> This only joy for which poor we were made
> Is grown, like play, to be an arrant trade.
> The rooks creep in, and it has got of late
> As many little cheats and tricks as that.
>
> [ll. 40–53]

99. Compare the fashionable fops in Swift's "Cadenus and Va-
nessa" who give "hints of who and who's together," and Mrs. Western
in *Tom Jones* 4:2, who knew "the world" and "Who and who were
together." The "grave discourse / Of who fucks who" ("St. James's
Park") may parody this cliché.

Vieth says, inaccurately I think, that Artemisia speaks here "self-righteously of the traditional spirituality of love." [100] I would say she is rather self-conscious than self-righteous; she makes no claims for her own kind of love; indeed, she generalizes as much as possible. As we have come to expect, she eschews moderation, inclining toward superlatives ("most generous," "softest") and absolutes ("the only blessing," "none") and a daring richness in metaphor: "cordial drop," [101] subsidies in lands of atheists. The former of these metaphors, perhaps suggested by a famous passage in Lucretius,[102] makes God a physician and perhaps a philosopher; the latter likens God to a constitutional monarch seeking funds. From metaphors which make love a sweetening drop and a blessing, she then surprisingly descends to metaphorical equivalence between love and "play," or gambling.[103] We are back, once more, in the world of satire, a world which, in one of Rochester's key metaphors, is nothing so much as a game of chance plagued by swindlers.

It is difficult to know how to orient this expression of an ideal within the poem and within Rochester's works as a whole. We suspect, I think, that Artemisia's voice still carries an edge of facetiousness; she realizes the highly dramatic value of this vivid juxtaposition of old ideal and present reality. The very richness of the passage should perhaps

100. *Complete Poems*, p. xl.

101. Rochester's couplet on the "cordial drop" was striking enough to be remembered and adapted by many eighteenth-century writers. See Pope, *Imit. Hor. Ep.* 1:6, ll. 126–127; *Walpole's Correspondence*, ed. W. S. Lewis *et al.* (New Haven, 1937–), vol. 31, p. 111; vol. 28, p. 331; Boswell's *Life*, ed. G. B. Hill, rev. L. F. Powell (Oxford, 1934), 3:386–387; Lady Mary Wortley Montagu's *Collected Letters*, ed. R. Halsband (Oxford, 1966–1967), 3:223.

102. Lucretius compares his doctrine set out in poetry to the physician's bitter medicine sweetened with honey. The "cordial drop" may have been a commonplace, but note that Rochester makes no claims for the beneficent qualities of the "nauseous draught."

103. Rochester puns quietly on the older senses of both "play," — "amorous disport, dalliance" — and "cordial," — "of or belonging to the heart."

warn us that this is neither the thematic center of the poem nor an expression of Rochester's deepest beliefs. On the other hand, the language seems to recall the conception of love in some of the songs, where love is a soft "refuge" for innocence, a director of youth, a haven of security, essentially a mother's arms.[104] Rochester seems to have been preoccupied, as I have suggested earlier, with the desire of all men for a place of security and rest — from the anxious and compulsive lovers, to the wits earlier in this poem who find no harbor and are "wrecked on the dull shore," to man as a species in the "Satyr Against Mankind" whose behavior is governed always by fear, by the wish "to make himself secure." Whatever the relative weight of Artemisia's slightly facetious and self-conscious spirituality on the one hand, and Rochester's deepest feeling about generosity and security on the other, we can neither discount this ideal of love as mere irony or exaggeration nor conceive of any way in which this ideal might be realized in the Hobbesian kind of world described in the rest of the poem.[105] Rochester is not, I think, measuring the corrupt present against a glorious past; he seems to say, rather, perhaps with some regret, that the old ideal is simply irrelevant to the way people are.

Just as the lines on the "cordial drop" seem to contain the spirit of Rochester's best songs, so the following contain the spirit of some of his best satire on affectation, fashion, and passionless love:

104. Compare the early love elegy, "The Submission": "There can be no danger in sweetness and youth / Where love is secured by good nature and truth" (ll. 13–14). Rochester seems to have remolded the earlier lines and given them a less sprightly tone.

105. Note that Hobbes's conception of love is wholly self-directed rather than "generous": "That which men desire, they are also said to love, and to hate those things for which they have aversion. So that desire and love are the same thing; save that by desire, we always signify the absence of the object; by love, most commonly the presence of the same" (Burtt, p. 149).

But what yet more a woman's heart would vex,
'Tis chiefly carried on by our own sex

. . . .

They call whatever is not common, nice,
And deaf to nature's rule, or love's advice,
Forsake the pleasure to pursue the vice.
To an exact perfection they have wrought
The action, love; the passion is forgot.
'Tis below wit, they tell you, to admire,
And ev'n without approving, they desire.
Their private wish obeys the public voice;
'Twixt good and bad, whimsey decides, not choice.
Fashions grow up for taste; at forms they strike;
They know what they would have, not what they like.
Bovey's a beauty, if some few agree
To call him so; the rest to that degree
Affected are, that with their ears they see.

[ll. 54–55, 59–72]

Perhaps more epigrammatic than Rochester's usual couplets, these lines show off his satire at its best: fluid and fast-moving, unerringly colloquial in diction and rhythm. Contrast between natural and unnatural is the theme of the passage, conveyed through the couplet rhetoric, particularly antithesis and the use of negatives: "private" and "public," "whimsey" and "choice," "fashion" and "taste," "ears" and (implicitly) eyes. The real unnaturalness of fashion, however, is suggested not through such standard contrasts as private and public, but through the use of opposed pairs of terms that we do not ordinarily think of as opposites.

Ordinarily we would not take "common" and "nice" to be true antitheses. But to the fashionable ladies, whatever is not "common" (i.e., fashionable, accepted by all competent judges) is "nice" (particular, over-refined).[106] Likewise, we

106. This difficult line, as I read it, makes the women of fashion prefer the common to the nice, "nice" here understood pejoratively. It is possible to turn the sense around: whatever is uncommon (i.e.,

normally assume that pursuing a vice would include pursuing pleasure, that desire would include approval, but, to the unnatural women of fashion, pleasure and vice, desire and approval, wanting and liking, are separate. The real perversity being attacked is the indulgence in "vice" not for the pleasure of it, but only because it is "vice." [107] These passionless women are only sexual machines, like the Corinna in "St. James's Park":

> But to turn damned abandoned jade
> When neither head nor tail persuade;
> To be a whore in understanding,
> A passive pot for fools to spend in!

Like Corinna, the fine women of fashion perfect the action of love and forget the passion. Action and passion in love are not usually thought of as true opposites; physical passion involves both. But the women of fashion contrive to make them opposite. Ironically, they reinstate "passion" as a passive submission to the "public voice," and reduce action to the mechanical observation of forms. Personal tastes are disregarded. Women no longer "strike at" (i.e., dazzle, impress, catch the admiration of) [108] men: they strike at "Forms" or ceremonies, the formalities of courtship. [109]

As an illustration of this charge against women, Artemisia

unusual, unnatural, contrary to nature's rule and love's advice) is held by the ladies of fashion to be nice (i.e., delicate, fashionable, appealing to fastidious minds).

107. Artemisia does not mean, I think, to suggest that sexual pleasure is immoral or a "vice." She uses the word ironically, or perhaps euphemistically. Is "the vice" (i.e., sexual pleasure) perhaps an unrecorded usage similar to "the sex" (i.e., women)? Note here an implicit link between the fine ladies and Artemisia, who says she writes *because* it is a "sin."

108. Cf. "Timon," p. 52, "She with her old blear eyes to smite began."

109. Perhaps with a pun on form, the disembodied outline of a man.

then vividly presents the arrival in town of a fine lady and
her humble knight:

> Where I was visiting the other night
> Comes a fine lady, with her humble knight,
> Who had prevailed on her, through her own skill,
> At his request, though much against his will,
> To come to London.[110]
> As the coach stopped, we heard her voice, more loud
> Than a great-bellied woman's in a crowd,
> Telling the knight that her affairs require
> He, for some hours, obsequiously retire
>
> . . . .
>
> "Dispatch," says she, "that business you pretend,
> Your beastly visit to your drunken friend!
> A bottle ever makes you look so fine;
> Methinks I long to smell you stink of wine!
> Your country drinking breath's enough to kill:
> Sour ale corrected with a lemon peel.
> Prithee, farewell! We'll meet again anon."
> The necessary thing bows, and is gone.
>
> [ll. 73–81, 85–92]

The domestic comedy is broad but deftly managed. The lady
and her knight both (the terms are probably carried over
from "my lady" and "th'unhappy knight" in the fragment,
"What vain, unnecessary things —") prove to be less genteel
than "fine" and "humble" would suggest. The knight is a
drunk, and the fine lady as coarse and loud as "a great-
bellied woman in a crowd." Her skillful domineering is revealed in a superb couplet, "Who had prevailed on her,
through her own skill, / At his request, though much against
his will," and her scornful comparison between her "affairs"
(she uses the French term) and his pretended "business." His
lowly status is witheringly summarized in Artemisia's phrase,

110. Skillful use of the half-line, contrasting, in rhythm and sense,
to the deviousness of the preceding couplet.

"the necessary thing," more contemptuous even than the "vain, unnecessary things" of the earlier fragment.

Once arrived, she delivers a set-piece of thirty-five lines in praise of fools as the best lovers. She begins with a rhetorical question, " 'How is love governed, love that rules the state, / And pray, who are the men most worn of late?' . . . ," which she never waits to hear answered. Her question, ironically, is similar to the one Artemisia offered to answer: "Y'expect at least to hear what loves have passed . . . what change . . . who and who's together." But while Artemisia is concerned with the practice of love, the fine lady, more remote from experience, asks about the theory of love. Note, too, that men are reduced to the equivalent of clothes or fashions, to be worn or displayed. She proceeds immediately to describe the reigning fashion "When I was married":

> fools were *à la mode.*
> The men of wit were then held *incommode.*
> Slow of belief, and fickle in desire,
> Who, ere they'll be persuaded, must inquire
> As if they came to spy, not to admire.[111]

Ironically, the fine lady criticizes the wits for the same thing ladies themselves, according to Artemisia, are guilty of: " 'Tis below wit, they tell you, to admire." Her case against the wits, however, seems well argued. Her principle is, roughly, "ignorance is bliss," a variety of the antirationalism in affairs of love which Quaintance has found to be a characteristic of much court poetry of the Restoration.[112]

> With searching wisdom, fatal to their ease,
> They still find out why what may, should not please;

111. An unexpected remembrance of *Gondibert* 2. 5.16, a description of the House of Astragon where men study nature: "Others with Optick Tubes the Moons scant face / (Vaste Tubes, which like long Cedars mounted lie) / Attract through Glasses to so near a space / As if they came not to survey, but prie."

112. See the chapter in Quaintance on "Artemisia to Chloe" and antirationalism.

> Nay, take themselves for injured when we dare
> Make 'em think better of us than we are,
> And if we hide our frailties from their sights,
> Call us deceitful jilts and hypocrites.
> They little guess, who at our arts are grieved,
> The perfect joy of being well deceived.
>
> [ll. 108–115]

Her argument is not that the exercise of mental faculties impairs sexual performance, but that what men do not know of women's frailty will not hurt them. The tradition of the cuckold's "perfect joy" has been traced by Quaintance through Ovid, Chaucer, the *Praise of Folly*, *Othello*, Denham, and (in the Restoration) William Walsh, Wycherley, Aphra Behn, and Prior.[113] To his list may be added La Rochefoucauld and Butler.[114] Among the many formulations of this amatory paradox, Rochester's is perhaps the most felicitously phrased. Significantly, it is to Rochester that Swift later turned for his version of the commonplace.[115]

Not only does a wit create his own "certain woe" (recalling that pattern of self-destructive acts Artemisia found in wits, men and maids, and herself), he also destroys the illusion that a woman seeks to foster, hurting thereby both himself and her:

> Women should these, of all mankind, avoid,
> For wonder by clear knowledge is destroyed.

113. See especially Walsh, "The Reconcilement": "I grant 'tis Folly to believe a cheating wife; / But 'tis by this Folly I vast Pleasures gain, / While you, with all your Wisdom, love in pain." *Letters and Poems*, 1692, p. 92; Aphra Behn, tr. of La Rochefoucauld, Maxim 387: "I am more happy in being deceived by Lysander than in being undeceived."

114. La Rochefoucauld, Maxim 441: "Dans l'amitié comme dans l'amour, on est souvent plus heureux par les choses qu'on ignore que par celles que l'on sait." Butler, *Hudibras*, part 2, 3:1: "Doubtless, the pleasure is as great, / Of being cheated, as to cheat, / As lookers on feel most delight, / That least perceive a Juglers slight; / But still the less they understand, / The more th'admire his slight of hand."

115. See Chapter VI.

> Woman, who is an arrant bird of night,
> Bold in the dusk before a fool's dull sight,
> Should fly when reason brings the glaring light.
> [ll. 119–123]

In the context of the fine lady's antirationalist argument, the lines are apt as well as richly visual.

What the fine lady wants is a man who, like the wit, conspires, in effect, against himself, but whose folly enhances rather than interferes with a woman's joy. She wants, in short, a fool:

> But the kind, easy fool, apt to admire
> Himself, trusts us; his follies all conspire
> To flatter his, and favor our desire.
> Vain of his proper merit, he with ease
> Believes we love him best who best can please.
> On him our gross, dull, common flatteries pass,
> Ever most joyful when most made an ass.
> Heavy to apprehend, though all mankind
> Perceive us false, the fop concerned is blind,
> Who, doting on himself,
> Thinks everyone that sees him of his mind.
> These are true women's men.
> [ll. 124–135]

The rhyme words — "admire," "desire," "ease," "please" — repeated in these lines from the lines on the wits (ll. 105–109), secure the parallel and contrast. It is striking that the fine lady is quite candid about the "frailties" of her sex. Like Artemisia, she implicitly calls herself "arrant" (ll. 24, 121), and admits to "gross, dull, common flatteries," even to falseness. Note, too, that she makes no claims about the superiority in sexual potency of fops over wits. Her argument is less profound, epistemologically, than Quaintance suggests. Essentially, it defines a well-devised practical strategy for securing sovereignty in love.

Having demonstrated her wit and wisdom, the fine lady

then exposes her own foolish side, embracing her "much esteemed dear friend, the monkey." [116] Her theory may be sound, but her practice is ridiculous:

> The dirty, chattering monster she embraced,
> And made it this fine, tender speech at last:
> "Kiss me, thou curious miniature of man!
> How odd thou art! how pretty! how japan! [117]
> Oh, I could live and die with thee!"
>
> [ll. 141–145]

If we had developed sympathy or admiration for the fine lady, it is here severely qualified. Artemisia too finds the mixture of wisdom and folly very puzzling:

> I took this time to think what nature meant
> When this mixed thing into the world she sent,
> So very wise, yet so impertinent:
> One who knew everything; who, God thought fit,
> Should be an ass through choice, not want of wit.
>
> [ll. 147–151]

Like her victims, the fine lady seems an "ass." Like the wit, the fop, and Artemisia, she exposes her own folly. Curiously, Artemisia at first thinks that "nature" and "God" planned this lady's excellent foppery, but then contradicts herself:

> Nature's as lame in making a true fop
> As a philosopher; the very top
> And dignity of folly we attain
> By studious search, and labor of the brain,
> By observation, counsel, and deep thought:
> God never made a coxcomb worth a groat.
>
> [ll. 154–159]

116. Quaintance is right, I think, in suggesting (p. 37) that this is "a smack at the characteristic libertine esteem for unreasoning, instinctual animal life. . . . Rochester is satirizing the overzealous endorsement of an attitude he himself had advanced in his 'Satyr.'"

117. Not clear. Perhaps a reference to the contemporary fashion for Oriental miniatures.

Her final judgement, though seemingly just, is only partly right:

> An eminent fool must be a fool of parts.
> And such a one was she, who had turn'd o'er
> As many books as men; loved much, read more;
> Had a discerning wit; to her was known
> Everyone's fault and merit, but her own.
> All the good qualities that ever blessed
> A woman so distinguished from the rest,
> Except discretion only, she possessed.
>
> [ll. 161–168]

True, she is discerning (in judging others) rather than discreet (discerning about human conduct). But does she not see and admit her own frailties and know her own strengths? It seems, then, that she does not act on the basis of her own best knowledge. This, of course, distinguishes her from no other character in the poem except the fools. (They, too, choose their folly, but do so out of ignorance.)

The fine lady realizes that she is thought to be foolish. Her words implicitly answer Artemisia's criticism:

> You smile to see me, whom the world perchance
> Mistakes to have some wit, so far advance
> The interest of fools, that I approve
> Their merit, more than men's of wit, in love.
>
> [ll. 171–174]

She now offers another pragmatic reason in favor of fools: they can and often do repair the damage done by a witty lover: "But, in our sex, too many proofs there are / Of such whom wits undo, and fools repair" (ll. 175–176). No matter how ruined, a woman who finds a fool can still be "revenged on her undoer, man." The story of Corinna is offered as an example, set within the fine lady's speech just as the story of the fine lady is set within Artemisia's letter.

The sixty or so lines that comprise the episode are some of the best satirical narrative of the Restoration. Guided by Artemisia and by Rochester behind her, we witness the rise, fall, and recovery of Corinna, exploited by wits and exploiter of a booby squire, in a spirit of sympathy that turns ultimately not into satiric judgment but amoral tolerance of the way of the world.

Corinna's first flash and diseased decline present a grave spectacle:

> That wretched thing Corinna, who had run
> Through all the several ways of being undone,
> Cozened at first by love, and living then
> By turning the too dear-bought trick on men —
> Gay were the hours, and winged with joys they flew,
> When first the town her early beauties knew;
> Courted, admired, and loved, with presents fed;
> Youth in her looks, and pleasure in her bed;
> Till fate, or her ill angel, thought it fit
> To make her dote upon a man of wit,
> Who found 'twas dull to love above a day;
> Made his ill-natured jest, and went away.[118]
> Now scorned by all, forsaken, and oppressed,
> She's a *memento mori* to the rest;
> Diseased, decayed, to take up half a crown
> Must mortgage her long scarf and manteau gown.
> Poor creature! who, unheard of as a fly
> In some dark hole must all the winter lie,
> And want and dirt endure a whole half year
> That for one month she tawdry may appear.
> [ll. 189–208]

This portrait might stand next to that of Wolsey or the scholar in the "Vanity of Human Wishes," equal to them in laconic solemnity. "Gay were the hours" — the cliché comes to life when we see they were only hours that now have

118. This "man of wit" is the sole exception to the rule that "men work their own woe."

flown. "Early beauties" releases its power when we see her decaying, tawdry later beauty. Her end comes abruptly and inexplicably. Once rejected by a man of wit, who "Made his ill-natured jest, and went away," she is suddenly forsaken by everyone, perhaps (no other reason is offered) because in doting on the wit she violates an unwritten rule of the game of love. Reduced at last to a dirt-born fly, she glitters for a single month. "Poor creature!" is not needed to evoke our sympathy.

Now the tone shifts markedly with the introduction of the booby squire. Corinna's fortunes immediately look promising; we are invited to laugh at the country clown —

> From pedagogue and mother just set free,
> The heir and hopes of a great family;
> Which, with strong ale and beef, the country rules,
> And ever since the Conquest have been fools.
> And now, with careful prospect to maintain
> This character, lest crossing of the strain
> Should mend the booby breed, his friends provide
> A cousin of his own to be his bride.
>
> [ll. 211–218]

— who comes to town and is won by the lost Corinna. Ruthlessly Corinna plays on his credulousness and innocence, flattering his prejudice against "the lewdness of the times." On his part, the Squire is "grateful for favors. . . . Believes, then falls in love, and then in debt." The zeugma yokes not so much an incongruous pair as (given the nature of the social world) a cruelly inevitable one. His conception of love — " 'Tis better than good sense, than power or wealth, / To have a love untainted, youth, and health" (ll. 238–239) — ironically recalling Artemisia's praise of the "safe director of unguided youth," proves to be not only inadequate but positively harmful to him in a world of experience. Unknowingly, he is condemned to repeat Corinna's own errors. She began with "Youth in her looks, and pleasure in her bed," and he "fresh in his youth, and faithful in his love." Parallel syntax secures the parallel in sense. Just as her doting leads to financial ruin (she must mortgage her scarf and gown), so love leads him to near bankruptcy (he must mortgage all). Like Corinna, like Artemisia and the wits, he brings his ruin on himself. His end, his "Fate" (l. 248), like hers (l. 197) is abrupt and total:

> And when t' th' height of fondness he is grown,
> 'Tis time to poison him, and all's her own.
> Thus meeting in her common arms his fate,
> He leaves her bastard heir to his estate,
> And, as the race of such an owl deserves,
> His own dull lawful progeny he starves.
> [ll. 246–251]

Perhaps because a woman is telling Corinna's story, we are left with lighter feelings than at Corinna's own fall. The fine lady has little pity for the booby, a "kind keeping fool" whose function is "To patch up vices men of wit wear out" (l. 255). Artemisia neither assents to nor dissents from this judgment. She comments:

> Thus she [i.e., the fine lady] ran on two hours, some grains of sense
> Still mixed with volleys of impertinence.
> [ll. 256–257]

We cannot be sure which, in her view, is folly and which is sense. I suspect the uncertainty is designed. The poem as a whole, when we step back from it, does not actively condemn Corinna. She does what she must do in order to survive. The booby squire, toward whom we feel little pity, gets what he deserves. The gravity and horror, powerfully evoked in the description of Corinna's fall, are at the fall of the booby squire dissipated into a kind of amorality. This is the way, the satirist says, the world turns: men and women are willing victims (undoing themselves and being undone) or exploiters (undoing others). In such a world, fools are of course the best lovers (i.e., victims). They are worn (l. 102) like fashions, and then "worn out" (l. 255) like old clothes, by the fine lady (who seems to have married a country booby) or Corinna (herself worn out by the men of wit).

The poem concludes by restoring the two narrative frames. The fine lady points her moral (ll. 252–255), and Artemisia speaks depreciatingly (perhaps disingenuously) of her own writing:

> But now 'tis time I should some pity show
> To Chloe, since I cannot choose but know
> Readers must reap the dullness writers sow.
> By the next post such stories I will tell
> As, joined with these, shall to a volume swell,
> As true as heaven, more infamous than hell.
> But you are tired, and so am I.
>
> Farewell.
>
> [ll. 258–264]

Artemisia remains an ambiguous figure. Just as we are unsure of her attitude toward Corinna or the fine lady, so we are unsure of her attitude toward herself. Typically, she exaggerates, perhaps ironically: "As true as heaven, more infamous than hell." What do her true and infamous stories make her — a satirist or a gossip? [119]

We begin and end with Artemisia, but we are not with her throughout the poem; she represents no norm who judges for us or by which we judge. Indeed, the poem contains no single view of experience. It offers, perhaps, the par-

119. We should not forget that many of Rochester's letters to Savile ask for or pass on the latest gossip about politics, court business, and amatory scandals.

tial view that consistent exploitation of folly and weakness insures social success. Yet exploitation does not bring love. Corinna, left a rich widow, had forced herself into a loveless marriage for profit. The fine lady, following her own advice, has married a country fool, but appears to derive no happiness from him. Artemisia, like Artemis or Diana, whose name she bears, seems to have little to do with men. Her "cordial drop" (curiously sexless [120]) remains a remote, unworldly ideal. Fruitful relations between men and the three women of the poem seem to have broken down altogether. Significantly, perhaps, for a man who seems to have found them threatening, women play the dominant and aggressive roles. Artemisia, like her other namesake who commanded a ship for Xerxes at Salamis, is somewhat masculine. The fine lady bullies and brutalizes her "humble knight" and in effect prefers the monkey, a "miniature of man," as a sexual partner. One might almost say she makes monkeys — and miniatures — of men. Corinna easily makes a fool of an "o'ergrown schoolboy." The only aggressive and successful male in the poem is the absent "man of wit," a Don Juan figure who "found 'twas dull to love above a day" and perhaps embodies Rochester's fantasies of effortless sexual conquest.

Yet the poem does not attack exploitive women. It extends sympathy, satire, and finally just tolerant recognition toward Artemisia, the fine lady, and Corinna. Literally, Rochester adopts the women's point of view: we look at the booby from Corinna's point of view, at Corinna from the fine lady's, at the fine lady from Artemisia's. Like much of Rochester's poetry, this poem upsets our expectations and our standard responses. It does not simply praise wits and condemn fools; nor does it praise generous love and condemn self-interest. Perhaps it condemns women of fashion, but not,

120. Unless we should associate it with the women who "drink up" men in earlier songs and satires. In any case the "cordial drop" (cf. the "dram of sperm") is swamped by the "nauseous draught" (cf. the "vast meal of nasty slime").

unequivocally, the fashion of taking fools as lovers. It leaves us puzzled about the mixture of folly and sense in the fine lady, and about the mixture of gossip and moral fervor in Artemisia. It envisions the paradoxical possibility that, given such a world, perhaps fools, who know only "the perfect joy of being well deceived," are the happiest and most successfully adjusted of men. It leaves us, in short, with a clear idea of a world, but with little assurance of the best way for man or woman (short of exploitation or folly) to survive in it.

"Artemisia to Chloe" is Rochester's most comprehensive and complex treatment of women and love. But the poem has wider concerns, as we have seen, and close affinities with Rochester's entire oeuvre. Positing, like the "Satyr Against Mankind," a bifurcated world of dupes and cheats, it posits, too, a gap between the actual and ideal. Just as Rochester himself admitted to "a sense of what the methods of my life seem utterly to contradict," [121] and was unable to achieve the religious faith he could envision as comforting ("if a man says he cannot believe, what help is there?"), so in "Artemisia to Chloe" the gap between the actual behavior of man and whatever ideal can be imagined (the "cordial drop" of love) is simply too great to be bridged. The ideal-projecting voice gives way to an ironic, pragmatic, worldly-wise voice, just as Artemisia earlier recognized the danger in writing, but plunged ahead anyway, or as the lover in "Absent from thee," after contemplating his place of rest in his mistress's arms, imagines realistically how he will forsake that rest. The amused stance is that of "The Maimed Debauchee," who, "good for nothing else," looks on as spectator. In that poem, and (probably) in a number of others, Rochester writers about sexual impotence with artistic potency. In this poem (where men — except for Corinna's "man of wit" — are weak and exploited) we can perhaps see an

121. Hayward, pp. 290–291.

analogue to impotence: a sense of failure to match desire with performance. Indeed, the recurrent pattern in Rochester of a gap between ideal and actual is itself a kind of impotence. It is only in the observation of that gap, and in the masterful expression of it in art, that Rochester's poetry displays any sense of impotence overcome.

4 The Background to Rochester's "Satyr"

Although a psychological approach is suited to much of Rochester's work, especially the libertine satires and love songs, a broader approach is necessary to his most famous poem, the "Satyr Against Mankind." Although this poem no doubt reflects Rochester's experience, it also reflects, more than the others, a wide philosophical and literary background. There is nothing like the "Satyr Against Mankind" in English literature before Rochester, but it has long been recognized that the poem has literary and intellectual forebears in "Boileau's eighth satire ["Satire sur l'Homme"] . . . Hobbes, Montaigne, and the tradition of *le libertinage* generally," as Vieth's headnote to the poem conveniently observes.[1]

That Boileau was the first "source" to be recognized is suggested by Burnet's remark that Rochester's favorite poets were Cowley and Boileau, and by Johnson's dismissal of the poem's originality: "Of the Satire against Man, Rochester can only claim what remains when all Boileau's part is taken away." Johnson must have been repeating a popu-

1. *Complete Poems*, p. 94.

lar misconception remembered from years before and never questioned, for if he had compared the two poems, as some before him did, he would probably have produced a verdict more like Rymer's in 1691: "My Lord Rochester gives us another Cast of Thought, another Turn of Expression, a strength, a Spirit, and manly Vigour, which the French are utter strangers to. Whatever Giant Boileau may be in his own country, He seems little more than a man of Straw with my Lord Rochester." [2] Other eighteenth-century readers, Francis Lockier and Voltaire, compared the "Satyr" and Boileau's "Satire," noting important differences.[3] But the misconception persisted that Rochester was translating, even if improving, the French,[4] and it was not until the mid-twentieth century that the minimal nature of the debt was demonstrated in detail.[5]

That Rochester has debts to Montaigne and Hobbes has also been proposed. From the beginning, his poetry has been considered "Hobbist." Courthope's *History of English Poetry* (1911) repeats this general belief, though with less hostility than earlier critics: "He puts forward his principles moral and religious, such as they were, with living force and pungency, showing in every line how eagerly he had imbibed the opinions of Hobbes" (3:465).[6]

Montaigne's part in the background of the poem has been

2. Rochester's *Poems* (1691), Preface, n.p.

3. For Lockier, see Spence, *Observations, Anecdotes, and Characters of Books and Men*, ed. James Osborn, 2 vols. (Oxford, 1966), 1:293; for Voltaire, *Letters Concerning the English Nation*, tr. J. Lockman (London, 1733), p. 197.

4. "Rochester improves on Boileau by his English version." Pound, *A B C of Reading* (1934), New Directions, 1960, p. 156.

5. John Moore, "The Originality of Rochester's *Satyr Against Mankind*," *PMLA*, 58 (1943), 393–401. Paul C. Davies has recently reopened the question, and restated the case for Boileau's influence. See "Rochester and Boileau: A Reconsideration," *Comparative Literature*, 21 (1969), 348–355.

6. Since Courthope's time, both Pinto and Thomas Fujimura ("Rochester's 'Satyr Against Mankind': An Analysis," *SP*, 55 [1958], 576–590), as we shall see, have argued for Hobbes's influence.

urged most strongly by a critic who compares the ideas in the "Satyr" to those in the "Apologie for Raymond Sebond" as well as to La Rochefoucauld's in the *Maximes*, and to the writings of some French libertine poets, Theophile de Viau, Des Barreaux, and Claude le Petit.[7] His conclusion, that "there is scarcely an idea of major or minor importance in Rochester that is not present in Montaigne," is accompanied by his admission that this is still not "sufficient evidence to establish a source" (p. 73). There is need, then, for further examination of the background of the "Satyr." Many, but by no means all, of of the poem's specific debts have been pointed out; general debts need to be reassessed.[8]

The aim of this chapter is to describe the materials Rochester drew on, in order to enable the reader to understand both his debt to tradition and his originality, and how he altered and combined his "sources" to produce a poem that answered his own conception of life.

Traditions of Self-Disparagement

To sketch in the broadest context, the "Satyr Against Mankind" belongs to the long tradition of human self-disparagement. Although Rochester and Boileau were the first to indicate by an actual title that their target was man, they were preceded in other aspects by all those preachers, philosophers, railers, and satirists who have fulminated against the generic failings of human kind. Rochester takes his immediate impulse from some seventeenth-century

7. S. F. Crocker, "Rochester's *Satire Against Mankind*: A Study of Certain Aspects of the Background," *West Virginia University Studies*: 3. Philological Papers (vol. 2), [May 1937], pp. 57–73.

8. Moore develops Crocker's warning, concluding that "a single source for the content of the *Satyr* will be difficult to accept" ("The Originality of Rochester's *Satyr*," p. 401) . Indeed, despite the extensive work on the sources of the "Satyr" represented in articles by Crocker, Moore, Davies, and Fujimura, "there is little unanimity of opinion," as the last-named of these critics has written, "either as to its originality or its meaning" ("Rochester's 'Satyr' ", p. 576).

schools of thought, but these schools in turn rest on classical, biblical, and medieval foundations.

Pliny's *Natural History* is a *locus classicus* for that aspect of self-disparagement in which man is unfavorably compared to the animals:

man alone on the day of his birth [Nature] casts away naked on the naked ground, to burst at once into wailing and weeping. . . . On man alone of living creatures is bestowed grief, on him alone luxury, and that in countless forms and reaching every separate part of his frame; he alone has ambition, avarice, immeasurable appetite for life, superstition, anxiety about burial and even about what will happen after he is no more. No creature's life is more precarious, none has a greater lust for all enjoyments, a more confused timidity, a fiercer rage. In fine, all other living creatures pass their time worthily among their own species . . . fierce lions do not fight among themselves, the serpent's bite attacks not serpents, even the monsters of the sea and the fishes are cruel only against different species; whereas to man, I vow, most of his evils come from his fellow-man.[9]

The lines of continuity between this and Rochester — "Savage man alone does man betray" (l. 130) — are clear. Self-disparagement is older, however, than Pliny. Menander's Crato imagines he has the freedom to be reborn: "If some god should come up to me and say: 'Crato, you, after your death, shall again have being anew and you shall be whatsoever you desire — a dog, sheep, goat, man, horse — for you have to live twice. This is decreed. Choose what you prefer.' Forthwith, methinks, I'd say: 'Make me anything but human.'"[10] Somewhere, perhaps in a Latin translation or in the work of a Renaissance natural historian,[11] Rochester

9. *Naturalis Historia*, proem to 7, Loeb edition, 2:509–511.

10. *Menander*, Loeb edition, p. 357. Crato goes on to describe the happiness of animals and the misery of man.

11. Six editions of *Menander* had appeared in print by 1653, one of them in England. Neither Montaigne nor Charron (nor Gelli) refers to this fragment.

came across this fragment and adapted it for the famous beginning lines of the "Satyr":

> Were I (who to my cost already am
> One of those strange, prodigious creatures, man)
> A spirit free to choose, for my own share,
> What case of flesh and blood I pleased to wear,
> I'd be a dog, a monkey, or a bear,
> Or anything but that vain animal
> Who is so proud of being rational.

Yet more widely known than Menander was Plutarch, whose Gryllus (a man transformed into a hog) refuses the chance to become a man again, and maintains: "I scarcely believe that there is such a spread between one animal and another as there is between man and man in the matter of judgment and reasoning and memory." [12] Gryllus's remark alludes to a whole stream of thought — that animals enjoy the exercise of reason, or its equivalent — still strong in the seventeenth century.

The biblical tradition of self-disparagement or self-abasement dates from the Old Testament prophets, and from moralists like the Preacher, whose theme is the vanity of all things — riches, the works of men, wisdom: "I have seen all the works that are done under the sun; and, behold, all is vanity and vexation of spirit. . . . And I gave my heart to know wisdom, and to know madness and folly: I perceived that this also is vexation of spirit. For in much wisdom is much grief; and he that increaseth knowledge increaseth sorrow" (Eccles. 1:14, 17–18). St. Paul and the Church Fathers gave this stream of antirationalism (and hence self-disparagement) a distinctive direction through their warnings against "philosophy and vain deceit" (Coloss.

12. *Plutarch's Moralia*, Loeb edition, 12:509. Plutarch's dialogue was frequently imitated in the Renaissance, most famously in G. B. Gelli's *Circe* (see below, p. 165).

2:8) .[13] Medieval authors such as Augustine and Bernard of Clairvaux cautioned against speculation; others, Innocent III, for example, preached *De Contemptu Mundi*, thus broadening the Christian antirationalism of the patristic writers into a tradition of self-abasement on all accounts, not simply pride of intellect.

These traditions, classical and Christian, flowed into the sixteenth and seventeenth centuries, where they took various forms. Cornelius Agrippa's popular *De Incertitudine et Vanitate Scientiarum et Artium atque Excellentia Verbi Dei Declamatio* (c. 1530) [14] extended the stream of skeptical antirationalist thought. Other religious writers, not only the Calvinists, preached the universal depravity of man. Puritans and Anglicans alike vividly reminded their audiences of man's corrupted nature: "how poore, and inconsiderable a ragge of this world, is man! . . . for man is so much lesse than a worm, as that wormes of his own production, shall feed upon his dead body in the grave." [15] Godfrey Goodman, in a systematic survey of man's fallen nature, asks, "In what course or condition of life would you suppose man, wherein you should not finde an evident proofe of his corruption?" and cites man's numerous miseries as "punishment justly inflicted on man for his sinne." [16] Samuel Purchas, in an equally gloomy survey of human vanity and degradation, concludes, "thus . . . have we followed Man downe the Descents of his Fall, the Degrees of his Degradation, and found that he is Universa, Omnimoda Vanitas,

13. See Howard Schultz, *Milton and Forbidden Knowledge* (New York, 1955).

14. Translated into French in 1582 and 1608, into English in 1569.

15. Donne, *Complete Verse and Selected Prose*, ed. Hayward (London, 1962), pp. 593–594. See R. M. Frye, "Swift's Yahoos and the Christian Symbols for Sin," *Journal of the History of Ideas*, 15 (1954), 102–117, for numerous examples of analogous self-abasement.

16. *The Fall of Man, or the Corruption of Nature Proved by the Light of Our Natural Reason* (London, 1616), pp. 207, 107 ff.

Altogether Vanitie." [17] Both Goodman and Purchas throughout compare man unfavorably to beasts (with respect to
senses, infirmities, miseries) — "in regard of the corruption
of his flesh, his condition is equall, if not inferiour to the
beasts of the field" [18] — thus illustrating how the classical
and Christian traditions of self-abasement might be merged.

The Immediate Background

With these varied traditions of abasement and disparagement of man Rochester was doubtless generally familiar.
He was probably more specifically familiar with what we
can now see as the immediate intellectual and literary background to his "Satyr" — three heterodox traditions of abasement, with classical roots, that flowered in the late Renaissance and seventeenth century as skepticism, theriophily,
and sensationalism. By denying the uniqueness or the excellence of human reason and the superiority of man over
the animals, these bodies of thought ranged themselves
against the official position of the Anglican and Catholic
churches on man's peculiar potential for (if not achievement
of) excellence.

Skepticism, as Rochester would have known it, derived
from Pyrrho of Elis, reputed founder of a sect in the third
century B.C. which taught the vanity of all attempts to discover truth, and indifference to all philosophical proposi-
tions. Pyrrho left no writings, but his teachings were trans-
mitted by Sextus Empiricus (c. A.D. 200), whose Pyrrhonic
Hypostases were frequently translated in the sixteenth and
seventeenth centuries,[19] popularized in Thomas Stanley's
History of Philosophy (1655–1661), and disseminated by

17. *Purchas his Pilgrim. Microcosmus, or the Historie of Man* (London, 1619), pp. 403–404.

18. Goodman, *The Fall of Man*, p. 107, and Part 2, *passim*; Purchas,
Purchas his Pilgrim, passim.

19. Into Latin (1569), French (1615–1670), English (by Raleigh,
1651).

works like Montaigne's well-known "Apologie de Raymond Sebond" (c. 1580)[20] and the *Sagesse* (1601) of Montaigne's disciple, Pierre Charron.[21] The themes in the skeptical tradition with the most direct bearing on Rochester's "Satyr" are the weakness of reason, the feebleness of the senses, and man's presumption in the face of these disabilities. In Montaigne's "Apologie" he might have found an attack on "curiosity": ". . . curiosity is in a man a naturall and originall infirmity. The care to increase in wisdome and knowledge was the first over throwe of mankind: It is the way whereby man hath headlong cast himselfe downe into eternall damnation."[22] Yet reason, as Montaigne and Charron repeatedly warn, "hath so many Tricks and Turnings, is so flexible in its Arguments, and so disguis'd in its Forms, that any thing may be made plausible from it."[23] Furthermore, reason often gives way under the influence of passion, sickness, or prejudice.[24] The senses are no more trustworthy; they, too, are altered by passion or by age, or by each other, so that "nothing comes unto us but falsified and altered by our senses."[25] If man saw himself clearly, he would see

a Creature made up of these Four things; Vanity, Weakness, Inconstancy, and Misery . . . the Prey of Time; The Sport and Geugaw of Fortune; The Image of Inconstancy; The Pattern, nay rather the Prodigy of Weakness; the Balance of Envy and Misery; a Dream; a Phantome; Dust and Ashes; a Vapour; a Morning-Dew; a Flower that presently fadeth, in the Morning

20. Montaigne's *Essais*, frequently printed from 1595 to 1635, were translated into English by John Florio in 1603, and Charles Cotton in 1685.

21. Also frequently reprinted in the 17th century, and translated into English by Samson Leonard in 1606 (frequently reprinted) and George Stanhope in 1697.

22. *Essayes*, 2:199.

23. *Of Wisdom*, tr. Stanhope (3rd ed., 1729), 1:346.

24. *Essayes*, 2:277–279.

25. *Ibid.*, 2:321. "The Weakness and Uncertainty of our Senses is the great Cause of our Ignorance and Error, and all sort of Misapprehension." *Of Wisdom*, 1:95.

Green and growing up, in the Evening cut down, dry'd up, and withered; a Wind; Grass; a Bubble; a Shadow; a Leaf born away by the Wind; a Sponge full of Excrements in his Beginning; a a Bundle of Infirmities and Miseries in the Middle State; Rottenness and a Nuisance, and Food for Worms, in his Latter End. In a Word, the Most Despicable, the most Calamitous Part of the whole Creation.[26]

So writes Charron in his "general Draught of Man," as thorough a satire on mankind as preacher, philosopher, or satirist ever wrote. But man does not see himself for what he is:

Who hath persuaded him, that this admirable moving of heavens vaults; that the eternal light of these lampes so fiercely rowling over his head; that the horror-moving and continuall motion of this infinite vast Ocean, were established, and continue so many ages for his commoditie and service? Is it possible to imagine any thing so ridiculous, as this miserable and wretched creature, which is not so much as master of himselfe, exposed and subject to offences of all things, and yet dareth to call himselfe Master and Emperour of this Universe.[27]

With this may be compared Rochester's denunciation of reason — reason

<blockquote>
that makes a mite
Think he's the image of the infinite,
Comparing his short life, void of all rest,
To the eternal and the ever blest.
[ll. 76–79]
</blockquote>

Pyrrhonic skepticism and attacks on human presumption led Montaigne and Charron, and others like them, to a second Renaissance tradition of self-disparagement, theri-

26. *Of Wisdom*, 1:322–323. In completing his picture, Charron cites the authority of Job and Pliny.

27. *Essayes*, 2:139. Charron paraphrases Montaigne, *Of Wisdom*, 1:409. See also Montaigne, "Of Presumption," *Essayes*, 2:355–390.

ophily — the argument that in many respects man is no better or better off in this world than the beasts. Theriophily, as George Boas has shown in *The Happy Beast*, was much discussed and disputed in the seventeenth century, particularly in France,[28] not only by followers and enemies of Montaigne, but by zoologists, philosophers, and theologians alike. Theriophilists argued either that animals are able to reason — to demonstrate which Montaigne and Charron cited a series of hoary examples from the classics [29] — or that, guided by a lower degree of reason or instinct, animals are wiser and happier than man. Thus in Gelli's *Circe* (1549), a popular storehouse of theriophilist ideas, the Dog observes to Ulysses that what is called prudence in man and instinct in animals comes to the same thing: "This instinct or direction of nature, if it guides us more regularly than your prudence does you, is better, and consequently we are more perfect than you." [30] Rochester makes the same point with Jowler the Dog:

> Those creatures are the wisest who attain,
> By surest means, the ends at which they aim.
> If therefore Jowler finds and kills his hares
> Better than Meres supplies committee chairs,

28. Some of the French writers were translated into English. See Marin Cureau de la Chambre, *A Discourse of the Knowledge of Beasts, wherein all that hath been said for and against their Ratiocination is Examined*, "translated by a person of quality" (London, 1657). Rochester could have discovered La Chambre through Boileau, who names him in *Satire* 8, l. 117.

29. Montaigne, "Apologie de Raymond Sebond." Charron, *Of Wisdom*, 1, ch. 34.

30. G. B. Gelli, *Circe*, tr. Tom Brown, ed. R. Adams (Ithaca, 1963), p. 137. *Circe* is a series of dialogue between Ulysses and various Greeks whom Circe has transformed into beasts. Gelli, who draws freely on both Plutarch (for his basic idea) and Pliny, is a satirical but orthodox moralist who ultimately has Ulysses convince a beast that it is preferable to be a man than an animal, but his work (since the animals argue so well against Ulysses) might easily be turned to skeptical purposes. It was often translated and imitated in the Renaissance.

Though one's a statesman, th'other but a hound,
Jowler, in justice, would be wiser found.

[ll. 117–122] [31]

On other grounds too, "dominion," "perfect liberty," and "virtue," alleged advantages of man over beast were disputed.[32] Beasts, some theriophilists claimed, do not kill others of the same species; only men, among all living creatures, enslave or kill their fellows.[33] Others, like Gelli, drew a different distinction, arguing that "no beast will prey on another of the same kind unless urged on by hunger, love, jealousy, or some similar cause," while men kill each other out of ambition and "dread . . . of one another." [34] Rochester, who makes the same distinction, may well remember Gelli in writing, "For hunger or for love they fight and tear, / Whilst wretched man is still in arms for fear" (ll.139–140). His emphasis on fear ("The good he acts, the ill he does endure, / 'Tis all from fear, to make himself secure") may derive from Gelli's Goat, who argues that man's principle miseries (none of them shared by animals) are all species of fear: "the insecurity of the present good, the terror of the future, mistrust of his own kind, and fear of

31. Cf. *Of Wisdom,* 1:34; Pierre Chanet, *Considerations sur la Sagesse de Charron* (1643).

32. Compare also La Chambre's assertion that beasts know "the End and the Means": "We cannot doubt but the Dog knows the Hare as the prey which he would take, and that when he runs after it, and useth so many endeavours and so many slights to catch it, is not likely but he knows that they are means he must use to attain that end." (*A Discourse of the Knowledge of Beasts,* p. 243).

33. Aristotle, *Politics,* 1:2; Montaigne, "Apologie"; Juvenal, *Satire* 15; Boileau, *Satire* 8; *Of Wisdom,* 1:34; Denham, "Friendship Against Love": "The Wolf, the Lyon, and the Bear / When they their prey in pieces tear, / To quarrel with themselves forbear . . . / But Man's that Savage Beast, whose mind / From Reason to Self-Love declin'd / Delights to prey upon his Kind."

34. *Circe,* p. 75. Cf. Milton's description of animals after the Fall: "Beast now with beast gan war, and fowl with fowl, / And fish with fish." *PL* 10:710–711.

the laws." [35] Where Rochester differs from Gelli — and this seems to be his particular contribution to the theriophilic tradition — is in his emphasis not on human savagery or human fear, but on gratuitous human treachery:

> Birds feed on birds, beasts on each other prey,
> But savage man alone does man betray.
> Pressed by necessity, they kill for food;
> Man undoes man to do himself no good
>
> . . . .
>
> With voluntary pains, works his distress,
> Not through necessity, but wantonness.
>> [ll. 129–132, 137–138]

Both Montaigne and Charron, and doubtless others too, after conceding that some men display nobility and excellence and that men on the whole surpass the animals, fall back on Plutarch's Gryllus:

Plutarke saith in some place, That he findes no such great difference betweene beast and beast, as he findeth diversitie betweene man and man. He speaketh of the sufficiencie of the minde, and of internall qualities. . . . I could finde in my heart to endeare upon Plutarke; and say there is more difference betweene such and such a man, than there is diversitie betweene such a man, and such a beast.[36]

Somewhere, either in Plutarch or his Renaissance imitators, or in Montaigne, Charron, or one of their disciples, Rochester came across this idea, and adapted it for the famous

35. *Circe*, p. 70. Gelli may recall Plutarch's Gryllus: "all your courage is merely the cowardice of prudence and all your valour merely fear that has the good sense to escape one course by taking another" (*Moralia* [n. 12 above], 12:531).

36. Montaigne, "Of the Inequalitie that is Betweene Us," *Essayes*, 1:294. Charron paraphrases Montaigne, *De La Sagesse* (1621 ed.), pp. 162–163.

final line of his "Satyr": "Man differs more from man than
man from beast."

A third strain of Renaissance heterodoxy forming the immediate background to Rochester's "Satyr" is sensationalist
epistemology. Though not offered by its proponents — neo-
Epicureans and Hobbist materialists [37] — as self-disparagement, this was nevertheless understood as such by the orthodox, who saw an attack on man through the devaluation of
his distinctive excellence, reason, and an attack on God
himself through the denial of the realm of spirit.

"Of Sense," the opening chapter of *Leviathan*, announces
Hobbes's sensationalist bias: every thought, says Hobbes, is

> a representation or appearance, of some quality or other accident
> of a body without us, which is commonly called an object. Which
> object worketh on the eyes, ears, and other parts of a man's body,
> and by diversity of working produceth diversity of appearances.
> The original of them all is that which we call sense, for there
> is no conception in a man's mind which hath not at first, totally
> or by parts, been begotten upon the organs of sense.[38]

The Epicureans, in Stanley's account of their thought, go
beyond even Hobbes to claim that sense is infallible. The
four "canons of sense" set forth their creed:

> 1) Sense is never deceived; and therefore every Sensation, and
> every perception, of an Appearance is true. . . . 2) Opinion fol-

37. Hobbism and Epicureanism were popularly associated by their
common enemies in the seventeenth and eighteenth centuries for obvious reasons: in physics, both schools of thought were materialistic in
holding matter rather than spirit the prime reality; in epistemology,
both derived knowledge from the senses; in ethics, both were hedonis-
tic, Epicurus prescribing the quest for pleasure, Hobbes simply describing how, in a state of nature, men seek to attain private pleasures.
Important differences, of course, remained: in physics, Hobbes denied
the existence of an Epicurean void; in psychology, he denied the Epicurean free will. See further, Thomas F. Mayo, *Epicurus in England,
1650–1725* (Austin, Texas, 1934).

38. Burtt, p. 131. See also Burtt, p. 140.

lows upon sense, and is superadded to sensation, and capable of Truth or Falsehood. . . . 3) All Opinion attested, or not contradicted by the evidence of Sense, is True. . . . 4) An opinion, contradicted or not attested by evidence of sense, is false.

[*History of Philosophy*, 1701 ed., pp. 549–552]

In Hobbes, reason begins with sense, proceeds to the names of things perceived, thence to assertions connecting those names, to syllogisms, and finally to knowledge.[39] Reason eventually discovers the laws of nature: "A law of nature, lex naturalis, is a precept or general rule, found out by reason, by which a man is forbidden to do that which is destructive of his life, or taketh away the means of preserving the same; and to omit that by which he thinketh it may be best preserved" (Burtt, p. 163). Reason, in other words, without reference to any universals, ideals, or to God, determines in the state of nature what is good and ill for each man, according, as Hobbes says in the following chapter, to the measure of his "private appetite."[40] The broad similarity to Rochester's conception of right reason is apparent:

> That reason which distinguishes by sense
> And gives us rules of good and ill from thence,
> That bounds desires with a reforming will
> To keep 'em more in vigor, not to kill.
>
> [ll. 100–103]

Somewhat closer to the "Satyr" is the description of the operation of right reason in Stanley's section on the Epicureans: "There is in us a free or arbitrary power of reason,

39. *Leviathan*, ch. 5.
40. Burtt, p. 173. In other works Hobbes discusses right reason, but it is unreasonable to expect that Rochester read more than *Leviathan*. If he did, he would have found material to strengthen, and to complicate, the case he thought Hobbes was making. In *De Cive* right reason concerns actions that affect a man's neighbors, not just himself (*Works*, ed. W. Molesworth, 16 vols. [1839–1845] 2:16). Elsewhere Hobbes warns against "deceptions of sense" (*Works*, 4:24) and defines right reason as "the natural, moral, and divine law" (*Works*, 2:166).

that is, a faculty elective and prosecutive of that which reason hath judged good, and of avoiding and shunning what it hath judged ill" [*History of Philosophy*, 1701 ed., p. 610]. Rochester no doubt derived his conception from the climate of free thought all around him, in which Hobbism and Epicureanism were prominent.[41] Since the poem alludes throughout to complex philosophical ideas, it is impossible to say whether the allusions are specific or general.[42]

For the principle that desires ought to be bounded to keep them more vigorous, a sophisticated sort of hedonism, Rochester was probably indebted to Epicureanism, in particular to the third "canon of Affection": "All Pleasure, which either hindreth a greater pleasure, or procureth a greater pain, is to be shunned."[43] While the Stoics argued that all desire be extinguished (in Rochester's word, "kill[ed]"), the Epicureans, like the speaker in the "Satyr," advised avoidance of the sort of pleasure that led to subsequent greater pain (to kill pleasure through overindulgence would be as painful as to kill it through abstinence). Rochester adopts the Epicurean argument: he seeks to moderate desire, not in order to avoid the inevitable pains of desire, but to keep desire strong and unsated, and pleasure at a maximum.[44] He diverges from Epicureanism, however, and shows his Hobbist coloring in failing to observe the distinction, clearly announced in Stanley, between the higher

41. Perhaps Rochester knew Walter Charleton's *Epicurus' Morals* (1656), whose first page emphasizes that action is the end of speculation (cf. "Thoughts are given for action's government") and that ethics consists of "plain and certain rules" for acquiring happiness. But these ideas are Epicurean commonplaces.

42. For the demotion of the Christian humanist conception of right reason from "the total mind operating upon a complex and fully representative human experience" to "only those mental operations that the mathematician and the scientist employed or any operation analogous there," see S. L. Bethell, *The Cultural Revolution of the Seventeenth Century* (New York, 1951), p. 57, and Robert Hoopes, *Right Reason in the English Renaissance* (Cambridge, Mass., 1962).

43. Stanley, *History of Philosophy* (3rd ed.; London, 1701), p. 554.

44. *Ibid.*, pp. 615–617.

pleasures of rest ("placability, calmness, and vacuity, or immunity from trouble and grief") and the lower pleasures
of motion ("sweet movement, as in gladness, mirth, and
whatsoever moveth the Sense delightfully, with a kind of
sweetness and titillation").[45] Rochester's appetites and desires are clearly "of motion," and bring his position closer
to that of the Cyrenaics (also described in Stanley), who
prefer the bodily pleasures of motion to the mental pleasures
of rest, and to that of Hobbes, for whom "motion" is the
principle of all human activity. Rochester, however, may
have thought he was drawing on Epicurean thought, sharing
with most of the seventeenth century, despite Stanley's
careful distinction, a misconception about Epicurean
ethics.[46]

Having offered Rochester the groundwork of an epistemology and ethics, the sensationalist tradition, like the
skeptical, offered him as well a comparison between man
and the animals. While Montaigne was more interested in
the rationality of beasts, Hobbes, denying that beasts could
reason,[47] was most concerned with their social conduct, and
perhaps helped shape Rochester's thinking in the lines on
man's treachery. In chapter 17 of *Leviathan*, Rochester
could have found careful distinctions made between man
and the other social animals (bees and ants) which could
be adapted to his own comparison of man to the hunting
animals. Hobbes argues that men, unlike social animals, are
"continually in competition for honor and dignity," which

45. *Ibid.*, p. 608.
46. First pointed out by Mayo, *Epicurus in England*, pp. 174–175.
47. In chapters 2–6 of *Leviathan*, Rochester could find Hobbes declaring the ways in which man is like and unlike a beast. Thus, "It is
not prudence that distinguishes man from beast. There be beasts that
at a year old observe more, and pursue that which is for their good
more prudently, than a child can do at ten" (ch. 3, Burtt, p. 139).
Compare Rochester's Jowler. Rochester was probably not familiar with
Hobbes's lesser known *Questions Concerning Liberty, Necessity, and
Chance* (1656), which declares than man excels the animals in his
knowledge and his use of right reason.

leads to envy, hatred, and finally war; that among such animals the common good does not differ from the private good, that animals neither find fault with nor deceive each other.[48]

While Rochester could not find here the description of animal savagery, he would have found an analysis of the gratuitous violence and treachery of which only man is capable.[49] He may have been indebted further to chapter 13, "Of the Natural Condition of Mankind, as concerning their Felicity, and Misery," together with Gelli, for the lines on fear which immediately follow those on treachery:

> For fear he arms, and is of arms afraid,
> By fear to fear successively betrayed;
> Base fear, the source whence his best passions came:
> His boasted honor, and his dear-bought fame.
>
> . . . .
>
> The good he acts, the ill he does endure,
> 'Tis all from fear, to make himself secure.
>   [ll. 141–144, 155–156]

As has already been pointed out,[50] Rochester here modifies the interpretation of human motivation in Hobbes, who finds that quarrels arise between men for three reasons — the desire for gain, the desire for safety and the concomitant fear of other men, and the desire for glory.[51] Rochester stresses the element of fear, making it the true motive behind the apparent desires for gain and glory.[52] In so doing,

48. Burtt, p. 176.
49. He may have taken hints, too, from the description in Boileau's *Satire* 8 of the chicanery and judicial injustice of which man, despite his civil laws, is always capable (ll. 123–160).
50. Fujimura, "Rochester's 'Satyr,' " (n. 6 above), p. 586.
51. Burtt, p. 160.
52. C. F. Main argues, mistakenly I think, that the departure from Hobbes's analysis is "due to the conventions of satire [i.e., the need to simplify] rather than to divergent philosophies." "The Right Vein of Rochester's *Satyr*," in *Essays in Literary History Presented to J. M. French*, ed. R. Kirk and C. F. Main (New Brunswick, N.J., 1960), p. 107.

I suspect, he sought to stress what he understood to be the essential characteristics of Hobbes's state of nature, described in a famous passage (from which I have already quoted) directly following the more complex analysis of human motive: "where every man is enemy to every man . . . wherein men live without other security than what their own strength and their own invention shall furnish them withall. In such condition there is . . . worst of all, continual fear, and danger of violent death; and the life of man, solitary, poor, nasty, brutish, and short." [53] Strictly then, if Rochester departs from Hobbes, he may in his own mind have thought he was following him the better.

Le Libertinage

Still another tradition of heterodoxy and self-disparagement — French *libertinage* — forms part of the contemporary literary context, as opposed to the intellectual background to the "Satyr." The *libertin* poets, themselves Montaignian skeptics, writing in the first half of the seventeenth century — Theophile de Viau, Mathurin Regnier, Jean DeHenault, Antoine Baraby de La Luzerne, Jacques Vallée Des Barreaux, and their literary descendant Boileau — often chose as the target of their satire man as a species.

Although little external evidence survives to prove that Rochester had read these satirists, they were certainly part of the available climate in the Restoration. There is ample reason to believe that a casual familiarity with *libertinage* was part of every wit's "education" at the Court of Charles II. [54] In the work of the libertines could be found recurrent treatments of familiar heterodox themes: theriophily, hedon-

53. Burtt, p. 161. With this passage Rochester perhaps combined the beginning of chapter 17, which stresses repeatedly man's desire for "security." Burtt, pp. 174–175. It is less likely that he knew the discussion of fear among the weak in *De Corpore Politico*, 1:1 (*Works*, 4:82).

54. See Underwood, ch. 1.

ism in ethics, antirationalism, the relativity of values, and human presumption.[55] Rochester would have had adequate opportunity in London or Paris to read the work of Regnier,[56] in whom he may have become interested because Boileau, whom he already admired, in turn admired and owed much to Regnier. Some of the later writers — Des Barreaux, DeHenault, La Luzerne — were still living when Rochester visited Paris in 1662 and again 1669. It has even been suggested that he is likely to have met Des Barreaux.[57] In addition to these probabilities, we have more certain internal evidence; in several poems Rochester fairly clearly draws on the words of Des Barreaux and (what has not, I think, been pointed out) Regnier.

Rochester almost certainly read Regnier's *Satire* 10 (1609), "Le repas ridicule," dealing with a traditional theme in formal satire. Rochester's "Timon," chiefly an adaptation of Boileau's third satire, which in turn draws on Regnier, shows in one instance that Rochester used a detail from Regnier rather than Boileau. At the end of the meal, the satirist in "Timon" flees in disgust: "I ran downstairs, with a vow nevermore / To drink bear-glass and hear the hectors roar" (ll. 176–177). At the same point in the action Boileau has "J'ai gagné doucement la porte sans rien dire" (l. 230), while Regnier has "Je cours à mon manteau, *je descends l'escalier*" (l. 401, emphasis added).

Knowing *Satire* 10, then, Rochester very likely knew the

55. No single one of these themes appeared in the works of all the libertines, nor did any one libertine incorporate all the themes in his work. As Alan Boase has pointed out, the libertines were not a single unified group; they included Christians, Deists, and pagans. What united them was their interest in Montaigne and Charron, their distinction between religion and ethics, their toleration for diversity, their ethics based on reason, with an acknowledgment of the limits of reason, and their principle of following one's own nature. *The Fortunes of Montaigne* (London, 1935), pp. 135–163.

56. Published in 1608, 1609, 1612, 1613, and 1654.

57. E.-D. Forgues, "John Wilmot: Comte de Rochester," *Revue des Deux Mondes*, 10 (1857), 826.

mockery of mankind in *Satire 2* — "Voyez que c'est du monde
et des choses humaines! / Tous jours à nouveaux maux nais-
sent nouvelles peines"[58] — and the full-scale satire on man
in *Satire* 14:

> J'ay pris cent et cent fois la lanterne en la main,
> Cherchant en plain midy parmy le genre humain
> Un homme qui fust homme et de faict et de mine
> Et qui peust des vertus passer par l'estamine;
> Il n'est coin et recoin que je n'aye tanté
> Depuis que la nature icy bas m'a planté;
> Mais tant plus je me lime et plus je me rabote,
> Je croy qu'à mon avis tout le monde radote,
> Qu'il a la teste vuide et sans dessus dessous,
> Ou qu'il faut qu'au rebours je sois l'un des plus fous.
>
> [ll. 1–10][59]

Regnier alludes of course to Diogenes, who went about in
the daylight with a lantern, looking for an honest man.
Rochester glances scornfully at the other well-known tale
about Diogenes (that he lived in a tub, "Satyr," ll. 90–91),[60]
but would seem to endorse Regnier in the passage on the
search for one just man — "In Court a just man, yet unknown to me . . . If so upright a statesman you can
find . . ." (ll. 179ff).

Between Regnier and Boileau a number of libertine satirists tried their hands at poetic satire on man. Théophile de
Viau's first satire and Cyrano de Bergerac's *Histoire des
Oiseaux* compare man unfavorably with animals.[61] One of
the constant themes of La Luzerne [62] is human folly:

58. *Oeuvres Complètes*, ed. G. Raibaud (Paris, 1958), p. 152.
59. *Ibid.*, p. 189.
60. Available in Stanley's *History*, (n. 43 above), p. 282.
61. Théophile, *Satire 1*, "Qui que tu sois, de grace escoute ma sa-
tyre," esp. ll. 1–42. Cyrano, in *Les Estats du Soleil, Oeuvres Libertines
de Cyrano de Bergerac*, ed. Frederic Lachèvre (Paris, 1921), 1:147 ff.
62. La Luzerne (1617–1679), who expresses, in Boase's words (*The
Fortunes of Montaigne*, p. 155) a "liberal Catholicism," first published
satire in his *Essais poetiques* (1638).

Rien n'est si peu sage que l'Homme,
Noë fit le fol en buvant,
Adam en mangeant la pomme,
Et moi, possible, en écrivant.

In a prose commentary on these lines La Luzerne acknowledged his debt to Charron and, indirectly, to Pliny:

Nous avons commencé ce livre par le discours de la Sagesse, l'Amour et la crainte de Dieu: nous le clorrons par ce théorème general de la folie des hommes et de la mienne propre. Je suis homme, et comme tel inseparable de ces cinq: vanité, faiblesse, inconstance, misère, présomption. *Nihil superbius homine ac miserius* au discours de Pline qui est bien vrai.[63]

The poets so far considered satirize man's universal folly without attacking his reason. For the poetic treatment of antirationalism we must turn to Des Barreaux. Much of his work, written in the period 1658 to 1664, was published in a 1667 collection, *Recueil de quelque pièces nouvelles et galantes tant en prose qu'en vers. Second Partie,* which Rochester possibly saw. In this collection were published three antirationalist sonnets by Des Barreaux, as well as a pair of poems, "Jouissance Imparfaite" and "Jouissance Parfaite," that Rochester very likely had in mind when writing "The Imperfect Enjoyment." It is the sonnets that concern us here, for they are similar in theme and in some cases very close in wording to the "Satyr." The first of them, entitled in the *Recueil* "Homine nullum animal aut miserius aut superbius (Pline)" — after the same pasage in the *Natural History* to which Charron and La Luzerne allude — is in another collection of the same year called "Sonnet X, sur l'Homme":

63. *Sentiments Chrétiens, Moraux, et Politiques, Maximes d'Etat et de Religion illustrées de paragraphes selon l'ordre des Quatrains* (1654), pp. 202, 205, quoted in Boase, *The Fortunes of Montaigne,* p. 161.

L'Homme a dit en son coeur sot et audacieux
Je suis maistre absolu de la terre habitable,
Des plus fiers animaux je suis victorieux
Et ma raison sur tout me rend considerable.
Que pour te regarder tu prens de mauvais yeux
Animal fastueux que miserable!
Connois tes propres maux, et plus judicieux
Ne *te vante* point *tant d'estre si raissonable.*

Le regret du passé, le peur de l'avenir,
Le chagrin du présent, penser qu'il faut finir,
Qui nous livre en vivant les assauts les plus rudes,
Les crimes que commet le fer et le poison,
Les larmes, les soupirs, et les inquietudes,
Ce sont des beaux présents que te fait la raison.[64]

The ideas in this poem do not require comment. Rochester need not have read it to find them, but it seems possible that he had the poem in mind while writing of "that vain animal / Who is so proud of being rational" (ll. 6–7).[65]

On the same page of the *Recueil* (p. 204) Rochester would have found the following sonnet "Sur le même sujet (que le précédent)":

Maistre sans contredit de ce globe habité
Ayant assujetty toute autre creature,

64. For information on publication of this and the following poems, see Lachèvre, *Jacques Vallée Des Barreaux: Sa Vie et Ses Poesies* (Paris, 1907), pp. 197–204. The sonnets are printed on pp. 161–164 and also in Lachèvre's *Disciples et Successeurs de Theophile de Viau* (Paris, 1911), pp. 146, 243–244.

65. See also Dryden's preface to *Aureng-Zebe* (1675): "I have observed, says Montaigne, that when the body is out of order, its companion is seldom at his ease. An ill dream, or a cloudy day, has power to change this wretched creature, who is *so proud of a reasonable soul,* and make him think what he thought not yesterday." Dryden refers probably to the "Apologie," *Essayes,* 2:278, 280, which mentions the effect of "the ayre itself," and of a "melancholy humour," on the judgment.

C'est l'Homme qui fait voir, en sa noble figure,
Un précieux éclat de gloire et dignité.

Mais ne nous flattons point et disons verité
Cet animal forme d'admirable structure,
Ce petit Roytelet de toute la nature
Ce chef-d'oeuvre dernier de la Divinité,

Que fait cet Homme ayant la raison pour partage,
Et qui du Dieux vivant est la vivante image?
Toujours moucher, cracher, éternuer, tousser,

Se lever, se coucher, dormir, manger et boire,
Et puis roter, dormir, peter, chier, pisser;
Oh! le brave animal que l'Homme, O voire, voire.

Again, Rochester did not need to know this poem to be
scornful of human pride in reason, but lines in the "Satyr"
are remarkably similar. In each poem praise of "glorious
man" — "l'Homme . . . en sa noble figure / Un précieux
éclat de gloire et dignité . . . du Dieux . . . la vivante
image,"

> Whom his great Maker took such care to make
> That from himself he did the image take
> And this fair frame in shining reason dressed
> To dignify his nature above beast
> ["Satyr," ll. 62–65]

is countered by scorn for the mite, the "brave animal," who
"thinks he's the image of the infinite" ("Satyr," l. 77).

A third sonnet might have given Rochester a hint for his
conception of right reason. It is entitled in the same *Recueil*
(p. 208) "Sonnet. Qui multiplicat intellectum multiplicat
afflictionem": [66]

66. Apparently a paraphrase of the Vulgate of Eccles. 1:18, "Qui
addit scientiam addit et laborem," itself the epigraph for another sonnet on the next page of the *Recueil*, in which appear the lines: "Je

Mortels, qui vous croyez quand vous venez à naistre,
Obligez à Nature, o quelle trahison!
Se montrer un moment, pour jamais disparaistre,
Et pendant que l'on est, voir des maux à foison.

Tenant plus de néant que l'on ne fait de l'estre,
Je l'ay dit autre fois et bien moins en saison,
Estudions-nous *plus à jouir* qu'à *connoistre,*
Et nous servons des sens plus que de la raison.

D'un sommeil éternel ma mort sera suivie,
J'entre dans le néant quand je sors de la vie.
O déplorable estat de ma condition!

Je rénonce au bon sens, je hay l'intelligence,
D'autant plus que l'esprit s'élève en connoissance,
Mieux voit-il le sujet de son affliction.

What Rochester might have taken from this poem, aside from the suggestion that man trust his senses more than his reason, is the epigrammatic linking of *jouir* and *connoistre:* "His wisdom did his happiness destroy / Aiming to *know* that world he should *enjoy*" (ll. 33–34).

One further French libertine literary influence is a matter more of spirit and method than substance. La Rochefoucauld's *Maximes* (1664), almost surely familiar to Rochester, would have provided a model for cynical commentary on man's nature and motives. Rochester's tone in

> Look to the bottom of his vast design,
> Wherein man's wisdom, power, and glory join:
> The good he acts, the ill he does endure,
> 'Tis all from fear, to make himself secure
> [ll. 153–156]

me dégrade de raison / Je veux devenir un oison / Et me sauver dans l'ignorance. / En beuvant toujours du meilleur / Seluy qui croit en connoissance / Ne fait qu'accroistre sa douleur."

sounds much like that of La Rochefoucauld, who continually uncovers self-love, weakness, or pure chance from beneath those actions apparently noble, altruistic, or rational.

Libertinage, originally a French phenomenon, colored English literature as well. The libertine rake, of course, cuts a central figure in Restoration comedy. So, too, does the freethinking railer, like Wycherley's Manly, to remind us of the close connection between libertinism and self-abasement.[67] Railing satire, too, directed not at classes or individuals, but at the species, seems to have gained popularity in the Restoration.

Sometime during the 1670s Butler wrote his satires "Upon the Imperfection and Abuse of Human Learning," "Upon the Licentious Age of Charles II" —

> 'Tis a strange Age we've liv'd in, and a lewd
> As 'ere the Sun in all his Travels view'd;
> An age as vile, as ever Justice urg'd,
> Like a fantastic Letcher, to be scourg'd.

— and "Upon the Weakness and Misery of Man" arguing, much like Rochester, that man preys on man, and (what is worse) on himself — "Unhappy Man takes Pain to find plagues / T'inflict himself upon his Mind" — particularly through curious speculation, "hypothetic dreams and visions . . . everlasting Disquisitions." Not printed until 1759, these poems, similar in theme to the "Satyr Against Mankind," may possibly have influenced Rochester, or been influenced by him.[68]

67. For the relations of Rochester's poem and contemporary drama, see below, ch. VI.

68. The poems, printed in *Satires and Miscellaneous Poetry and Prose*, ed. R. Lamar (Cambridge, 1928), may have circulated in manuscript before Butler's death in 1680. If so, they might well have been seen by Rochester, perhaps by way of Buckingham, with whom Butler collaborated on *The Rehearsal* (1673). On the other hand, it is possible that Butler's satires were composed after 1675, in which case the flow of any possible influence would be from Rochester to Butler. In the 1680's, Oldham imitated Boileau's "Satire sur l'Homme,"

It is too strong to say that Rochester drew on the skeptical, theriophilist, sensationalist, or libertine traditions in any specific ways. Though much has been made of his debts to the "Apologie" and *Leviathan*, the one clear borrowing (the "Satyr's" final line) cannot with certainty be traced to any particular writer. The relation of Rochester's reading to his writing is illuminated by a comment from Burnet: "Sometimes other men's thoughts mixed with his composures, but that flowed rather from the Impressions they made on him when he read them, by which they came to return upon him as his own thoughts, than that he servilely copied from any" (p. 22). If Burnet here repeats what Rochester truthfully said to him, we may deduce that he drew not on any particular writer whose works lay open before him, but rather on his combined memories of their writings, and on the intellectual climate of the age.

Much in each tradition, of course, he would not as libertine have found useful. He sloughed off from the skeptical tradition Montaigne's stress on the need for faith in an incomprehensible God, radical distrust of the senses, and the idea that animals use reason.[69] From the sensationalists he discarded Hobbes's political philosophy and the Epicurean principle of indolence. In so doing, he simply followed libertine precedents, as Underwood (p. 28) has described them.

drawing occasionally on Rochester's "Satyr" for details. Robert Gould, a friend of Oldham and of Rochester's daughter, wrote a five-part "Satire on Man" (1689–1709), of which Part 1 is apparently inspired by Rochester's attack on mankind. Wycherley's poem "Upon the Impertinence of Knowledge, the Unreasonableness of Reason, and the Brutality of humanity; proving the Animal Life the most Reasonable, since the most Natural, and most Innocent," written sometime between 1661 and 1696, though a tired collection of fashionable clichés, serves nonetheless to illustrate the popularity of the theme of self-disparagement down to the end of the seventeenth century.

69. The very vastness and heterogeneity of Montaigne's *Essais*, and particularly of the longest of them, the "Apologie," invited the piecemeal quotation which was its fate. This encyclopaedic work was quoted in the seventeenth century by atheistic libertines, devout fideists, and a wide range of humanistic Christians in between. See Boase, *The Fortunes of Montaigne* (n. 55 above).

Rochester's sincerity in voicing current heterodox notions is a matter for dispute. As a casual reader and gentleman scholar, who allowed himself only "intermittent fits" of study, he cannot be expected, perhaps, to show rigor or consistency in his thinking. We will err as much, however, in supposing that Rochester's heterodoxy is simply a fashionable pose of the day, adorned with sentiments from appropriate texts, as in supposing that all his thought derives from introspection and deep conviction. On the one hand, he was very likely interested in delighting his friends and shocking his broader audience with whatever outrageous heterodoxy might serve. On the other, Rochester's satire often carries a note of disgusted conviction, as if it springs from his own honest appraisal of experience. In making fear the prime motive of all human behavior (ll. 139–156) Rochester may, as suggested, follow Gelli or give his understanding of Hobbes's argument. Just as likely, however, he stresses fear because he honestly recognizes it as a powerful force within himself.

Orthodoxy and Optimism

Whatever the disturbing and disillusioning effect in the seventeenth century of the varied traditions of disparagement, of the discoveries in geography and astronomy,[70] there remained as orthodoxy in Rochester's day a strong current of enthusiastic optimism about man's capacities for understanding the world and God's will through the exercise of the divine gift of reason in conjunction with faith, and in man's ability and willingness to act, in accordance with his understanding, with nobility and dignity. The new Restoration orthodoxy, like the older Renaissance equivalent, represented an alliance of science and religion, the

70. See the bibliography in Douglas Bush, *English Literature in the Earlier Seventeenth Century, 1600–1660* (2nd ed., Oxford, 1962), pp. 476–477.

Royal Society on the one hand, and the Anglican Church, the Cambridge Platonists, and even some Dissenters on the other. To be sure, no Christian advocated an unbridled rationalism or asserted the perfection or perfectibility of man;[71] on the contrary, all men joined in condemning "mere speculation" and in asserting man's fallen nature.[72] Nevertheless, there remained schools of thought in Rochester's time which continued to claim, in the face of skepticism, Hobbism, Epicureanism, and theriophily, the glory and dignity of rational man.[73] It is against these schools, not merely against their spokesmen in the Church, that Rochester's "Satyr" is directed.

The traditions of optimistic self-praise, like those of self-disparagement, have both a long history and a vigorous seventeenth-century life.[74] In Rochester's time the key notions were still those of the Renaissance:

> What a piece of work is a man! How noble in reason!
> How infinite in faculties, in form, and moving how
> express and admirable, in action how like an angel,

71. See, however, the Cambridge Platonists on man's deiform nature, in C. A. Patrides, *The Cambridge Platonists* (London, 1969), introduction, pp. 18–23, and selections, esp. pp. 70, 101, 167.

72. See Robert Boyle's critique of the pretense of physical certainty made by the new natural scientists, *Excellence of Theology* (1673), in *Works* (London, 1744), 3:432. Compare also Ralph Cudworth's endorsement not of pure "dry" reason, but of reason dedicated to God. *The True Intellectual System of the Universe* (1678), ed. Thomas Birch (London, 1820), 1:63–64. See also Joseph Glanvill, *The Vanity of Dogmatizing* (1661), reprinted and addressed to the Royal Society in 1664 as *Scepsis Scientifica*. Though he endorsed the methods of the new science in forming hypotheses rather than dogmas as a means toward attaining "real and useful knowledge," Glanville was far more affected by philosophical skepticism than many Anglicans.

73. See, for example, Walter Charleton, who popularized Epicureanism in *Epicurus' Morals* (1656) yet exalted man's reason and his superiority over animals in *The Immortality of the Human Soul* (1657).

74. For an account of the idea of human dignity in classical antiquity, the Middle Ages, and the Renaissance, see Herschel Baker, *The Image of Man* (New York, 1961), first published as *The Dignity of Man* (Cambridge, Mass., 1947).

> in apprehension how like a god: the beauty of the
> world, the paragon of animals . . .
>
> [*Hamlet*, 2:2: 312–316]

and in the words of La Primaudaye, "a creature made of God after his own image, just, good, and right by nature"; [75] that he stands preeminent over the animals in an ordered, hierarchical world (a commonplace given almost universal currency by popularizers such as Du Bartas); [76] and that this preeminence is due to man's godlike faculty of reason.

The third of these notions took a variety of forms in Rochester's day. The old medieval Aristotelian synthesis, constructed under Aquinas, of faith and speculative reason, still strong in the universities, was vital enough to provoke attacks in Bacon's *Novum Organum*, Hobbes's *Leviathan*, and Butler's *Hudibras* against the "absurd speeches . . . without any signification at all, from . . . deceived and deceiving schoolmen." [77] Rochester joins them in ridiculing the speculative reason:

> This busy, puzzling stirrer-up of doubt
> That frames deep mysteries, then finds 'em out,
> Filling with frantic crowds of thinking fools
> Those reverend bedlams, colleges and schools
>
> .   .   .   .
>
> 'Tis this exalted power, whose business lies
> In nonsense and impossibilities.
>
> [ll. 80–83, 88–89]

His attack on reason, however, is comprehensive, directed not only against the Schoolmen, but against the more mod-

---

75. Pierre de la Primaudaye, *The French Academie* (1618), p. 5, an encyclopaedia of Renaissance lore and piety, first translated into English in 1577 and frequently reprinted. Quoted in Baker, *The Image of Man*, p. 224.

76. Sylvester's translation of *The Divine Weeks and Works* (1605) was one of the most popular books of the seventeenth century.

77. *Leviathan*, ch. 3.

erate anti-Aristotelian rationalism of the Anglicans, whose
views, favorable to experimental scientists and inductive
reason, Cowley and Dryden (before his conversion) may
represent. Dryden, denouncing the tryanny of Aristotelian-
ism, pays tribute to Bacon and the Royal Society:

> The longest tyranny that ever sway'd
> Was that wherein our ancestors betray'd
> Their free born reason to the Stagirite
> And made his torch their universal light
>
> . . . .
>
> Among th'assertors of free reason's claim,
> Th' English are not the least in worth or fame
>
> . . . .
>
> The world to Bacon does not only owe
> Its present knowledge, but its future too.
> ["To My Friend, Dr. Charleton"]

Cowley, too, in a Pindaric ode "To Mr. Hobs," deplores
the mere "words" and "empty air" of the Schoolmen, but
shows in "Reason: the Use of it in Divine Matters" that
Anglicans continued to believe in the cooperation of faith
and reason:

> Reason within's our onely Guide,
> Reason, which (God be prais'd!) still walks, for all
>   It's old Originall Fall
> And since it self the boundless Godhead joyn'd
>   With a Reasonable Mind
> It plainly shews that Mysteries Divine
>   May with our Reason joyn.
> [ll. 26–32]

And while Faith, says Cowley, is necessary,

> Yet Reason must assist too, for in seas
> So vast and dangerous as these,

Our course by Stars we cannot know
Without the Compass too below.
[ll. 37–40]

Still a third form of contemporary Christian rationalism, at odds on some accounts with the Anglicans, took a Platonic cast with the group of seventeenth-century divines — Benjamin Whichcote, Nathanael Culverwell, Ralph Cudworth, John Smith, and Henry More — known as the Cambridge Platonists.[78] Holding that God is pure reason, they found no conflict between human reason and faith. ("What is most spiritual is most rational.")[79] God, said Culverwell, "hath set up a distinct lamp in every soul that men might make use of their own light."[80] This lamp, "the spirit of man," they called "the candle of the Lord" (a phrase from Proverbs 20:27 that they never tired of quoting), meaning not the light of grace or a private inner light, but the godlike faculty of reason. "To blaspheme reason," Culverwell wrote in *A Discourse of the Light of Nature* (in effect a commentary on the Proverbs phrase which stands at its epigraph), "is to reproach Heaven itself, and to dishonour the God of reason, to question the beauty of his image."[81] Or as Whichcote said simply: "To go against Reason is to go against God."[82] The candle of the Lord, More called a lantern to guide man's way. Comparing reason to torches or

78. While sympathetic, like many Anglicans, with the experiments of the Royal Society, the Cambridge Platonists resisted the reduction of earthly experience to sense-perception. They in their turn were reproached by Anglicans as "Latitude-Men" for tendencies toward Arminianism and sympathies with pagan Platonism. For a full discussion, see Ernst Cassirer, *The Platonic Renaissance in England*, tr. Pettegrove (Austin, Texas, 1953), esp. pp. 25–85, and Patrides, *The Cambridge Platonists*, pp. 1–41.

79. Whichcote, *Moral and Religious Aphorisms* (London, 1753), sec. 1183, n.p.

80. *Discourse of the Light of Nature* (1652), ed. John Brown (Edinburgh, 1857), p. 206.

81. *Ibid.*, p. 17.

82. *Aphorisms*, sec. 76.

lanterns, "convenient lights," he held that men who deny the use of reason in religion are like those who break a lantern on the ground in the middle of the night, "with hazard of knocking their noses against the next tree they meet, and tumbling into the next ditch."[83]

Rochester clearly would have found this kind of rationalism vain and misguided. His famous lines on reason as an "ignis fatuus" (perhaps with Whichcote's aphorism — "Passion before, or without Reason, is as Bad for a Guide as an Ignis Fatuus"[84] — in mind) may be his mocking parody of the "candle of the Lord":

> Reason, an ignis fatuus in the mind,
> Which, leaving light of nature, sense, behind,
> Pathless and dangerous wandering ways it takes
> Through error's fenny bogs and thorny brakes;
> Whilst the misguided follower climbs with pain
> Mountains of whimseys, heaped in his own brain,
> Stumbling from thought to thought, falls headlong down
> Into doubt's boundless sea . . .
>
> [ll. 12–19]

Implicitly controverting More, Rochester claims that the light of reason leads men into ditches; controverting Culverwell, he claims that the true "light of nature" is sense, not reason.

In the Cambridge Platonists, Rochester also would have found foolish the exaltation of man as "the glory of God's creation," "the Masterpiece of God's workmanship," "fit for attendance upon God, and conversation with Angels,"[85] an exaltation which went so far as to assert man deified: "the

83. *Enthusiasmus Triumphatus* (1656), sec. 54, in *Phil. Works*, 2:214, quoted in Cassirer, *The Platonic Renaissance*, p. 40.

84. *Aphorisms*, sec. 412.

85. Whichcote, *Select Discourses*, ed. J. Jeffrey (London, 1702), 2:25–50. Quoted in Patrides, *The Cambridge Platonists*, (n. 71 above), p. 38.

Gospel is nothing else, but God descending into the World in our Form, and conversing with us in our likenesse; that he might allure, and draw us up to God, and make us partakers of his Divine Form." [86] The satirist of mankind would have mocked such claims for man's divinity, as well as those for his humanity. Whichcote declares that God has created man with "a secret Genius to humanity; a Bias that inclines him to a Regard of all his own kind," a fact, says Whichcote, which leads man to "detest and reject that Doctrine [i.e., Hobbes's] which saith, that God made man in a State of War." [87] The Cambridge Platonists, indeed, as Rochester would have noted, opposed Hobbes at almost every point: "He posited a universe permeated by matter, they believed in a world palpitating with spirit. . . . He was never conscious of the transcendental, they were never without 'the delicious sense of the Divine.' . . . He claimed that man is motivated by fear, they asserted that man is instinct of love." [88]

To represent in his poem these various optimistic rationalist tendencies, Rochester somewhat arbitrarily chooses three minor religious figures of his day — Nathaniel Ingelo, Simon Patrick, and Richard Sibbes — with whom he associates the spokesman for orthodoxy who has challenged the satirist's attack on man and reason. "What rage ferments in your degenerate mind," asks the optimist,

> To make you rail at reason and mankind?
> Blest, glorious man! to whom alone kind heaven
> An everlasting soul has freely given.
> Whom his great Maker took such care to make
> That from himself he did the image take

86. Culverwell, *A Sermon Preached Before the House of Commons, March 31, 1647*, repr. in Patrides, *The Cambridge Platonists*, p. 101.

87. Whichcote, *Select Sermons*, ed. Anthony, Earl of Shaftesbury (London, 1698), pp. 381, 382. Quoted in Patrides, *The Cambridge Platonists*, p. 38.

88. Patrides, *The Cambridge Platonists*, p. 28.

And this fair frame in shining reason dressed
To dignify his Nature above beast.
[ll. 58–64]

To this the satirist replies:

Hold, mighty man, I cry, all this we know
From the pathetic pen of Ingelo,[89]
From Patrick's *Pilgrim*, Sibbes' soliloquies.
[ll. 72–74]

Previous critics have not paid enough attention to the adversarius's speech. A recent critic suggests that the "mighty man" is only a "straw man":

He is a smug prelate, a self-styled idealist of the kind that regards all satirists as degenerates. He believes in the dignity of man, in man's essential difference from the beasts, and in man's ability to pierce the infinite, and thereby attain ultimate knowledge. These notions are the commonplaces of Renaissance optimism, but never in the Renaissance were they mouthed so complacently and so glibly. The adversarius is a proud man defending Pride, a mock Christian who has conveniently forgotten the Fall. Again Rochester has offended the pious by making this facile optimist their spokesman.[90]

This is well said, yet it does not go far enough; it dismisses too readily the possibility that the adversarius, as I have suggested, indeed fairly represents current notions about mankind and reason. Nor have previous critics done more than take for granted the general aptness of Ingelo, Patrick, and Sibbes in Rochester's argument. No one, curiously, has shown specifically what in these religious writers Rochester ridicules.

89. "Pathetic," "producing an effect upon the emotions; moving, stirring, effecting" (*OED*, sense 1).
90. C. F. Main, "The Right Vein of Rochester's *Satyr*," (n. 52 above), pp. 103–104.

Nathaniel Ingelo (c. 1621–1683) would have been known to Rochester as the author of *Bentivolio and Urania,* a long religious-allegorical romance first published in 1660 and reprinted several times prior to 1675.[91] Also a Doctor of Divinity and Fellow of Eton College, Ingelo was probably singled out for scorn in the "Satyr" for two reasons: first, for his high estimate of man's potential for good, and second, for his attack on "Atheists, Epicureans, and Skeptics." On both grounds, he sounds like Rochester's "band and beard."

In the preface to Book 1, Ingelo speaks against those "who entertain themselves with things which correspond not with the Dignity of Reasonable Souls; instead of perfecting those rare capacities with which their Natures are invested, by a generous endeavour to obtain that Happiness which God doth not envy us, they lessen themselves . . . and make them degenerate into a brutish incapacity" (p. 62). In the preface to Books 5 and 6, likewise, he speaks of man's capacity for dignity, nobility, and glory. The goal is difficult but attainable, and he has ventured therefore

to describe Noble Examples in which Holy Rules appear practicable, that I might both engage and assist Imitation in all Capable Souls; and I made choice of this way, knowing that we ought as Plato hath told us . . . to act looking upon beautiful and divine images set before us. . . . It is the glory of men to conform their lives to the Eternal Reasons of Goodness, whose Indispensable Principles are Connate with our Souls. [pp. 65–66]

It is clear what Rochester would have objected to, both in his prefaces and in his hero, Bentivolio, or Good Will: "When Bentivolio appear'd to the astonishment of the de-

91. Originally published in four books, and later (1664) in six. *Cambridge Bibliography of English Literature* records editions in 1660 (twice), 1664, 1673, 1682. I have consulted a copy in the Yale University Library designated as the "2nd edition," dated 1669 [sic]. *Cambridge Bibliography of English Literature,* 1:698; 2:24, 598.

generate world, which could not remember to have seen any gentleman equal to him in Complexion or Stature, he was so perfectly made up, that one might easily perceive Wisdom, Goodness, and Courage to have done their utmost in his Composure" (p. 1). Ingelo's estimate of "Blest, glorious man" and his potential for virtue make him a natural target for the satirist of mankind.

Ingelo offends Rochester not only by exalting man, but also by attacking Epicurus and the Skeptics. In the preface to Books 5 and 6 the Skeptics are quickly dismissed for their "stupid unbelief" (Sigs. [b4–b5]) [92] and the Epicureans berated, at greater length, for their "beastly Philosophy" and "brutish Voluptuousness" (Sig. [bf]), Ingelo understanding no more than his contemporaries the distinction between pleasures of motion and of rest. In Book 5 the attack is more elaborate:

That he [Epicurus] debas'd Humane Nature, is prov'd already; for what can be more unworthy of a Man, then to use his Reason to make him more perfectly a Beast? That the extirpation of all Religious Observance of God was his Design, is manifest both by the acknowledgment of his greatest Disciples, and by the nature of his discourse. [pp. 63–64]
Lucretius, who took the pains to put [Epicurus's] philosophy into Verses, hath recorded it as his Immortal glory, that he was the *first that ventur'd to set his face against Heav'n, durst disclaim Religion*, and brought Arguments against it into the field of Disputation, which made Devotion tremble and flie out of the soules of men, *and trample under his victorious feet* that which durst resist him, and *then triumph'd over it.* [p. 64, emphasis added]

With the charge that Epicurus sought to extirpate all religion, Rochester set out to have fun. The italicized lines in the second passage are paraphrased from those lines in *De*

92. Antitheus ("an Atheist"), Diaporon ("one who doubts," and a devotee of Epicurus), and Apronaeus ("one who denies Providence") figure notoriously in Book 5.

Rerum Natura where Lucretius praises Epicurus for conquering man's superstition of the gods, especially "a man of Greece was the first that dared to uplift mortal eyes against her [i.e., Religion], the first to make stand against her. . . . Wherefore Religion is now in her turn cast down and trampled underfoot, whilst we by the victory are exalted high as heaven." [93]

Perceiving the ironic congruity between Lucretius's praise of the bold, reasoning, godlike Epicurus, and Ingelo's praise of reasoning, godlike Christian man, Rochester makes his "formal band and beard" approvingly allude to the same passage in Lucretius. Rochester has:

> Reason, by whose aspiring influence
> We take a flight beyond material sense,
> Dive into mysteries, then soaring pierce
> The flaming limits of the universe,
> Search heaven and hell, find out what's acted there,
> And give the world true grounds of hope and fear.
> [ll. 66–71]

Lucretius has: "Therefore the lively power of his mind prevailed, and forth he marched far beyond the flaming walls of the heavens, as he traversed the immeasurable universe, in thought and imagination; whence victorious he returns bearing his prize, the knowledge what can come into being, what can not." [94] The joke is not dwelt on, but the point must have been obvious to Rochester's educated readers, who would recognize at once the irony of having the pious "band and beard" quote from the pagan and atheistic Lucretius. If they happened to know Ingelo's attack on Epicurus, their pleasure in the irony would be the greater. [95]

---

93. *De Rerum Natura*, 1:66–67, 78–79, in the Loeb translation.
94. *Ibid.*, pp. 72–76.
95. Note, too, that the adversarius's line, "Whom his great Maker took such care to make" (l. 62), conflicts with the Epicurean view that the gods are remote and uninterested in men, and, presumably, with

Simon Patrick's *Parable of the Pilgrim* (1664), recounting like Bunyan's later *Pilgrim's Progress* (1678) the passage of the Christian pilgrim from this world to the heavenly city, was probably chosen as a victim of Rochester's "Satyr" (1675) because it was a popular devotional manual (reaching a sixth edition by 1687) somewhat old-fashioned in its simple piety. Exaltation of man, furthermore, is implicit in the very idea of the earthly pilgrimage to heaven. The dangers of such a journey, set forth in chapter 19, "Of many other devices to discourage him in his Journey; Especially if he should chance to get a fall," Rochester may parody in his own lines on the "misguided follower" of reason. Patrick warns against stepping aside from the direct path, stumbling and falling, and even drowning, all through the tricks of one's enemies. Rochester's pilgrim stumbles and falls through the tricks of his own guide, reason: "Stumbling from thought to thought, falls headlong down / Into doubt's boundless sea, where, like to drown. . . ." Upon arrival in heaven, Patrick's pilgrim "becomes noble," "in so much that the meanest Pilgrim on the Earth that is found worthy by reason of his virtuous disposition and generous Spirit to be admitted a Citizen of Jerusalem instantly becomes noble, and is enrolled among the Princes of Heavenly Progeny" (p. 96). While yet on earth, too, the pilgrim's mind, by meditation, "being abstracted from, and elevated *beyond things of corporeal sense*, is brought to a converse and familiarity with heavenly notions":

Meditation furnishes our understanding with right opinions, and noble thoughts. . . . This, it is manifest, is the natural and true use of these devout exercises meditation and prayer: to dispose our

Rochester's view (he translated a famous passage from *De Rerum Natura* to this effect — *Complete Poems*, p. 35 — and expressed to his wife a disbelief in providence) but reflects Ingelo's own theme of God's infinite goodness and care for humanity: "to say that anything is too little for his care is to reproach him for labour ill bestow'd in the making of it" (pp. 65–66).

souls by drawing them away from these inferiour enjoyments, *to receive communications from above, and to be made partakers of a Divine Nature.* [p. 153, emphasis added]

Here again are phrases which Rochester may well have had in mind when he made his optimist praise reason in the Lucretian terms described just above.[96]

Richard Sibbes is also directly represented by the adversarius. A Puritan lecturer in divinity at Cambridge, and publisher of many volumes of sermons and devotional works, he had urged, in *The Soul's Conflict with Itself*, chapter 13 ("Of Imagination, sin of it, and remedies for it"), as a form of remedy for sin, a "soliloquy" in which a man meditates by asking himself questions. For example:

we should ask of ourselves upon what ground we entertain such a conceit [i.e., anything imagined], whether we shall have the same judgment after we have yielded to it as now we have?

Here, therefore, is a special use of these soliloquies, to awake the soul and to stir up reason cast asleep by Satan's charms, that so scattering the clouds through which things seem otherwise than they are, we may discern and judge of things according to their true and constant nature.[97]

Why Rochester should have singled out Sibbes's "soliloquies" is puzzling.[98] This is the only mention of them in

96. To be sure, Rochester does Patrick some injustice by caricaturing his position, and by ignoring the qualifications in his praise of the human mind "rightly disposed" (pp. 153–154) and his disapproval of the metaphysical learner explaining spiritual matters in obscure and bombastic language (p. 146).

97. *Works*, ed. Grosart, 7 vols. (1862–1864), 1:191. Cf. Joseph Hall's *Soliloquies: or Holy Self-Conferences of the devout Soul*, in *Works* (Oxford, 1863), 8:22.

98. Puzzling, too, to some early scribes who substituted "S—— [or "Stillingfleets"] replies" in the Huntington Library copy of the *Poems* (1680) and in the *Gyldenstolpe MS* and Yale MS version. Edward Stillingfleet (1635–1699), a Latitudianarian, popular London (and Court) preacher, and controversialist for Anglican rationalism (and later Bishop of Worcester) wrote a number of polemical works, including

Sibbes's complete works, and there appear to be no references to them in the poetry of the period, or in the standard
works on Puritanism, all of which suggests that they held
no position of prominence in the religious life of the times.
On the other hand, Rochester may have wanted to extend
his attack to include a Puritan divine (to match the Anglican Patrick). It is possible that Rochester as a child had been
force-fed Sibbes by his pious Puritan mother, and carried
with him a distasteful memory. He may have remembered,
too, what Sibbes said of reason:

for reason is a beam of God . . . God having made man an
understanding creature, guides him by a way suitable to such a
condition. . . . Faith is an understanding grace; it knows whom
it trusts, and for what, and upon what grounds it trusts. Reason
of itself cannot find what we should believe, yet when God hath
discovered the same, faith tells us there is great Reason to believe
a sanctified instrument *to find out God's grounds,* that it may
rely upon them. He believes best, that knows best why he should
believe.[99]

and what he said of the likeness between the soul and God:
"Sometimes in a clearer state of the soul, faith hath not so
much use of reason, but upon near and sweet communion
with God (as it shall be in heaven), and by reason of some
likeness between the soul that hath a divine nature stamped
on it and God, it presently, without any long discourse,

A Rational Account of the Ground of Protestant Religion (1665),
along with numerous "Answers" and "Replies" to theological opponents. K. F. Paulson has recently demonstrated that Stillingfleet would
have made an appropriate victim for Rochester's satire: in February
1674 he preached before Charles II a sermon that appears to attack
the "Satyr." See "The Reverend Edward Stillingfleet and the Epilogue to Rochester's *A Satyr against Reason and Mankind,*" *PQ,* 50
(1971), 657–663. Paulson's argument that "Stillingfleet's replies" was the
original reading seems to me not fully convincing.

99. *Works,* 1:245, emphasis added. Compare Rochester's: "Search
heaven and hell, *find out* what's acted there / And give the world true
grounds of hope and fear (ll. 70–71).

runneth to God, as it were, by a supernatural instinct." [100] It is against such presumptions about the power of man's reason and the godlike nature of his soul that the "Satyr" is written.[101] Doubtless Rochester meant to belittle his optimistic opponents — panegyrists of mankind, whether poets, scientists, or churchmen — by associating them with such minor religious writers. At the same time it is now clear (for the first time, I think), that Ingelo, Patrick, and Sibbes, while representing a whole range of orthodox optimistic opinion, were singled out not simply as insignificant spokesmen of a general position, but for their concrete formulations of current attitudes.

100. *Works*, 1:245. Compare Rochester: "Whom his great Maker took such care to make / That from himself he did the image take . . . / This supernatural gift . . . (ll. 62–63, 76).

101. Rochester was probably not familiar with Sibbes's own warnings about reason's limited use: "we must not stand to look for reason too much, nor trust the reason or wit of any man, but divine authority especially," and his attack on man's pride in reason "that will make their own apprehensions and conceits of things the measure of divine truth." *Works*, 4:159; 5:467.

∘5 A Reading of the "Satyr Against Mankind"

Backgrounds, intellectual and literary, of course tell only part of the story. The power and appeal of Rochester's "Satyr" depend less on its derived philosophical content than on its vigorous surge and flow (what Voltaire called Rochester's "Energy and Fire")[1] and the consequent ambiguity of its argument. We need now to look at the effect of paradox, style, and thematic inconsistency, in order to discover the poem's true originality.

The Theme of Paradox

At first reading we are aware that the poem is a vigorous and provocative utterance by a self-conscious speaker, directed, as it were, at "mankind." We have no suggestion of a specific audience until line 46, when the speaker introduces a second person, the "formal band and beard," who

1. *Letters Concerning the English Nation,* tr. J. Lockman (London, 1733), p. 203.

undertakes to comment. After twenty-four lines, he recedes into the background, though kept in the speaker's mind (and ours) by occasional references to a second person (e.g., "Thus, sir, you see . . .").[2] The satirist then resumes his attack, until in the closing lines we have as little consciousness of a second person as at the beginning.

The structural affinities with formal verse satire are obvious. In one of its various forms, less a narrative of past events than a musing on or casual contemplation of any given topic, the satirist will imagine what "someone will say" in answer to his own thoughts (a favorite practice of Boileau). In another form, the satiric monologue becomes a fully dramatic dialogue; a second person breaks in unannounced from time to time, his speeches probably marked typographically with "A." (Adversarius or Amicus). Although we might at first have placed the "Satyr" in the latter category, it belongs in fact, like Boileau's eighth satire, in the former, the imaginary conversation: "But now, *methinks*, some formal band and beard takes me to task. Come on, sir; I'm prepared" (ll. 46–47).[3] Rochester's adversarius is clearly only imagined to speak.

Several suggestions have been advanced by previous critics concerning the poem's structure or division into parts. Thomas Fujimura has maintained[4] that the poem ought to be considered a philosophical discourse, of which lines 1–112 deal with epistemology, and lines 113–221 with ethics. But this proposal meets with difficulties, for the poem surely discusses ethics at lines 100–101: "That reason which distinguishes by sense / And gives us rules of good and ill from thence." "Good and ill" apart, "distinguishes" is an

---

2. Lines 72, 104, 106–110, 113, 123, 126.

3. It would have been easy for Rochester to give the adversarius fully independent status, simply by writing, for example, "But now, I see, this formal band and beard. . . ." But he clearly chooses otherwise.

4. "Rochester's 'Satyr Against Mankind': An Analysis," *SP*, 55 (1958), 576–590.

ethical (recognizes as different in order to choose) as well as an epistemological (makes out, sees) term. In lines 114–122 the poem discusses both epistemology and ethics:

> 'Tis evident beasts are, in their degree,
> As wise at least, and better far than he.
> Those creatures are the wisest who attain,
> By surest means, the ends at which they aim.
>
> [ll. 115–118]

Indeed, the poem shows that distinctions between knowledge and action and conduct are false: ". . . thoughts are given for action's government; / Where action ceases, thought's impertinent" (ll. 94–95). The conception of right reason presented by the poem insists on our considering epistemology and ethics together.

A more recent critic, C. F. Main, has rightly criticized Fujimura's structural analysis and offered one of his own. He sees the poem as essentially a formal satire, unified in accordance with the theory that Dryden was later to set forth (based on classical practice and Renaissance theorists) in the *Discourse concerning the Original and Progress of Satire* (1693). Satire, Dryden wrote, "ought only to treat of one subject; to be confined to one particular theme; or at least, to one principally. If other vices occur in the management of the chief, they should only be transiently lashed." [5] Main belives that Rochester's "Satyr" is a unified attack on pride: pride in reason (ll. 1–28), in wit (ll. 33–45), in learning (ll. 72–113), and in "accomplishment" (ll. 117–173).

While it is true that the poem continually lashes pride (the word and its derivatives occur nine times in the poem), it is not true, I think, that this is the only basis of the poem's design. If we insist that the "Satyr" is a poem against pride, we are forced to read long passages on the deceptiveness of reason or on fear being man's ultimate motive as elabora-

5. *Of Dramatic Poesy and other Critical Essays*, ed. Watson, 2:145.

tions of or digressions from the main theme. At several points in the poem, the speaker seems more interested in working out details of his comparison of men to animals than in scoring points against man's pride. It is possible, however, to discern in the "Satyr" some aspects of the characteristic two-part structure of a formal verse satire,[6] the attack on a vice and (at least implicit) praise of a corresponding virtue. The poem attacks pride in reason, and the brutality of human nature. It commends explicitly a modest kind of "right reason . . . which distinguishes by sense," and implicitly the instinctual, untreacherous life of animals, and (perhaps) the godlike "meek, humble man of honest sense," though the satirist doubts to find such a man on earth. Indeed, as we shall see, the poem finally suggests that all commendations and ideals are after all irrelevant to the behavior of mankind.

The "Satyr Against Mankind," then, is in some respects a philosophical discourse proposing a particular course of action, and in some respects a formal attack on pride. But I wish to suggest that we will better understand the poem's full and various implications and its peculiar tone if we view it primarily as a discourse of four parts in which a speaker presents and defends the paradox that it is better to be an animal than a man. Before examining the "Satyr" as a paradox, let us note briefly what the term meant for Rochester.

An ancient rhetorical form, the paradox became a favorite with the Renaissance humanists, the most famous example being Erasmus's *Encomium Moriae*. As H. K. Miller has shown, "the term 'paradox' was very broadly construed throughout the seventeenth century, when," as he says, "it was at the peak of its popularity as a form of argumenta-

6. As described by Mary Claire Randolph, "The Structural Design of Formal Verse Satire," *PQ*, 21 (1942), 368–384; and Howard Weinbrot, "The Pattern of Formal Verse Satire in the Restoration and Eighteenth Century," *PMLA*, 80 (1965), 394–401.

tion." [7] Two senses of the term were current in the Restoration: (1) "A statement or tenet contrary to received opinion or belief," and (2) "A statement seemingly self-contradictory or absurd, which upon examination, may prove to be either well-founded or in fact self-contradictory after all" (*OED*). Rochester's poem is paradoxical, I think, in both senses: it presents a statement antithetical to orthodox opinion (it is better to be an animal than a man) and a statement which is seemingly absurd but in fact not self-contradictory. As is characteristic of Rochester, however, the poem is more interested in the negative face of the coin (to be a man is loathsome) than in the positive (it is better to be an animal).

The purposes of paradoxes, in accordance with their broad definition, were various. Many, Donne's *Paradoxes and Problems* (1633) perhaps included, were written simply as displays of rhetorical ingenuity, or, in the terms of the title of another collection, "to exercise yong wittes in difficult matters." [8] On the other hand, several critics have suggested that Donne's purpose was not simply to display wit. In a letter to a friend, enclosing some paradoxes, Donne wrote that "their function is to make the reader find better reasons against them," and that "they are rather alarums to truth to arm her, than her enemies." [9] Third, paradoxes might be used to advance opinions unorthodox and serious against those vulgar and mistaken. As Miller has shown, many paradoxes, representing the author's true opinion, were written on such various topics as the advantages of the short sword over the rapier, the benefits of colonization, a call for political moderation ("The Paradoxical Encomium,"

7. H. K. Miller, "The Paradoxical Encomium: With Special Reference to its Vogue in England, 1600–1800," *Modern Philology*, 53 (1956), 145–178.

8. *Ibid.*, pp. 158–160.

9. E. M. Simpson, *A Study of the Prose Works of Donne* (1948), p. 316. Discussed by A. E. Malloch, "Techniques and Functions of the Renaissance Paradox," *SP*, 53 (1956), 191–203. Charles Estienne specifies the same purpose in the "Au Lecteur" prefaced to his translation of Ortensio Landi's *Paradossi*.

pp. 157–158). What would probably have proved most interesting to Rochester, however, were the writings of the paradoxical theriophilists. The address "To the reader" by the English translator of La Chambre's *Discourse of the Knowledge of Beasts* (1657) speaks of "the probability of La Chambre's paradoxes" (Sig. A2ʳ). La Chambre himself writes, in the *Discourse*, of Chanet's *Instinct and Knowledge of Beasts*, a work attacking his own theriophilic conclusions, that beasts possess a lower "sensual and corporeal reason": "As soon as his Discourses came to my hands, I fancied him to be some Hero of the Schools, and some new Hercules, whose commission was to damn paradoxes, and to maintain Vulgar opinions" (p. 8).

Just as paradoxes had no single purpose, so they were written in no single style or form.[10] They might take the form of paradoxical encomium, following more or less closely the rules set down for the encomium by classical and Renaissance rhetoricians.[11] Rochester's familiarity with this form is clearly demonstrated by his own "Upon Nothing." They might also take the form of the *vituperatio*, blame or censure, surely familiar to Rochester in the "Against Fruition" poems of the Cavalier poets and his fellow Restoration writers. Third, a paradox might take the form of a defense, distinguishable rhetorically from the encomium. While a paradox might well combine praise, blame, and defense, it is the third of these forms, I think, which is the structural principle of Rochester's poem.

The defensive paradox is related to the scholastic *quaestio*, or disputed question, with which Rochester may have been familiar from his brief training at Oxford, where exercises were still set for young students, to train them in the arts of the trivium.[12] That these university exercises often

10. Rosalie Colie, *Paradoxia Epidemica* (Princeton, 1966), p. 5.
11. Miller, "The Paradoxical Encomium," pp. 152–154.
12. A student's commonplace book dating from 1685 containing a list of themes for disputation is quoted in *Hudibras*, ed. John Wilders (Oxford, 1967), p. 323 n.

involved defenses of paradoxical opinions is suggested by the topic of the First Prolusion of Milton, delivered at Cambridge some sixty years earlier, "Whether Day or Night is the More Excellent."

By the sixteenth and seventeenth centuries the form of the *quaestio* had changed markedly from its medieval predecessor. Originally an oral performance by two students before a *magister* who decided the winner, the *quaestio* later consisted typically of four parts and involved a single student: the disputant (in writing) began with a thesis, offered a series of proofs, then reported any possible objections, and answered them. As Malloch writes, "what was once a true dispute [both orally and in written form] has become a one-man show" ("Renaissance Paradox," p. 200 n). We can see already the similarity between the Renaissance *quaestio* and the satires of Boileau and Rochester, with their primary speaker and imagined *adversarius*.

Boileau's satire shows the distinct influence of the scholastic dispute. The satirist begins by stating his thesis that "Le plus sot animal, c'est l'Homme" (l. 4). After imagining an exchange with another speaker, he proceeds to set up a formal *quaestio* (such as was currently practiced at the Sorbonne) to *prouver* his *propos* to the satisfaction of the theological "Docteur de Sorbonne" to whom the poem is addressed, recognizably Dr. Claude Morel, a famous Paris anti-Jansenist theologian and therefore an appropriate antagonist for a disputant attacking human nature.

> "Ces propos," diras tu, "sont bons dans la Satire,
> Pour égayer d'abord un Lecteur qui veut rire.
> Mais il faut les prouver. En forme." — J'y consens.
> Répons-moi donc, Docteur, et mets-toi sur les bancs.
> [ll. 15–18]

The satirist apparently sets up a fictional scene of oral disputation, with the *Docteur* presumably on the student's rather than the magister's "bench," preparing to answer the satirist's arguments.[13] In fact, however, only one voice speaks, imagining possible objections [14] and answering them.

Rochester perhaps takes over from Boileau the structure built on a *quaestio* and the idea of the comparison between man and animals, the latter familiar to him from other sources. But he takes some pains to alter the structure of Boileau's poem, bringing it more in line with a formal written disputed question or defense. His thesis, to begin with, is changed from "Le plus sot animal, c'est l'Homme" to

> Were I . . .
> A spirit free to choose, for my own share,
> What case of flesh and blood I pleased to wear,
> I'd be a dog, a monkey, or a bear,
> Or anything but that vain animal
> Who is so proud of being rational.

Rochester leaves out Boileau's explicit indications of oral disputation between two persons,[15] and inserts in the "Satyr" some references to the process of disputation or formal debate which have no equivalent in Boileau:

> . . . some formal band and beard
> Takes me to task. Come on, sir; I'm prepared.
> [ll. 46–47]

13. The structure of the imaginary disputation is clear in Oldham's translation of Boileau. The "Argument" reads: "The poet brings himself in, as discoursing with a Doctor of the University upon the subject ensuing." For Boileau's lines 15–18, Oldham has: "(Dr.) 'You must make [your thesis] appear / By solid proof.' Believe me, Sir, I'll do't: / Take you the Desk, and let's dispute it out." *The Works of Mr. John Oldham*, (final rev. ed. 1722), 2:5, 6.

14. "Poursuis-tu" (l. 60), "diras-tu" (l. 161), "dira-quelqu'un" (l. 97), "dit-on" (l. 119).

15. Rochester's adversarius, the "you" of the poem, is addressed in imagination only. Unlike Boileau's Monsieur M., he is not given a name or a title. The advantage is clear. The "Satyr" addresses not a historical individual, but all of mankind through the person of its panegyrist.

This plain distinction, sir, your doubt secures.[16]
[l. 110]

I'll ne'er recant, defend him if you can.
[l. 113]

Be judge yourself,[17] I'll bring it to the test.
[l. 127]

And all the subject matter of debate
Is only: Who's a knave of the first rate?
[ll. 172–173]

If upon earth there dwell such God-like men,
I'll here recant my paradox to them.
[ll. 216–217]

This last quotation is, of course, the clearest proof that Rochester considered his own poem a paradox, and, in the light of other references to debating, judging, and testing, a paradoxical defense of a heterodox opinion. Rochester departs from Boileau, too, by condensing the imagined objections of the adversarius into one speech of twenty-four lines, while Boileau scatters some forty lines of objection throughout his poem. His modification brings the poem closer to the *quaestio* model. Then, too, he deals with fewer topics than Boileau's wide-ranging poem, so that the "Satyr," as a defense, may be said to consist of four parts: (1) the statement of the thesis (ll. 1–45), (2) the imagined objections by the adversarius (ll. 48–71), (3) the reply to the objections, concerning first reason (ll. 72–111) and then mankind, both with respect to his "wisdom" (ll. 112–122) and "human nature" (ll. 123–173), and (4) an epilogue, containing a summary (ll. 174–178) and peroration, in which the speaker con-

16. I.e., "ought to convince you," "ought to dispel your doubt."

17. Gelli's dialogue may also have contributed to the form of the "Satyr." Ulysses disputes with a series of animals the question "whether it is better to be a man than a beast." The goat, for example, says, "You may judge for yourself. Only give me a fair hearing, and I will make out every particular so evident and plain that you shall give sentence against yourself." *Circe*, tr. Tom Brown, ed. R. Adams (Ithaca 1963), p. 142.

ditionally recants (ll. 179–219) and conditionally reformulates his paradox (ll. 220–221).

The advantages of such a structural analysis of the "Satyr," in comparison with suggestions that the poem has two parts, or one part, are fourfold; it notices the rhetorical form of the imaginary dialogue; it takes into account the references to debate and to paradox; it corresponds with the division of the poem into verse paragraphs in the 1680 editions; [18] and it helps tie Rochester's poems to still another traditional literary and rhetorical form, advancing the thesis that far more in his work than has previously been thought may be better understood if viewed in relation to existing ideas and conventions. Rochester's purpose in writing a paradox is not to call forth arguments against his statement that it is better to be an animal than man, not to express the whole of his personal feelings (i.e., he would not, in fact, want to be a monkey), and not, as with Montaigne's skeptical and theriophilic paradoxes, to urge complete faith in God. Doubtless he intended, instead, to display his wit and skill as a poet and rhetorician, to chastise mankind's pride, and to shock his readers by making them realize how nearly true is his outrageous suggestion.

The Flowing Tide

Structurally then, the "Satyr" is a combination of formal satire and formal defense of a heterodox opinion. The eclecticism is successful, for the conventions of satire (the adversarius, the combination of attack on vice and praise of a corresponding virtue) are integrated into the larger design of the paradox. The style, too, is eclectic, but tends to work

18. The printer, it is true, may not have been following Rochester's instructions. The first paragraph contains lines 1–45 (part 1); the second, lines 46–47, the introduction of the adversarius; the third, lines 48–71 (part 2); the fourth, lines 72–173 (part 3). The so-called "epilogue" (ll. 174–221) — possibly written later — was divided into five brief paragraphs.

against integration and formal unity. Its eclecticism produces not variety within unity, but nervous (in both the
modern sense and the eighteenth-century sense of "vigorous, forcible") ebb and flow that prevents the steady pro-
gression of an argument. Its essential feature is its energy, a
term that has lost its precision for modern critics, but remained a precise and useful word for Rochester's contemporaries, who found "energy" a prominent characteristic
of Rochester's poetic style.[19] Johnson defines the term (in
its literary use) as "strength of expression; force of signification; spirit; life." The first of these phrases refers to "a particular stylistic quality which is forceful because it succeeds
in communicating the active, the living, the moving in all
the 'energy' of its original actuality."[20] The second phrase
extends "energy" to include thought as well as expression,
and refers, in Puttenham's words, to forcefully wrought
ideas that inwardly work "a stirre to the mynde."[21] Both
senses are appropriate to Rochester's poetic style, which conveys its pictures with vigor and force, communicating, above
all, the energy of the mind's restless movement to a reader,
whose mind is equally moved or "stirred." Rochester's "energy" is perhaps nowhere better displayed than in the poem's
opening lines.

The poem begins suddenly and remarkably. The bold
opening lines (1–7) are unsettling, both intellectually and
syntactically. Their function is to make a provocative state-

19. For Voltaire's comment, see n. 1; Hume (Rochester's poetry discovers "energy of style"), *History of Great Britain* (1757), 2:453; Joseph
Warton ("he has much energy in his Thoughts and Diction"), *Essay on
the Genius and Writings of Pope* (1756) (5th ed.; London, 1806), 2:46.
"Vigour" is a related term of praise: see Burnet ("a strange vivacity of
thought, and vigour of expression"), p. 27; Rymer, see above, p. 157;
Johnson ("in all his works there is sprightliness and vigour"), *Lives*,
1:131.

20. Jean Hagstrum's helpful gloss in *Samuel Johnson's Literary
Criticism* (Minneapolis, 1952), p. 51.

21. *Arte of English Poesie*, 3:3, quoted in Hagstrum, *Samuel Johnson's Literary Criticism*, p. 51.

ment — "I'd rather be any animal than a man" — with force
and disgust, and also to alert the reader about what kind of
discourse the poem will be, not measured, judicious, coolly
rational, but fitful, exaggerated, impassioned. Consider only
the first three lines, an epitome both stylistically and thematically of the whole poem.

We begin with the mere sign of a conditional phrase,
"Were I . . . ," that asks for immediate completion: "Were
I" plus infinitive, adjective, or noun. Instead, a parenthesis
cuts across our expectations, interrupting one syntactic path
and opening another: "Were I (who to my cost already am)."
The second syntactic path is itself puzzling. Taken together
with "Were I," it offers what appears to be the immediate
fulfillment of an unnamed condition: "Were I . . . who already am," a syntactic expectation that is not frustrated even
when we proceed to line 2, "who already am / One of those
strange prodigious creatures, man." The latter part of this
phrase has its own surprise, however. After "strange, prodigious creature" we might expect the name of a strange or
monstrous animal (is the poem going to be a beast fable or
fantasy?), or perhaps some human creature traditionally
thought of as strange or prodigious (Smithfield freak? City
merchant? Frenchified fop? poet?), but surely not plain
generic "man." As if this were not puzzling enough, we do
not find out until late in the poem how and why it is to
the speaker's "cost" to be a man. Proceeding to line 3 we are
caught up short again. If we are not reading attentively, or
if we (with some justification) consider that the condition
announced by "were I" has been fulfilled ("who already am
a man"), then we will expect a "then" clause and not the
predicate, "A spirit free to choose . . . ," which we now see
completes the condition.

The grammatical sense now proceeds fairly smoothly
through line 7, and we get the completion of the formal
statement: "if I were free to choose . . . I'd be anything but
a man." In fact, however, our experience of reading Roches-

ter's lines is nothing like that of reading my paraphrase of
them. What the paraphrase leaves out is the interruptive
parenthesis, which unsettles us syntactically and also intellectually: "If I were free to choose — but I'm not — I'd
be. . . ." The poem becomes a futile, gratuitous gesture.
The speaker is on the one hand a commentator on the human condition, and at the same time imprisoned in it, a
point made effectively by the distorted syntax which runs
"A spirit free to choose" hard up against "strange, prodigious creature, man." A possibility for change or freedom is
offered, only to be taken away immediately. The whole
poem operates in this fashion, as surprise and frustration,
an illogical pattern always working against the clear logic
of the poem's four-part structure.

Syntactic dislocations are perhaps never again so strong
as they are here, but the poem continues to display dislocations of a larger kind. Note, for example, the sudden shifts
from one level of discourse and couplet style to another.
After moving through several lines (8–11) of colloquially
stated popular philosophy (about senses, instinct, reason),
the speaker suddenly at line 12 starts a long, metaphoric,
even emblematic narrative about erring reason:

> And before certain instinct, will prefer
> Reason, which fifty times for one does err;
> Reason, an ignis fatuus in the mind . . .
> [ll. 10–12]

We begin line 12 expecting some amplification of the preceding statement, but are hardly prepared for the loaded phrase
"ignis fatuus," or for the little morality play enacted for us
in the following eighteen lines.

> Which, leaving light of nature, sense, behind,
> Pathless and dangerous wandering ways it takes
> Through error's fenny bogs and thorny brakes;

Whilst the misguided follower climbs with pain
Mountains of whimseys, heaped in his own brain;
Stumbling from thought to thought, falls headlong down
Into doubt's boundless sea, where, like to drown,
Books bear him up awhile, and make him try
To swim with bladders of philosophy;
In hopes still to o'ertake th'escaping light,
The vapor dances in his dazzling sight
Till, spent, it leaves him to eternal night.
Then old age and experience, hand in hand,
Lead him to death, and make him understand,
After a search so painful and so long,
That all his life he has been in the wrong.
Huddled in dirt the reasoning engine lies,
Who was so proud, so witty, and so wise.

[ll. 13–30]

This passage is perhaps the most powerful in the entire
"Satyr." I have called it a "morality play" not only because
of the personified abstractions — reason, old age, experience,
and death [22] — but also because of its starkness and univer-
sality, its speed and its horror. The presentation of the hero
to death by old age and experience recalls the general design
of the old Summons of Death plays,[23] yet the device of the
allegorical journey is, of course, not peculiar to the medieval
morality play. Spenser's Wood and Den of Error, and Bunyan's Slough of Despond and Hill Difficulty are, like Rochester's "error's fenny bogs and thorny brakes" and "mountains of whimseys," part of a broad allegorical tradition, still
active in the seventeenth century in works like Patrick's
Pilgrim and Ingelo's romances, or simply as a habit of

22. In the 1680 Huntington Library copy the abstractions are incon-
sistently capitalized: Reason, Whimseys, Old Age, but errors, doubts,
experience, death.

23. I know of no specific morality play that supplied Rochester with
details. He draws perhaps on the morality tradition as it filtered into
the seventeenth century and merged with religious allegory, and on
the theme of the chastening of the Everyman or Juventus figure.

mind.[24] As in *The Faerie Queene* and *The Pilgrim's Progress*, the immense, emblematic landscape, however much visualized, is really an internal one. Rochester literally places the scene within the "brain" of the misguided follower:

> Reason, an ignis fatuus *in the mind* . . .
> Whilst the misguided follower climbs with pain
> Mountains of whimseys, heaped *in his own brain*.

The action unfolds in a suddenly changing, partly dreamlike scene. As in Vaughan's "Regeneration," where the mountain and its mysterious pair of scales appear and then disappear, so in Rochester's poem the mental wanderer suddenly passes from bog and brake to mountain, thence to a boundless sea. When darkness comes, the sea disappears, and the wanderer finds himself "huddled in dirt."

The figurative language, too, derives from an older tradition. Reason was widely conceived of as a light or guide. Boileau's Docteur de Sorbonne protests that reason is man's "flambeau, son pilote fidele" (*Satire* 8, l. 235).[25] Rochester, however, drawing on popular tradition for the metaphor, and probably reversing, as we saw earlier, the Cambridge Platonists' "candle of the Lord" (with a mocking glance at the "inner light" of the Puritans), makes reason a false light. Though he no doubt had seen a will-o'-the-wisp (the popular name), he could have read in John Swan's popular *Speculum Mundi* (1643) the definition of the ignis fatuus as

a fat and oily Exhalation, hot and drie . . . often seen in Fennes and Moores . . . [which the] much terrified, ignorant, and superstitious people . . . deemed . . . walking spirits. They are no

24. Temptations to suicide by drowning, as Maynard Mack points out, are standard in morality-related literature. *King Lear in our Time* (Berkeley, 1965), pp. 61–62.

25. Butler calls reason the "Helme of the understanding" and "the only Cumpas Man ha's to Sayl by." *Characters and Passages from Notebooks*, ed. A. R. Waller (Cambridge, 1908), p. 336.

spirits, and yet lead out of the way, because those who see them are amazed, and look so earnestly after them that they forget their way; and then . . . wander to and fro, sometimes to waters, pits, and other dangerous places. [pp. 88–89]

Though Rochester seems to have been the first to call reason an *ignis fatuus*,[26] previous poets (following contemporary writers on meteorology) [27] had realized the usefulness of the term as a metaphor for deception. Milton's simile, in Book 9 of *Paradise Lost*, antedates Rochester's by less than ten years:

> As when a wand'ring Fire,
> Compact of unctuous vapor, which the Night
> Condenses, and the cold invirons round,
> Kindl'd through agitation to a Flame,
> Which oft, they say, some evil Spirit attends,
> Hovering and blazing with delusive Light,
> Misleads th' amaz'd Night-wanderer from his way
> To Bogs and Mires, and oft through Pond or Pool
> There swallow'd up and lost, from succor far.
> So glister'd the dire Snake . . .
> [ll. 634–643]

Some five years earlier Butler had described, with the same metaphor, the sectarian Ralpho's "new light" of divine inspiration:

> 'Tis a dark-Lanthorn of the Spirit,
> Which none see by but those that bear it.
> A Light that falls down from on high,
> For Spiritual Trades to cozen by:
> An Ignis Fatuus that bewitches,
> And leads men into Pools and Ditches,

26. Cowley makes delusive hope an ignis fatuus when it prevails over reason: "When thy false Beams o'er Reasons Light prevail / By Ignes Fatui for North-Stars we sail." "Against Hope," *Works* [of Mr. Abraham Cowley], 2 vols., 11th ed. (London, 1710), 1:123.

27. Kester Svendsen, *Milton and Science* (Cambridge, Mass., 1956), pp. 108–109.

To make them dip themselves, and sound
For Christendom and dirty pond.
        [*Hudibras*, Pt. 1 (1662), Canto 1, ll. 499–506]

At about the same time Davenant found the ignis fatuus an apt metaphor for human "knowledge" in his skeptical poem "The Philosopher's Disquisition to the Dying Christian," known popularly as "Faith and Reason":

Our glim'ring knowledge, like the wandring Light
    In Fenns, doth to incertainties direct
The weary progress of our useless sight;
    And only makes us able to suspect.
        [st. 66] [28]

Rochester's simile is a variation of what was developing into a topos.[29] His metaphor retains the combination, characteristic in popular lore, of qualities homely and rural, yet grave and universal.

Traditional, likewise, is the use of wandering, stumbling, falling as a metaphor for losing one's way morally or intellectually. Rochester's lines owe something to Montaigne's description of straying mortal nature: "how little soever she stray from the ordinary path . . . traced and measured out by the Church, how soone she loseth; entanglith, and confoundeth her selfe; turning, tossing, and floating up and downe in this vast, troublesome and tempestuous sea of man's opinion." [30] And he clearly draws on Boileau:

28. First published in Davenant's *Works* (1673), p. 332, but mistakenly attributed to Rochester by a contemporary. See three letters by Pinto in *The Times Literary Supplement* (London), 22 November, 6 and 13 December, 1934, pp. 824, 875, 895.

29. Congreve probably thought of Rochester and of Dryden's *Religio Laici* in writing of "Reason, the power / To guess at Right and Wrong; the twinkling Lamp / Of wand'ring Life, that winks and wakes by turns, / Fooling the Follower, betwixt Shade and Shining." *The Mourning Bride*, 3:1.

30. *Essayes*, 2:225. See also "This troublesome and vaste ocean of

Mais L'Homme sans arrest, dans sa course insensée,
Voltige incessament de pensée en pensée,
Son coeur toujours flottant entre mille embarras,
Ne scait ni ce qu'il veut, ni ce qu'il ne veut pas.
[*Satire* 8, ll. 35–38]

But where Boileau's point is only that man, foolishly inconstant, does not know what he wants, Rochester, whose wanderer "stumbling from thought to thought, falls headlong down / Into doubt's boundless sea" (ll. 18–19), finds man not wandering aimlessly, but actively misled, following in vain after Reason with far worse consequences.

Rochester's severity makes his tone less like Boileau's good-natured amusement than the gloomy warnings of the religious moralists. Compare Calvin: "For the dulness of the human mind renders it incapable of pursuing the right way of investigating the truth; it wanders through a variety of errors, and groping, as it were, in the shades of darkness, often stumbles, till at length it is lost in its wanderings; thus, in its search after truth, it betrays its incapacity to seek and find it." [31]

The Catholic skeptic Thomas Fitzherbert describes the same process of wandering and falling into doubt: "And therefore no marvaile if the wisest men of the world doe many times goe astray, stumble, and fal into the obscuritie of the manifold, and intricate doubtes, questions, controversies, perplexities, and uncertaine eventes that daylie occurre in humaine affaires." [32] Fitzherbert's image of a fall inevitably calls up man's first fall. Rochester's image of the

Physicall errours," *ibid.*, 2:269. See also the spiritual groper in Francis Quarles's Bk. 3, emblem 1: *Quarles' Emblems* (London, 1886), pp. 134–136.

31. *The Institutes of the Christian Religion*, tr. John Allen (1936), 2, 2:12.

32. *Treatise concerning Policy and Religion*, 1606, 1610, repr. 1615, 1652, 1696, quoted in Louis Bredvold, *The Intellectual Milieu of John Dryden* (Ann Arbor, 1934), p. 26.

proud reasoner's fall adverts likewise to Eden, but the language recalls Satan's rather than Adam's fall.[33]

Even the phrases "doubt's boundless sea" and "bladders of philosophy" build upon the figurative language of earlier moralists. Rochester perhaps combined a memory of Montaigne's "tempestuous sea of man's opinion" with what may have been a traditional metaphor — doubt as drowning. A Cambridge Protestant, ten years after the "Satyr," wrote contemptuously of a convert to Catholicism: "Something that looked like to a demonstration against the immortality of the soul had so confounded him, that he was up head and ears in the water all soused, and plunged in the doubt, and whether he is yet out of it we know not."[34] Add to this the belief that the ignis fatuus often led men into ponds, and the temptation to drowning in the morality tradition, and we can see how Rochester was able to combine fruitfully several disparate but related elements to produce a powerful metaphor solidly grounded in traditional thought and language.

Bladders, too, had been used before the "Satyr" in a figurative-moral context, chiefly as a metaphor for pride, in popular tracts, sermons, and poems alike.[35] The figure of

33. For the pattern "stumble-fall-headlong down-bottomless/boundless deep" see *Paradise Lost* (which Rochester may have read), 1:44-47, 177, 750; 2:271-272, 374, 890-891.

34. Thomas Bambridge, *An Answer to a Book Entitled Reason and Authority* (London, 1687), p. 1, quoted in Bredvold, *The Intellectual Milieu*, p. 96. The metaphor may originate in biblical commentary. Patrick, discoursing on Diffidence in the *Parable of the Pilgrim* ([London, 1664], p. 486), instances St. Peter walking on the water of the sea with Christ (Matt. 14:28-31). Peter becomes fearful, loses faith, and begins to sink. When he cries out, Christ saves him, but chides Peter "because he doubted."

35. Montaigne, "Of Democritus and Heraclitus": "Diogenes . . . accompt[ed]us but flies, and bladders puft with winde." *Essayes*, 1:344; Spenser, "Colin Clout," l. 717: "Bladders blowen up with wynd, that being prickt do vanish into noughts"; Donne, *Satire* 4: "Such as swells the bladder of our court." Evidence from *OED* suggests that figurative uses are confined to the sixteenth and seventeenth centuries.

the moralized swimming-bladder, though rarer, is not original with the "Satyr." Shakespeare strikingly anticipated Rochester's use in *Henry VIII*, when fallen Wolsey recalls his overweening life:

> I have ventur'd
> Like little wanton boys that swim on bladders,
> This many summers in a sea of glory,
> But far beyond my depth: my high-blown pride
> At length broke under me, and now has left me
> Weary and old with service, to the mercy
> Of a rude stream that must for ever hide me.
>
> [3:2:358–364] [36]

Bladders are an obvious and traditional symbol of pride, particularly pride of intellect, but it required the genius of a poet with a gift for concrete, humanized metaphor (the "little wanton boys") to imagine the swimming-bladder, suggesting not only wind-swollen pride, but the grave consequences when the proud man falls. Rochester's vividly imagined scene, evoking the hollow comfort of vain philosophy, demonstrates his gift — modest to be sure when compared to Shakespeare's — for apt and dramatic metaphor.

The closing lines of the passage demonstrate, too, the way in which Rochester builds on traditional moral discourse, and perhaps the way in which he draws eclectically on his reading for verbal hints and parallels in thought:

> Till, spent, it leaves him to eternal night.
> Then old age and experience, hand in hand,
> Lead him to death, and make him understand,

36. Compare some canceled lines from *Hudibras*, Part 2: "Whether the Ganza's, or a Scarab / Or Mahomets Hors, by birth an Arab, / Did *beare him up*, or that he flew / *With bladders* of Attracted Dew, / Since Authors mention to the moon, / Men only those four ways have gone." Canto 3, ll. 37ff., in Butler, *Satires and Miscellaneous Poetry and Prose*, ed. R. Lamar (Cambridge, 1928), p. 455; emphasis added.

> After a search so painful and so long,
> That all his life he has been in the wrong.

"Search so painful and so long" was perhaps inspired by Montaigne's "tout l'acquest qu'il a retiré d'une si longue poursuite, c'est d'avoir appris à reconnoistre sa foiblesse." [37] Elsewhere in the "Apologie" Rochester would have found a quotation from *De Rerum Natura*, of which he had himself already translated two short passages:

> The minde in bodies sicknesse often wandring strayes
> For it enraged raves, and idle talke outbrayes:
> Brought by sharpe lethargy sometime to more than deepe,
> While eyes and eye-lids fall into eternal sleepe.
>
> [2:262]

The wanderer here falls into "eternal sleepe" (compare Rochester's "eternal night"), a parallel in thought only. Davenant's "Faith and Reason" supplies a similar parallel:

> Fraile Life! in which, through Mists of humane breath,
>   We grope for Truth, and make our Progress slow;
> Because, by passion blinded, till by death,
>   Our Passions ending, we begin to know.
>
> [st. 8, p. 335]

But the idea of knowledge coming only in death (or through "experience") is too traditional to allow us to name Davenant (or anyone else) as Rochester's specific "source."

The broad arc of human experience represented by the ignis fatuus episode is quickly traversed, and the mind is left alone: "Huddled in dirt the reasoning engine [38] lies, /

37. Suggested by Pinto, *Poems*, p. 216.
38. There may be a hint of "ingenuity" in "engine"; the words are related etymologically, and "engine" itself meant "ingenuity" and "wit" up to about 1630 (*OED*). Pinto believes, on too little evidence I think, that Boyle's description of men as "engines endowed with wills" suggested Rochester's phrase (*From Dryden to Johnson*, ed. B. Ford

Who was so proud, so witty, and so wise" (ll. 29–30). The phrase "reasoning engine" marks a change in tone from a grave and lofty, even sympathizing, view of painfully self-deceived humanity to contemptuous dismissal. "Huddled in dirt" may mean wretched, debased and humiliated, groveling in the dust, or, more likely, dead in a fresh grave.[39] The couplet may thus be read as a supremely sardonic epitaph ("here lies a reasoning engine . . ."), a reminder (like an epitaph) of man's mortality as well as his proud folly.

But Rochester unexpectedly does not let the reader pause here:

> Pride drew him in, as cheats their bubbles catch,
> And made him venture to be made a wretch.
> His wisdom did his happiness destroy,
> Aiming to know that world he should enjoy.
>
> [ll. 31–34]

The first couplet is clearly meant to serve as commentary on the previous episode and as transition to the next movement. Rochester then takes up one at a time each term in "so proud, so witty, and so wise," to show that on each account, pride, wit, and wisdom, man works his own woe. Pride lures man to follow reason, to his ultimate regret, into disastrous ventures, as cheats, with the unwitting cooperation of their foolishly proud victims, lure their "bubbles" — the

[1957, rev. 1963], pp. 149, 155n). But compare the anti-theriophilist Descartes's description, in the *Discourse on Method*, of the human body as a "fabrick" [i.e., a machine or "engine"] made by God and differing from an invented man-machine [i.e., a robot] and from animals in being able to converse and to reason. From the first English translation (London, 1649), pp. 91–93. Robert Hooke's praise of Bacon's inductive method as an "engine" which regulates the actions of the human intellect "so that it shall not act amiss" quoted in J. C. Crowther, *Francis Bacon* [London, 1960], p. 8) was not published until 1705, but Rochester possibly heard of similar comments by boosters of the Royal Society.

39. For "huddle," *OED* cites Fuller (1655): "The obscurity of his burial (huddled into his grave at Langley)."

metaphor is something of an anticlimax after the somberly vivid passage on the ignis fatuus, and also a sharp change in level or style of discourse. The couplet is epigrammatic and "pointed," carrying us from a landscape within the mind to the streets and fairs of London. The cheat-bubble metaphor ends at line 32, and the following couplet, on wisdom, develops the third term, "so wise," in language abstract rather than concrete. Rochester then turns to the second term, "so witty," and in eleven lines describes how

> wit was his vain, frivolous pretense
> Of pleasing others at his own expense,
> For wits are treated just like common whores:
> First they're enjoyed, and then kicked out of doors.
>
> [ll. 35-38]

The scene has become firmly established as London. The following lines, crowded with wits, whores, and fools, carry us from medieval, or Bunyanesque, morality to Restoration comedy of manners. The language, always colloquial, is less figurative, less condensed: seven lines (more than one feels necessary) develop rather lamely and confusingly the idea (a commonplace in contemporary drama) that fops fear and hate wits.

At this point the "band and beard" breaks in. The problem of transition sidestepped, we hear the animated language of a would-be satirist of wit and panegyrist of reason and man, comically spluttering with self-important indignation and then, finding his true theme, hymning in one long sentence the glories of godlike man. His lines, designed by Rochester to recall the ignis fatuus passage, employ the same pattern of amplification:

> And this fair frame in shining *reason* dressed
> To dignify his nature above beast;
> *Reason,* by whose aspiring influence

> We take a flight beyond material sense,
> Dive into mysteries, then soaring pierce
> The flaming limits of the universe.
>
> [ll. 64–69; emphasis added]

They answer the imagery of wandering, climbing with pain, stumbling, and falling, with their own pattern of aspiring, flying, diving, piercing, and soaring.[40]

At the end of the panegyric there is another sharp break as the satirist rudely interrupts with a passionate tirade against "this very reason," heralded by a puzzling flurry of proper names — "Ingelo . . . Patrick's *Pilgrim*, Sibbs's soliloquies" — puzzling stylistically because the rest of the satire (with the exception of line 120) is free of all particular references to time, place, or person. The tirade itself answers the passion and some of the imagery of the adversarius's panegyric. Although the passage cannot help repeating some of the ideas already developed in the ignis fatuus episode, its style and tone are far different. Where the earlier passage was a sober and somber narrative about a sole "misguided follower" of reason, this Butler-like tirade is more shrill, more vehement, filled with foolish reasoners and rhetorically a series of denunciations, built, like Pope's character of Sporus,[41] on the repeated use of the contemptuous demonstrative:

> And 'tis *this* very reason I despise:
> *This* supernatural gift, that makes a mite
> Think he's the image of the infinite,[42]

40. Rochester's imagery of diving and soaring to describe mental excesses was already traditional by his time.

41. "Let Sporus tremble — 'What? *that* Thing of silk, / Sporus, *that* mere white Curd of Ass's milk? . . .' / Yet let me flap *this* Bug with gilded Wings, / *This* painted Child of Dirt that stinks and stings." "Epistle to Arbuthnot," ll. 305–306, 309–310.

42. "Mite" to answer "mighty man" (l. 72). Compare Dryden, *Religio Laici*: "How can the less the greater comprehend? / Or finite reason reach infinity? / For what could fathom God were more than He . . . /

Comparing his short life, void of all rest,
To the eternal and the ever blest;
This busy, puzzling stirrer-up of doubt
That frames deep mysteries, then finds 'em out,[43]
Filling with frantic crowds of thinking fools
Those reverend bedlams, colleges and schools;
Borne on whose wings, each heavy sot can pierce
The limits of the boundless universe;
So charming ointments make an old witch fly
And bear a crippled carcass through the sky.
'Tis *this* exalted power, whose business lies
In nonsense and impossibilities,[44]
This made a whimsical philosopher
Before the spacious world, his tub prefer,
And we have modern cloistered coxcombs who
Retire to think, 'cause they have nought to do.

[ll. 75–93]

These lines of angry contempt are followed, in one sense appropriately, by a calmer, steadier passage of philosophical exposition on how man ought to act:

But thoughts are given for action's government;
Where action ceases, thought's impertinent.
Our sphere of action is life's happiness,
And he who thinks beyond, thinks like an ass.
Thus, whilst against false reasoning I inveigh,

Dar'st thou, poor worm, offend Infinity?" (ll. 39–41, 93). One of the answers to the "Satyr," attributed to a Dr. Pocock or a Mr. Griffith (the poem beginning "Were I to chuse what sort of Corps I'd wear") defends the idea that man is "an image of the infinite," arguing that the image need not equal the original in all respects. *An Answer to the Satyr against Mankind* (?1679), p. 2.

43. Compare *Hudibras*, Part 1, 1:161–164: "He could raise scruples dark and nice / And after solve 'em in a trice; / As if divinity had catched / The itch on purpose to be scratched" and the "Satyr on the Weakness and Misery of Man": "Is busy in finding Scruples out, / To languish in eternal Doubt" (ll. 179–180).

44. Compare Butler, "The Elephant in the Moon" (c. 1676): "When one, who for his deep Belief / Was virtuoso then in chief, / Approv'd the most profound and wise, / To solve impossibilities" (ll. 27–30)

I own right reason, which I would obey:
That reason which distinguishes by sense
And gives us rules of good and ill from thence,
That bounds desires with a reforming will
To keep 'em more in vigor, not to kill.
Your reason hinders, mine helps to enjoy,
Renewing appetites yours would destroy.
My reason is my friend, yours is a cheat;
Hunger calls out, my reason bids me eat;
Perversely, yours your appetite does mock:
This asks for food, that answers, "What's o'clock?"
This plain distinction, sir, your doubt secures:
'Tis not true reason I despise, but yours.

[ll. 94–111]

The stylistic change is marked: now, instead of charged, figurative language — "this busy, puzzling stirrer-up of doubt," "frantic crowds," the reasoner likened to an "old witch" and a "crippled carcass" — comes language more plain and bare — "thoughts," "action," "life's happiness," "false reasoning," "sense," "rules of good and ill," "desires," "will," "appetites." The lines on right reason, clearly a doctrinal focus of the poem, are fittingly couched in calm, reasoned, almost prose-like language. The change in style perfectly mirrors the change in purpose, from the arousal of passionate indignation to the instruction in how to live.

The couplet style, too, is different from that of the preceding passage. While in lines 72 to 93 the couplets have a hurtling movement — with few full stops — here the couplets are more structured. Rochester employs frequent midline caesura to halt the flow, maintain steady pace, and to emphasize the recurrent antitheses — thought and action, right and wrong reason, renewing and destroying, friend and cheat. The same contrast between surging and marching couplets can be observed throughout the poem. The first thirty lines are essentially loose and flowing, with a number of lines closed by nothing stronger than a comma. Lines 31–45, which we have already noted to be stylistically different from those preceding, are strongly marked by caesura, balance, and antithesis — "wisdom" and "happiness," "know" and "enjoy," "others" and "own expense," "enjoyed" and "kicked out," "pleasure" and "doubt." Lines 46–93, the adversarius's hymn and speaker's contemptuous response, are built more loosely, with a good deal of enjambment. Lines 112–140, like lines 94–111, are in turn tighter, more end-stopped, using a series of antitheses appropriate to the extended contrast between animal and man. This contrast builds to the human motive of fear, whereupon the speaker's disgust explodes in a single twelve-line sentence. The looser style of couplet — reserved in the poem for more impassioned outbursts — runs to line 167. At that point the argument is summarized in the tighter, more balanced, couplets. The epilogue (ll. 174–221) continues in this vein, later to become even more formal and balanced ("raise his country, not his family," "who preaching peace, doth practice continence") . As a measure of their increased formality, they contain some eleven mild inversions of normal word order (always in order to place the verb in rhyme position), while in the preceding 203 lines only eight departures from the ordinary rhythm and word order of lively talk — Rochester's characteristic satiric mode — are to be found.

The effect of this and of other contrasts in style throughout the poem is, I think, to present a mind not calm and collected, but perplexed in the extreme, passionately engaged in its ideas, with emotions that ebb and surge violently, now vehement and belittling, now logically reasoning, in a "flowing tide," [45] which Rochester in "An Allusion to Horace" (ll. 21–22) recommended as the proper way to make one's style "rise." It is as if a clever libertine coolly set out to shock his readers with heretical notions about man

45. "Tide" may have been a traditional metaphor for eloquence. Cf. Pope, *Imit. Hor., Ep.* 2:2.171.

and reason, only to find himself caught up in his own rhetoric, unable to maintain the detachment required to execute a glib tour de force.[46]

Statement and Qualification

The greatest critical concern in the "Satyr Against Mankind" is not its structure or its style but the problem of distinctions and of standards by which the poem measures mankind. Eighteenth-century critics were later to complain that satires on man were too generalized, that, not distinguishing between good men and bad, they could be of no moral use.[47] Rochester was aware of the problem of distinguishing differences, as his language shows:

> This plain distinction, sir, your doubt secures:
> 'Tis not true reason I despise, but yours.
>
> .   .   .   .
>
> The difference lies, as far as I can see,
> Not in the thing itself, but the degree.
>
> .   .   .   .
>
> Man differs more from man than man from beast.
>
> .   .   .   .
>
> That reason which distinguishes by sense.

Yet when it comes to making those moral distinctions between good and bad and in establishing a moral hierarchy from most to least virtuous, Rochester is ambiguous as to whether, ultimately, all men are equally ridiculous, and whether men are any better or worse than, or merely differ-

46. It is difficult to say whether the variations in style are completely deliberate — as if Rochester set out to portray a perplexed libertine — or inadvertent — as if he himself is perplexed. Peter Thorpe argues for an "apparent indecision about style." "The Non-Structure of Augustan Verse," *Papers on Language and Literature*, 5 (1969), 240.

47. Bertrand A. Goldgar, "Satires on Man and 'The Dignity of Human Nature,'" *PMLA*, 80 (1965), 535–541.

ent from, the animals. As his ideas about moral hierarchy change, so do the standards by which he measures human and animal behavior, and the directions he points as our moral guide. If the first half of the poem (ll. 1–111) concludes with a defense of a libertine's "right reason" ("that reason which distinguishes by sense"), the second half (ll. 112–221) discovers that in a world of knaves nothing has value but knavery.

We have already seen how the stylistic dislocations in the opening lines have intellectual implications: possibilities are suggested, and then withdrawn. Note, too, how the opening lines are deliberately ambiguous in that they do not make clear whether men and animals belong to different orders of creation. "Prodigious creature" suggests perhaps something monstrous or unnatural, whether animal or not. Differences between man and "dog . . . monkey . . . or bear"[48] are blurred when man is called "that *vain* animal." Man is an animal, but distinguishable from other animals because of his vanity; he is not *animal rationale*, but an animal *proud* of being rational. By leaving the distinction muddled, Rochester gets double use of the phrase; he suggests both that man is only an animal, and also that man is not even as noble as an animal, for he is a *vain* or a monstrous animal.

The standard by which, initially, men and animals are judged in the "Satyr" is their dependence on reason and instinct as a guide to knowledge and conduct. Indeed, the opening lines, so forceful and apparently so definitive in their preference for "certain instinct" over "erring reason,"

48. A letter to Savile compares mankind and monkeys: "Most human affairs are carried on at the same nonsensical rate, which makes me (who am now grown Superstitious) think it a Fault to laugh at the Monkey we have here, when I compare his Condition with Mankind!" (*Letters*, p. 60). See also Butler's comparison of fights between "Dogs and Bears" with the savageness of fights between men (*Hudibras*, 1:1, 704, 731, 812), and the invidious comparison of Presbyterian synods to dogs and bears (1:3, 1095–1320).

have led one critic to think that Rochester wishes to set up instinct in place of reason as a guide for all living beings, man or animal.[49] The rest of the poem, however, does not bear out this conclusion. With that inconsistency in mind, we should look more closely at the disputed passage:

> The senses are too gross, and he'll contrive
> A sixth, to contradict the other five,
> And before certain instinct, will prefer
> Reason, which fifty times for one does err.
>
> [ll. 8–11]

In the first phrase Rochester's speaker mimics the vain animal's fastidious objection to the five senses. What Rochester intends by "sixth sense" is not clear.[50] He might allude to what was then also called "common wit" or "common sense," one of the five inward wits of medieval psychology: "Besides these Five particular Senses, the Organs whereof appear outwardly, there is another, which is call'd the Common Sensory within. Here it is that the several objects of every Sort, perceiv'd by the Corporeal Organs, make their Rendezvous: Hither they are brought to be examin'd, compar'd, sorted out, and distinguish'd asunder."[51] Rochester says, however, not that the sixth sense correlates the other senses, but that it contradicts them. Perhaps he engages in scornful polemical overstatement, adopting an existing term for his own purposes. Or he may have in mind something like the Cambridge Platonist John Smith's Plotinian conception of reason as "purified sense." In his discourse "Con-

49. Kenneth Murdock, "A Very Profane Wit," in *The Sun at Noon* (New York, 1939), p. 284.

50. *OED* does not record any usage of the phrase before Locke's *Essay* (1690), which speaks of a sixth, seventh, and eight sense only to discount their existence, giving as a meaning, however, a "faculty of perception supposed not to depend upon any outward sense" ("sense", sb. I d).

51. Charron, *Of Wisdom*, tr. Stanhope (3rd ed., 1729), 1 (ch. 9), p. 89.

cerning the True Way or Method of attaining to Divine Knowledge," Smith says:

> The soul itself hath its sense, as well as the Body, and therefore David when he would teach us how to know what the Divine Goodness is calls not for Speculation but Sensation, Taste and see how good the Lord is . . . . Divinity is not so well perceived by a subtile wit . . . as by a purified sense, as Plotinus phraseth it.

Reason itself, when raised by God, becomes a kind of sense:

> We must shut the Eyes of unpurified Sense, and open that Brighter Eye of our Understandings, that other eye of the Soul, as the Philosopher calls our Intellectual Faculty . . . when Reason once is raised by the mighty force of the Divine Spirit, into a converse with God, it is turn'd into Sense.[52]

The sixth sense, whatever its meaning in the poem, has nothing to do with "instinct," a blind, innate prompting common, as was known in the seventeenth century, to vegetables, animals, and man, and the literal antithesis of reason. Those who wished to decry instinct stressed its blindness; those who wished to elevate it stressed its origin in providence, its simplicity and direct operation, or, like Rochester's satirist, its certainty.

The opening lines of the "Satyr" appear to link the senses and instinct, juxtaposing them to both reason and the sixth sense. The syntax of the lines, particularly the simple connective "and" (l. 10), suggests that the second juxtaposed pair, instinct vs. reason, recapitulates the first, sense vs. sixth sense.[53] Thus the rationalist so disbelieves in the "gross senses" that (as a first step) he "contrives" another faculty to contradict them, reason, which the satirist scorns as a spurious (perhaps "purified") sixth sense, but which his oppon-

52. *Select Discourses* (1673 ed.), pp. 3, 10.
53. Perhaps the relation is proportional: instinct:reason::senses:sixth sense.

nent (as a second step) stubbornly prefers to the "certain" instinctive senses. This reading is possible. It assumes that Rochester adopted an existing term, "sixth sense," disposed of its established meaning, and applied it scornfully to reason, implying that reason, unlike the five senses, has no epistemological legitimacy. The poem makes more consistent sense, however, if we keep the juxtaposed pairs separate, and I think it is possible, from what follows, that Rochester meant them to be kept separate, but failed through loose or sloppy grammar.[54]

The sense of the lines in the alternate reading is that instinct and the speculative proud reason are to be imagined as polar opposites, with the senses somewhere in a middle ground. The rationalist, contradicting the testimony of the senses by means of a contrived sixth sense, spurns the middle ground and, choosing between two extremes, prefers reason to instinct. The satirist, on the contrary, if forced to choose, would at this point polemically prefer instinct, but argues later, as we shall see, for a position on the middle ground — "reason which distinguishes by sense" — midway between proud reasoning men and instinctual animals. What has confused critics is that the satirist, whether or not he distinguishes between instinct and senses, appears in these opening lines to have abandoned faith in reason of any kind, speculative or empirical.[55] And indeed he has — as a rhetorical gambit, a provocative opening blast whose purpose is to shock the orthodox. Later, this extreme statement, seemingly definitive, is qualified, a rhetorical strategy quite characteristic of the whole poem. This strategy has, I think, two purposes: first, to keep readers off balance by the calculated ambiguity of the poem's judgments, and second (hard to distin-

54. He tends to begin the first line of a couplet with "and" (seven times in the "Satyr"), at times lending to the verse a colloquial flow and a logical disconnectedness: "For all men would be cowards if they durst. / And honesty's against all common sense . . ." (ll. 158–159).

55. As in "Reason, an ignis fatuus in the mind, / Which, leaving light of nature, sense, behind" (ll. 12–13).

guish from the first) to convey a sense of a speaker, the satirist, uncertain in his own mind of his ideas about man and reason.[56]

In the following paragraph, too, the reader is caught off guard:

> Pride drew him in, as cheats their bubbles catch,
> And made him venture to be made a wretch.
> His wisdom did his happiness destroy,
> Aiming to know that world he should enjoy.
> And wit was his vain, frivolous pretense
> Of pleasing others at his own expense,
> For wits are treated just like common whores:
> First they're enjoyed, and then kicked out of doors.
> The pleasure past, a threatening doubt remains
> That frights th'enjoyer with succeeding pains.
> Women and men of wit are dangerous tools,
> And ever fatal to admiring fools:
> Pleasure allures, and when the fops escape,
> 'Tis not that they're belov'd, but fortunate,
> And therefore what they fear at heart, they hate.
> [ll. 31–45]

In the first two couplets all men, cheated by pride in reason, or by their own wisdom, are made equally wretched. In the next lines, however, a little surprisingly, the fops and fools (or at any rate some few of them) for once seem to get the better of the wits, acting as they do out of instinctual, prudent hatred of women and wits, and lacking the damning pride of wit and reason. The distinction between wits and fools proves ironically to be no distinction at all. Wits, tempted by pride to display themselves, are exploited by fools (who enjoy their company) and kicked out of doors when they have served their purpose. Fools, too, are tempted — by

56. As with the variations in style, it is difficult to decide whether Rochester's ambiguity is always calculated or unconscious. Since he is consistently ambiguous, I incline toward the former explanation.

the "pleasure [that] allures," i.e., the wits — almost always ("ever") with "fatal" results. Even those few fools that escape disaster do so, not because the wits admire them, but because, fearing and hating the wits, they are lucky.[57] Wits, in Rochester's metaphor, are analogous to poxed whores, dangerous but desirable. Fops are the whores' foolish customers. Thus, sexual pleasure allures the fops, and when they escape the pox, it is not because the whores love them and refrain from infecting them, but because they are simply lucky. Therefore, fops, though attracted to whores, fear them at heart and hate them.[58]

The movement of lines 31 to 45 is by no means as clear and logical as exposition makes it seem. We discover only gradually that fools, too, suffer, for at first they seem to be not unlike the exploitive cheats. Lines 40–41, for example, "Women and men of wit are dangerous tools, / And ever fatal to admiring fools," suggesting that tools can become two-edged, Rochester holds back until after we see the fools enjoy the wits and kick them out of doors. He then modifies the definitive "ever" by revealing that some fops escape. The obfuscation is deliberate, part of Rochester's plan of setting up false expectations through seemingly definitive statements, only to catch readers off guard with subsequent qualifications.

Part 1 of the poem begins, then, by suggesting that all men are equally ridiculous, and concludes by making distinctions between wits and fools which prove, in the end, to be no real distinctions, like the false distinction between whores and fops — each can be poxed, each hates the other. Part 2 (ll. 46–71), the speech by the adversarius, is also two-minded, but in a different manner, distinguishing between wit and reason. It begins, curiously, not by taking the satirist to task, as

---

57. For a more conventional expression of the wits' superiority over fools, see Rochester's "Epilogue" to *Circe, Complete Poems*, p. 140, esp. ll. 10–16.

58. I owe this suggestion to Brendan P. O Hehir.

readers expect ("Now . . . some formal band and beard [59] / Takes me to task"), but by agreeing with him in the attack on wit. In fact, the adversarius goes further than the satirist: he attacks wit itself, "this gibing, jingling knack," rather than just the foolishness of self-displaying wits. In the second half of his speech, however, praising "Blest, glorious man" and reason, he seems to forget that such a thing as wit exists. Thus, while the first half of the speech implicitly condemns a part of mankind for wit, the second half, as if distinguishing between man and man's faculties, condemns no one.

Part 3 (ll. 72–173) is equally ambiguous. Its opening denunciation of reason and reasoners seems to admit of no distinctions. But beginning at line 98, a new distinction is made between "false reasoning" [60] and "right reason," for which we have been imperfectly prepared. Distinction is made also between "me" and "you," between the satirist whose reason "distinguishes by sense" [61] and, presumably,

59. Vieth notes that "many Restoration clergymen wore Geneva bands" (*Complete Poems*, p. 96). "Formal" suggests rigorous observation of forms, precision, severity, qualities often attributed to Puritans, such as Sibbes, or more loosely to any clergyman. A band was also part of academic dress such as Ingelo and Sibbes would have worn. A beard, says Butler, was formerly the badge of the philosopher's profession. *Characters and Passages from Notebooks*, ed. Waller (Cambridge, 1908), pp. 57–58.

60. Compare Butler, *Hudibras*, Part 2: "So when your Speculations tend / Above their just and useful end, / Although they promise strange and great / Discoveries of things far fet, / They are but idle Dreams and Fancies" (3:777–781).

61. Compare Butler's "Satyr upon the Weakness and Misery of Man," and its attack on the man who "Grows positive and confident / In things so far beyond th'Extent / Of Human Sense, he does not know, / Whether they be at all, or no; / And doubts as much in Things, that are / As plainly evident, and clear; / Disdains all useful sense and plain, / T'apply to th'Intricate and Vain" (ll. 189–196).Compare also Shadwell, *The Libertine* (1675): "Nature gave us our Sense, which we please: / Nor does our Reason war against our Sense, / By Natures order, Sense should guide our Reason, / Since to the mind all objects Sense conveys. / But Fools for shaddows lose substantial pleasures, / For idle tales abandon true delight, / And solid joys of day, for empty dreams at night" (*Complete Works of Shadwell*, ed. Montague Summers [London, 1926], 3:26).

the adversarius, whose reason hinders desires and mocks appetites.[62] This distinction seems clear and unambiguous; we had been put on a wrong track carlier, but now see that some men are better (i.e., wiser, happier, less ridiculous) than others. The satirist seems here to have staked out that middle ground toward which he was hinting in the opening lines. Between the extremes of pure instinct and pure reason he defines a meeting place, "reason which distinguishes by sense," taking account in traditional fashion of man's higher and lower natures, reaffirming his position midway between brutes and angels. Those men who encamp on such a middle ground, says the satirist, are better than those who fly to either extreme.[63]

But the poem again surprises us, for the satirist turns around to attack all of mankind once more: "Thus I think reason righted, but for man, / I'll ne'er recant; defend him if you can" (ll. 112–113). We might well wonder why, if man is ultimately indefensible, the satirist ever bothered to "right" (that is, rectify) reason. He makes the same kind of curious distinction between worthless man and one of his noble faculties, right reason, as did the adversarius between noble man and one of his worthless faculties, wit. He proposes an ideal, but then, adding the qualifier, shows the ideal to be unrealizable, too remote from experience. This about-face marks a change of attention in the "Satyr," from "reason" to "man," for nowhere after line 112 does the satir-

62. Compare Boileau's *Satire* 4, ll. 113–128, and Hobbes: "Nor can a man any more live, whose desires are at an end, than he, whose sense and imagination are at a stand" (*Leviathan*, ch. 11, in *Works*, ed. W. Molesworth, 16 vols. [1839–1845], 3:85).

63. Rochester inverts John Smith's fourfold scheme of sense and reason, derived from Plotinus, in which the lowest form is "a knowledge wherein Sense and Reason are so twisted up together, that it cannot easily be unravel'd, and laid out to its first principles," and the highest true metaphysical contemplation and divine wisdom, in which the soul is separated from the body. *Select Discourses*, n. 52 above), pp. 17–21.

ist speak about true or false reason; he henceforth directs his attack at "man's wisdom" and "human nature." [64]

For the remainder of Part 3 no distinctions are made between men, now considered as a homogeneous group. Rochester might have averted the inconsistency by having his satirist stress that, with respect to animals, men are all alike, but no such stress is here laid. Just as distinctions established earlier are now blurred, so standards set earlier are now shifted from means to ends. In the comparison between Jowler [65] the hound and Meres the politician, the criterion by which wisdom and goodness are measured is the attainment of immediate ends, a desideratum which in this section of the poem looms larger than the maintenance of vigorous desires. It follows, then, that instinct is preferred not only to speculative reason, but apparently even to right reason; it is blind and direct. The conclusions drawn from this, however, are characteristically qualified.

We begin with a generalized comparison: " 'Tis evident beasts are, in their degree, / As wise at least, and better far than he" (ll. 115–116). The satirist, retreating a bit from the theriophily of lines 1 to 7, takes the more modest ground that beasts are, not wiser, but "as wise" as man; then, advancing again, he insists that animals are "better far" than man. But we are left uncertain whether beasts are absolutely better, or better only with respect to their own more limited capacities ("in their degree"). Next comes a firm statement of criterion for judgment: "Those creatures are the wisest who attain, / By surest means, the ends at which they aim" (ll. 117–118). But we conclude conditionally: "*If . . .* Jowler

64. It is very likely that this change of subject that prompted three early scribes, followed (against the majority of manuscripts and early printings) by Vieth, to entitle the poem "A Satyr Against Reason and Mankind" (*ARP*, pp. 371–372). In fact, the poem throughout satirizes man — attacking him first as a speculative reasoner, next attacking his wisdom and nature when unfavorably contrasted with the wisdom and nature of animals.

65. A quasi-proper name for a hunting dog.

finds and kills . . . , Jowler . . . *would be* wiser found."
The satirist does not affirm either that Jowler is or is not
wiser. It would have been a simple matter to write "since"
for "If" (l. 119) and "should" for "would" (l. 122), but the
satirist does not so choose, perhaps out of that same moral ambiguity, stating and qualifying, which we have been following. Nor does the summary — "You see how far man's wisdom
here extends" — commit the satirist to the superior wisdom of
beasts. Though man is potentially as wise as beasts, his wisdom does not habitually "extend" — witness Meres — so far.

Uncertainty, too, about human motivation marks the following section of Part 3 which examines "human nature."
The satirist begins with a series of indirect questions: [66]
"Look next" . . . if human *nature* makes amends for human
foolishness . . . look (i.e., tell me) who has the "most generous" and just principles, who has morals "you would sooner
trust" — man or beast? Generosity, we may conclude from the
recurrent honorific uses of the word "generous" in his
poems,[67] Rochester rated very highly, and in the "Satyr" de-
spairs of finding in man. Man only puts on a front of "smiles,
embraces, friendship" to mask treachery beneath: "Birds feed
on birds, beasts on each other prey, / But savage man alone
does man betray." [68] As John Moore has pointed out, Rochester here makes a significant alteration of Boileau's lines,
"L'Homme seul, en sa fureur extreme / Met un brutal hon-
neur à s'égorger soi-même" (*Satire* 8, ll. 151–152). While Boileau says animals live at peace with others of their species,
Rochester implies that they attack each other ("Birds feed on
birds") for food: "With teeth and claws by nature armed,

66. A more probable reading than to take "Whose" in lines 125 and
126 as relative pronouns referring back to man (l. 123), thus making
the lines a sarcastic comment on man's *allegedly* generous principles.

67. "St. James's Park," l. 98; "Artemisia to Chloe," l. 40; "Woman's
Honour," l. 11; "Prologue to 'The Empress of Morocco,' " l. 38.

68. Possibly parodying Waller's "Panegyric to My Lord Protector"
(1655), ll. 115–116: "Tigers have courage, and the rugged bear; / But
man alone can, whom he conquers, spare."

they hunt / Nature's allowance, to supply their want" (ll. 133–134). Boileau's emphasis, thematically and rhythmically, is on "L'Homme seul," man alone, who preys on his own kind. Rochester's emphasis, reinforced by its positioning at the end of the line, is on "betray." Human treachery is thus contrasted unfavorably with instinctive, straightforward animal savagery. Not only is man treacherous, he is wantonly so:

> Pressed by necessity, [animals] kill for food;
> Man undoes man to do himself no good
>
> . . . .
>
> Inhumanly his fellow's life betrays;
> With voluntary pains works his distress,
> Not through necessity, but wantonness.
> [ll. 131–132, 136–138]

In Rochester's sardonic pun, man "undoes" in order to "do" no good. "Wantonness" suggests unprovoked, capricious actions, reckless not only of justice and compassion, but of purpose, whether good or evil. Here, as elsewhere, Rochester seems to have been especially disgusted with such aimless, purposeless, passionless acts.[69] Once again, however, the definitive statement is qualified as the poem goes on: "For hunger or for love they fight and tear, / Whilst wretched man is still in arms for fear" (ll. 139–140).[70] Man's motive now is not wantonness, but fear.[71] Beasts, too, have been given a new

69. Compare Artemisia's lament that women nowadays forget passion (ll. 62–65), and the complaint against Corinna, who takes lovers aimlessly, without even the sanction of lust ("St. James's Park", ll. 98–102). Betrayal, like sex or writing libels in cold blood, is mechanical and "inhuman," as another pun stresses. In the words of one recent critic, the ugliest and most hateful possibility in Rochester's poems is to "become dehumanized through feeling nothing" (Ronald Berman, "Rochester and the Defeat of the Senses," *Kenyon Review*, 26 [1964], 367).

70. With possible puns on "still" ("always" and "motionless") and "arms" ("armor," "a protector's arms," or "a lover's arms [i.e., a place of refuge]).

71. Looking back, we might see "wantonness" as an expression of

motive, love. The satirist is not simply extending his comparison between man and beasts; he is changing the terms.[72] All man's actions and passions when examined closely in the cynical manner of La Rochefoucauld, turn out to derive from fear: [73]

> For fear he arms, and is of arms afraid,
> By fear to fear successively betrayed; [74]
> Base fear, the source whence his best passions came:
> His boasted honor, and his dear-bought fame;
> That lust of power, to which he's such a slave,
> And for the which alone he dares be brave;
> To which his various projects are designed;
> Which makes him generous, affable, and kind;
> For which he takes such pains to be thought wise,
> And screws his actions in a forced disguise,
> Leading a tedious life in misery
> Under laborious, mean hypocrisy.
> Look to the bottom of his vast design,
> Wherein man's wisdom, power, and glory join:
> The good he acts, the ill he does endure,
> 'Tis all from fear, to make himself secure.
>
> [ll. 141–56]

Rochester says not merely that honor, fame, and benevolence are hypocritically professed ideals, concealing power lust, he strips away yet another layer, uncovering more brutality,

fear (a reading more likely if "fear" had been named first) but it requires straining to find fear expressing itself in true (not just *apparent*) motiveless wantonness.

72. The change of terms is implicitly recognized by Thomas Lessey, whose answer to the "Satyr" seeks to refute the charge that "Man is compos'd of Cruelty and Fear, / From these his great, and his best actions are" ("A Satyr, in answer to the Satyr Against Man," *Poetical Recreations* [1688], p. 69).

73. It is surprising that Rochester does not say that man's religion is based on superstitious fear, an idea he would have discovered in Epicurus and Lucretius. Was it perhaps because he was painfully aware that his own ideas on religion were based on fear of the "vast power" of God?

74. Sardonically recalling "betrays," l. 136.

both in the human psyche and in the social fabric. Savage man is a slave to his own power lust but that lust, together with all human actions and reactions, is slave to fear. In Rochester's view, the commonwealth — Hobbes's system of political restraints and protections — is no less brutish or insecure than the state of nature it was designed to escape.

Not only does the poem change its mind about human motivation, it changes, too, its valuation of human appetites. While the lines on "right reason" endorse man's desires and appetites, urging that they be "bounded with a reforming will" not to extinguish them, but "to keep 'em more in vigor," to renew them, and keep them from being glutted, the lines describing man's savageness and treachery (130–138) implicitly condemn all human appetites as lawless and wanton. Perhaps, as one critic has suggested, Rochester should have clarified the relations between reason and appetite in order to remove any contradiction:

Perhaps the relation between the poet's conception of the reason "that bounds desires with a reforming will, / To keep 'em more in vigour, not to kill," as opposed to the reason that would destroy the appetites on the one hand, and to the lawlessness of appetites on the other, is not as clear as it should be. Rochester is probably fighting on two fronts at once: both defending the claims of appetite and attacking the ruthless pursuit of selfish pleasures.[75]

Yet such stating and qualifying, as we have seen, seems to be a hallmark of the "Satyr."

The final lines of Part 3 raise again the questions "Are all men alike?" and "By what standards ought men to be judged?"

> Merely for safety, after fame we thirst,
> For all men would be cowards if they durst.
> And honesty's against all common sense:

75. Irene Simon, " 'Pride of Reason' in the Restoration," *Revue des Langues Vivantes*, 25 (1959), 376n.

Men must be knaves, 'tis in their own defence.[76]
Mankind's dishonest; if you think it fair
Amongst known cheats to play upon the square,
You'll be undone.
Nor can weak truth your reputation save:
The knaves will all agree to call you knave.
Wronged shall he live, insulted o'er, oppressed,
Who dares be less a villain than the rest.

Thus, sir, you see what human nature craves:
Most men are cowards, all men should be knaves.
The difference lies, as far as I can see,
Not in the thing itself, but the degree,
And all the subject matter of debate
Is only: Who's a knave of the first rate?[77]

[ll. 157–173]

It requires more bravery and honesty to profess one's native cowardice than to dissemble bravery. But honesty, the poem hastens to add, is against all common sense.

On the one hand, furthermore, "Mankind's dishonest," "all men should be knaves": the difference between men is in the degree of knavery; on the other, "*most* men are cowards." How seriously, still further, are we to attend to the possibility that there exists among dishonest mankind a single honest man, addressed in imagination by the satirist as "you"[78] (ll. 161–165), who "play[s] upon the square"? It is

76. Compare Pepys' *Diary* (1661): "But good God, what an age is this and what a world is this, that a man cannot live without playing the knave and dissimulacion," ed. R. Latham and W. Matthews (Berkeley, 1970), 2:169; and Rochester's letter to Mrs. Barry: "take it for granted, that unless you can deceive them, they will certainly cozen you" (Hayward, p. 272).

77. Compare Boileau, *Satire* 4: "En ce monde il n'est point de parfaite sagesse. / Tous les hommes sont fous, et malgré tous leur soins, / Ne different entre Eux que du plus ou du moins" (ll. 38–40). For Boileau, all men are fools; for Rochester, knaves—a more serious charge.

78. The "you" of this part of the poem is presumably still the adversarius of lines 48–71. Whether arrogant and complacent (as before) or honest but naive (as here), in such a world he is a fool.

this hypothetical one just man who embodies a set of ideal moral standards — honesty, playing upon the square, truth — which are played off in this passage against the shrewd ethical pragmatism of "men must be knaves, 'tis in their own defence." The latter counsel carries far more weight here than the former idealistic notions, yet honesty and justice cannot be simply ignored, for they are to return with greater force in the epilogue.

The passage bears other marks of ambiguity. "Cowards" seems to be used in two different senses: "Most men are *cowards*" (l. 169) because they dare not *admit* that they are *cowards* (l. 159). Nor do we know the relation between knaves and cowards, in this part of the poem, and wits, fools, and fops in an earlier section. No useful distinction is made between dishonesty and knavery, but the terms are evidently not synonymous, for "Mankind's dishonest," (l. 16) while all men only "*should* be knaves." More serious yet is the flabby writing, the needless repetitions. Line 169, "all men should be knaves," only repeats line 160. The frequent use of "all" — "all men," "against all common sense," "the knaves will all agree," "all men should be knaves," "all the subject matter of debate," "All this . . . have I hurled" — in the space of less than twenty lines gives the impression that Rochester is substituting rhetorical emphasis for careful thought. On the other hand, such reckless exaggeration characterizes paradox — an outrageous claim that challenges refutation.

Epilogue

Part 4, or the epilogue, may have been written after the rest of the poem.[79] Thematically and stylistically, it bears some marks of an afterthought, still savagely indignant, but essentially a more conventional form of satire in balanced

79. The earliest printed text of the poem — a 1679 broadside — lacks lines 174–221. See further, *ARP*, pp. 370–374.

couplets on dishonesty and corruption in church and state. There is nothing in the epilogue, for example, about right reason or false reasoning, or (until the final couplet) about theriophily. But, in fact, the "epilogue" seems an integral part of the "Satyr"; it makes perfect sense within the poem's internal logic. A conditional recantation ("if there is a just statesman or churchman, then I'll recant my paradox that it is better to be an animal than a man") is offered only to make the satire more relentless. Rochester holds up another set of ideals (like "reason which distinguishes by sense") which we know to be unattainable and even irrelevant in the world of knaves described in the poem.

The opening lines are familiarly ambiguous:

> All this with indignation have I hurled [80]
> At the pretending part of the proud world,
> Who, swollen with selfish vanity, devise
> False freedoms, holy cheats,[81] and formal lies
> Over their fellow slaves to tyrannize.
> [ll. 174–178]

Setting aside for a time the interesting suggestion that the satirist conceives of himself — for the first time in the poem — as standing over and against the world, we see that the second line offers, and takes away again, the idea that only "part" of the world is bad. "Pretending part" implies for a moment that there is an "honest part," but "proud world" retracts the implication, condemning all men,[82] thus epito-

---

80. Hayman compares Waller's "Of Love": "All this with indignation spoke, / In vain I struggled with the yoke / Of mighty love" (*Poems*, ed. Thorn-Drury, 1:88). "An Image of the Sultan," *N & Q* 213 (1968), pp. 380–381.

81. "False freedoms" means here instances of deceptive frankness or openness in conversation, and thus aptly is linked with other kinds of hypocrisy, fraud disguised by piety, and lies disguised by form, ceremony, or puritan precision. Cf. *Hudibras*, 1:3.1145–1146: "When pious frauds and holy shifts / Are dispensations and gifts."

82. "World" means not the "great world" but all men, as does "rabble world," l. 219.

mizing the fluctuation of opinion characteristic of the whole poem. The pretenders, it is quickly specified, are selfish, vain, hypocritical tyrants, yet, as the cunning phrase "fellow slaves" indicates, enslaved just as much as their victims, perhaps to their own vanity, or to "that lust of power to which he's such a slave" (l. 145). The burden of these lines is thus that all men are slaves, just as all men are knaves — only some are more knavish and slavish than others.

The remainder of Part 4 does not significantly alter this conclusion. Essentially one long conditional sentence from line 179 to line 211, it leaves open the possibility — however slight — that somewhere, in state or church, there is one just man [83] who will disprove the paradox (that it is better to be an animal) and the cynical observation (that all men are knaves). Rochester clearly expects the conditions for his recantation to go unfulfilled, but we should recognize that the ostensible conditionality fits into the pattern of consistent refusal to make definitive moral statements without some subsequent qualification, retraction, or partial contradiction. The "Satyr," as we have seen, begins with a conditional sentence ("Were I . . . free . . ."), in which the condition itself is denied by the parenthesis: he is not free; he is already a man. Thus, the satire that follows is a hypothetical assertion. The same self-canceling effect is achieved at the opening of the epilogue — "But if in Court so just a man there be / (In Court a just man, yet unknown to me)" [84] — but here it serves another purpose, to make hypothetical not the satirical attack, but the one just man.

After sketching the hypothetical just statesman, an artful but not self-interested politician (ll. 179–90) , and the corrupt and worldly churchman (ll. 193–211), Rochester de-

83. Compare a letter to Savile, complaining of Portsmouth's unjust accusation of Rochester: "If there be upon Earth a Man of Common Honesty, who will justifie a Tittle of her Accusation I am contented never to see her." *Letters*, p. 35.

84. Cf. Fanshawe, tr. *Il Pastor Fido*, 1:3:675–676: "Faith in a woman (if at least there be / Faith in a woman unreveal'd to me)."

scribes an unworldly, even unearthly, pious man: the "meek humble man of honest sense" who practices what he preaches is "God-like" not in his power, glory, and rational knowledge (contrast the adversarius's panegyric on "blest, glorious man" made in the image of God, dressed in "shining reason") but in his Christ-like humility and piety. He believes (and his conduct proves it) "mysterious truths" through faith, not because he claims to have "conceived" them through the power of soaring, shining reason.

The hypothetical existence of such a man leads Rochester hastily to his conclusion:

> If upon earth there dwell such God-like men,
> I'll here recant my paradox to them,
> Adore those shrines of virtue,[85] homage pay,
> And, with the rabble world, their laws obey.
>   If such there be, yet grant me this at least:
> Man differs more from man, than man from beast.

The ending, especially the final couplet, is abrupt and condensed, not out of flippancy, but out of laconic mordancy. The meaning of the famous final line is ambiguous. Surely it does not carry the banal meaning that "man is various" or even "man resembles the beasts." Taken together with the picture of the "God-like men" and the "rabble world," the line seems to distinguish between two kinds of men, and sets them in relation to beasts. What is ambiguous is the order of the implied three-tiered hierarchy. Does the line mean that the difference between (1) "man" — God-like men, and (2) "man" — the rabble world, including wits, fools, cowards, knaves, and the satirist himself — is greater than the difference between (2) rabble man and (3) beasts? Such a reading ignores earlier implied hierarchies, in which animals were

85. Notably, Rochester returns in this conditional panegyric to the imagery of his earliest extant poem, an unconditional panegyric on Charles II, "Virtue's triumphant shrine." *Complete Poems*, p. 155. Vieth considers that the poem is "possibly by Rochester."

ranked as man's equal or superior, men of sense and of right reason were distinguished from speculative philosophers, and wits from fools, to say that the rabble is more like a beast than a god. Such a conclusion is hardly startling, and makes a second reading more likely: the difference between (1) God-like men and (3) the rabble is greater than the difference between (1) God-like men and (2) beasts; in other words, that beasts — generous, just, trustworthy, wise in their humble way — come closer to the ideal of God-like man than does the rabble. This more radical reading sharpens the satirical point. Rochester embarrasses proud man by showing how the beasts, traditionally man's irrational inferior, in fact measure up to man's own professed moral ideals better than he himself does.

The poem thus concludes on a sardonic note. Its high point — its highest estimate of man's potential — comes early in the lines on right reason. The few God-like men (whose relation to right reasoners is not made clear), if such exist, do not lift the rest of mankind with them. The final note is not the buoying ideal but the unpleasant reality. Of all the standards applied — right reason, animal instinct, orthodox Christian morality, and opportunistic knavery — man, in the end, measures up only to the last.

Real and Ideal

The "Satyr" as a whole, then, is a demonstrably ambiguous poem, stylistically and thematically. Although we may extract from one part of the poem a sensationalist ethic, in other parts we find that such an ethic does not produce good or happy men. As we have seen, standards and distinctions vary: men are, and they are not, the equal of animals. Are we to judge that Rochester carefully designed all the inconsistencies, or that he wrote badly, or is the explanation more complex?

Certainly parts of the poem are sloppily written. The passage on knavery (ll. 159–173) goes on too long, marked by superfluous repetitions. Some transitions are awkward, some shifts in style sudden and unmotivated. Some of the thematic inconsistencies may perhaps be charged to a mind not well equipped for synthesis or for systematizing consistency. On the other hand, Rochester shows a paradoxist's skill in managing an outrageous proposition, in allowing strategic qualifications while insisting on his main points. He adopted his design, we may reasonably conclude, partly by nature, partly by calculated choice.

He seems also, as we saw earlier, to have been a man for whom an unbridgeable gap existed between the ideal and the realizable, both in his own experience and in his poems. Artemisia imagines an ideal of love but describes a world in which such an ideal has no proper place. The "Satyr" exhibits the same gap; it urges at one moment that men be knaves in their own defense, at another laments that so few honest men remain. Rochester and his satirist envision an ideal, but cannot live it; the satirist thus includes himself with disgust among the rabble world. How different from Pope, who, envisioning horrors equal to Rochester's, firmly separates himself from the knaves around him:

> While Truth, Worth, Wisdom, daily they decry —
> "Nothing is Sacred now but Villany."
>
> Yet may this Verse (if such a Verse remain)
> Show there was one who held it in disdain.[86]

But there may well be other factors to explain a poem not solidly planted on firm moral ground. The middle years of the reign of Charles II found England in a state of flux, politically, religiously, morally. For the writers of the Court, standards of conduct were not clearly established, and powers of the mind not widely trusted. By Pope's time, the Tory

86. "Epilogue to the Satires," *Dialogue* 1:169–172. Only at one point (ll. 174–175) does Rochester seem to stand apart from the knavish world.

writers, whether in political ascendancy or in opposition, at least could share a set of ideas and values that guided their thought and life more firmly than was possible for the libertines of the 1670's. Skepticism left men more uncertain of their ideas under Charles than, sixty years later, under George II, when the Christian-classical tradition had absorbed (after being duly affected by) the traditions of skepticism and self-disparagement.

Add to this that formal verse satire was making a fresh start in England in 1675. Restoration satire, deriving from the classics not by way of the Elizabethans, but the French, had to feel its way toward the principle of unity enunciated by Dryden in 1693 and widely known and followed in the eighteenth century.[87] What is more, the satire on man was an untried form in English. Treading new ground, Rochester could not rely on precedent. Finally, however successfully a poem may imitate logical discourse, it is not to be responded to or judged as logical discourse. A poem inevitably supplies its own kind of emotional and sensuous logic.

No one factor suffices to account for the ebb and flow of statement and qualification which is such a marked feature of the "Satyr"; surely we should keep all factors in mind. The poem is not an Augustan satire in the Popean sense, either in its form or its content, and ought not to be judged as one. The "Satyr Against Mankind" is good, and will continue to be read, for its un-Augustan qualities — its unbridled vehemence and energy, its unsettling pessimism about the possibilities for knowledge and virtue, its presentation of a mind unable to establish for itself a firm and secure place in the universe.

87. Weinbrot, "The Pattern of Formal Verse Satire," (n. 6 above), pp. 397–398, 401.

6 Rochester and the Age

Analysis and comparison, said T. S. Eliot, are the tools of the critic. Analysis can illuminate the man and the poems, but such illumination alone can be too narrowly focused. By comparing Rochester with the great masters of his own and of the following age — Dryden, Pope, Swift, and the dramatists — we can perhaps gain a fuller measure of his distinctive achievement and of his place in the development of English literature. Analysis of the two poems — "An Allusion to Horace" and "Upon Nothing" — that the Augustans seem most to have admired and remembered may prepare the way for showing how Rochester, first as Horatian and next as Juvenalian, helped make possible the achievements of Pope and Swift. In the end, however, Rochester needs to be returned to the context of the Restoration, and set beside the comic dramatists and the age's acknowledged master, Dryden.

"An Allusion to Horace"

In "An Allusion to Horace," as with "Upon Nothing," the Augustans thought they found Rochester doing what they themselves did well. In the first instance they were nearer the truth than in the second. "An Allusion to Horace," an imitation of the tenth satire of Horace's first book, is Rochester's most Popean poem. Johnson, in the *Life of Pope*, honors Rochester and Oldham as the first practitioners of the form:

This mode of imitation, in which the ancients are familiarised, by adapting their sentiments to modern topics, by making Horace say of Shakespeare what he originally said of Ennius, and accommodating his satires on Pantolabus and Nomentanus to the flatterers and prodigals of our own time, was first practiced in the reign of Charles the Second by Oldham and Rochester; at least I remember no instances more ancient. It is a kind of middle composition between translation and original design, which pleases when the thoughts are unexpectedly applicable, and the parallels lucky.[1]

Other eighteenth-century admirers quoted from it because of the special kind of Horatian satire — essentially a piece of literary criticism — which Rochester imitated. Horace's poem dispensed judgment on the writings of Lucilius and of the poets of his own day. Rochester says of his contemporaries what Horace said of his;[2] the incisive and elegant judgments, particularly of Dorset, Sedley, and Wycherley, were often cited. Of Dorset, Rochester had said: "For pointed satyrs, I would Buckhurst choose: / The best good man with the worst-natured muse" (ll. 59–60). Sedley, he said,

> has that prevailing gentle art,
> That can with a resistless charm impart
> The loosest wishes to the chastest heart.
> [ll. 64–66]

And Wycherley, he said, was "slow" ("hasty Shadwell, and slow Wycherley," l. 43). Dryden, objecting to Rochester's

1. *Lives*, 2:192.
2. Rochester equates Dryden, an older contemporary, with Lucilius, who died almost forty years before Horace was born.

character of Dorset, the dedicatee of his own *Discourse on Satire*, called it "an insolent, sparing, and invidious panegyric,"[3] testifying to the currency of the description. Later writers, however, both minor (Peter Motteux, Tom Brown) and major (Pope, Boswell) found Rochester's words just, even proverbial, and quoted them often.[4]

The lines on Sedley were especially pleasing to Steele, who quoted them three times.[5] The character of Wycherley occasioned a minor controversy, many critics objecting that he was not a "slow" writer.[6] That the phrase remained popular, however, is evidenced by Pope, who in the "Epistle to Augustus" wrote of critics who talk

> Of Shakespear's Nature, and of Cowley's Witt;
> How Beaumont's Judgment check'd what Fletcher writ;
> How Shadwell hasty, Wycherley was slow.
> [ll. 83–85]

In a note to line 85, he commented further that the judgment was not to be taken as Horace's own, but as "the common Chatt of the pretenders to Criticism; in some things right, in others wrong." Accurate or not, the description of Wycherley had become in the eighteenth century, along with

3. *Of Dramatic Poesy and Other Critical Essays*, 2 vols., ed. G. Watson (London, 1962), 2:75.

4. Motteux, *Maria* (1695), p. 5; Brown, *Works* (9th ed., London, 1760), p. 27, and thrice paraphrased in *The Town Display'd* (1701), pp. 6, 14, 15; Pope, epitaph on Dorset; Walpole, *Catalogue of Royal and Noble Authors* (1759), in *Works* (1798), 1:425; Robert Shiels, author of "Cibber's" *Lives of the Poets* (1743), 3:256, who applies the line to Wycherley; and Boswell, *Life of Johnson*, ed. Hill, rev. Powell, 5:52, who applies the line to himself.

5. *Spectator* 91 and 400, and in a letter to Pope, *Pope's Correspondence*, ed. Sherburn (Oxford, 1956), 1:145. "Cibber" also quotes them in the *Lives of the Poets*, 3:97.

6. Lansdowne, *Character of Mr. Wycherley* (1712); "Cibber," *Lives*, 3:255–256; Pope, in Spence, 1:37. Rochester's words on Thomas Flatman were challenged by Dryden (*Of Dramatic Poesy*, ed. Watson, 2:230) and Boswell (*Life*, ed. Hill, rev. Powell, 3:29).

that of Sedley and Dorset, "common Chatt," and had attained the status of proverbial critical truth.

However much the Augustans admired and borrowed from "An Allusion to Horace," they were not quite right in thinking (if they shared Johnson's opinion) that Rochester and Oldham were the first to imitate the classical satirists. As H. F. Brooks has shown in "The 'Imitation' in English Poetry, Especially in Formal Satire, before the Age of Pope," [7] Rochester and Oldham were preceded in some ways by Wyatt and Hall, Cowley and Sprat, and perhaps even Etherege, in their adaptations of classical satire to their own time and place. In order to assess Rochester's contribution to an existing tradition, it is worth tracing, with Brooks's help, the progress of that tradition up to Rochester's time.

There is little reason to suppose that Rochester knew the work of Wyatt and Hall [8] or recognized them as his literary precursors. He probably would have known, however, about the restatements of a theory of free translation and modernization set forth in the 1650s by Denham and Cowley,[9] and first put into practice in earnest, so Brooks thinks, by Cowley and the other contributors to Alexander Brome's *Poems of Horace* (1666).[10]

But Brooks, I think, overestimates the importance of Brome's *Horace* in the development of the imitation. Brome's purpose in publishing was not to make Horace say of London what he said of Rome; rather he wanted, so he said, to make the Roman poet more open to English readers.[11] In his collection, modernization is restricted to the substitution of a few details (e.g., London for Rome). The

7. *RES*, 25 (1949), 124–40.

8. *Ibid.*, p. 126 and n.

9. Preface to *The Destruction of Troy* (1656); "To Sir Richard Fanshaw upon his translation of Pastor Fido" (1648); Preface to *Pindarique Odes* (1656).

10. Brooks, "The 'Imitation' in English Poetry," 127.

11. Sigs. [A$_5$v–A$_6$v].

poems remain essentially Roman.[12] Some of the imitations written during the 1670s — by Rochester and others — derive from this native tradition as modified by the example of Boileau.[13] Whereas the native school — Cowley, Sprat, and their followers — translated freely yet produced poems with no particularly English character, Boileau loosely modeled most of his satires on Juvenal or Horace yet managed to create poems very contemporary and very French. Boileau himself soon became a candidate for imitation, first, apparently, by Etherege in an unfinished translation which does not survive, yet was known to Rochester.[14] Rochester was Boileau's next imitator; his "Timon" (based freely on Boileau's third satire) and "Satyr Against Mankind" (based even more freely on Boileau's eighth) represent the first surviving imitations of Boileau in English, and the first imitations in the manner of Boileau — neither free translation nor mere substitutions of names, but an attempt to reproduce, in a second language, the equivalent for the spirit of the first. Pleasure in reading this kind of imitation derives not from recognition of parallels and discrepancies with the original (the imitation being far too loose for that) but in its contemporaneity.

"An Allusion to Horace" and Oldham's imitations in the early 1680s represent both an outgrowth of the existing theory and practice of imitation and (in important ways) "imitations" of Boileau — in being much more faithful to the consecutive sense as well as to the spirit of their originals. They differ from those of Cowley's school in two re-

12. Butler's translation of Boileau's second satire (written c. 1669, published after 1680) is likewise a free translation that remains French in spirit.

13. This point is made by Brooks, "The 'Imitation' in English Poetry," (p. 130n) in opposition to the contention by A. F. B. Clark (*Boileau and the French Neo-classical Critics in England* [Paris, 1925], p. 248) that Boileau was primarily responsible for the formal satire of the Restoration in England.

14. See a letter from Dryden to Rochester, July 1673, in *Works of Dryden*, ed. Scott, rev. Saintsbury (London, 1892), 18:94.

spects: (1) they are filled with English equivalents for the
names of people and places, whereas Cowley's and Sprat's
have only a handful of modernized details; and more important (2) they depend, as Cowley's did not, on an easy
familiarity with the Latin original, so that the reader derives the particular pleasure of recognizing parallels and
discrepancies. Rochester's imitation of Horace may further
be distinguished from the imitations by Oldham. Whereas
Oldham (in translating Juvenal, Horace, and Boileau) [15]
tended to modernize sentence by sentence — keeping extremely close to the original sense — Rochester in "An Allusion to Horace" modernizes paragraph by paragraph, thus
reproducing the spirit of the original with its consecutive
sense, yet producing a poem more original and more Eng-
lish-sounding.

After Rochester and Oldham, in the 1680s and 1690s,
came a flood of Horatian and Juvenalian imitations,[16] none
of them, however, as good as Rochester's "Allusion to Horace" or Oldham's imitations of Horace's *Satire* 1:9 and
Juvenal's third. When the great Augustan satirists — Swift,
Pope, and Johnson — perfected the form, it was in Rochester and Oldham that they found the best models. And as
Brooks points out ("The 'Imitation,' " p. 139), it was Rochester rather than Oldham whom the Augustans followed,
imitating paragraph by paragraph rather than sentence by
sentence.[17] Johnson recognized how well Rochester had suc-
ceeded: "perhaps few [imitations] will be found where the
parallelism is better preserved than in ['An Allusion to Horace']." [18] Although the poem was not printed side by side
with Horace's *Satire* 1:10 until 1714, it is very likely that
many readers before that date recognized, as Dennis did in

15. Juvenal, *Satires* 3, 13; Horace, *Satire* 1:9; Boileau, *Satire* 8.
16. For examples see Brooks, "The 'Imitation' in English Poetry,"
137–138.
17. *Ibid.*, p. 139.
18. *Lives*, 1:129.

1719,[19] how Rochester followed or altered Horace's words to fit his own time. Just how ingenious Rochester was in discovering apt parallels (and significant departures) is worth demonstrating in some detail.

His opening paragraph (ll. 1–7) gives good examples of parallelism and departure:

> Well, sir, 'tis granted I said Dryden's rhymes
> Were stol'n, unequal, nay dull many times.
> What foolish patron is there found of his
> So blindly partial to deny me this?
> But that his plays, embroidered up and down
> With wit and learning, justly pleased the town
> In the same paper I as freely own.

Compare now Horace's opening four lines:

> Nempe incomposito dixi pede currere versus
> Lucili, quis tam Lucili fautor inepte est,
> ut non hoc fateatur? at idem, quod sale multo
> urbem defricuit, charta laudatur eadem.
> (To be sure I did say that the verses of Lucilius
> run on with halting foot. Who is a partisan of
> Lucilius so in-and-out of season as not to confess
> this? And yet on the self-same page the self-same
> poet is praised because he rubbed the city down
> with much salt.)[20]

Rochester finds an equivalent for *incomposito pede* that reproduces ("unequal" rhymes, or false rhyme and broken meter) and extends ("stol'n . . . dull") Horace's sense to fit the circumstances of Dryden's early poetry and heroic plays.[21]

---

19. *Critical Works*, 2:169.
20. Loeb translation (which I use throughout).
21. Editors have been unable to identify the stolen and unequal rhymes which Rochester censures. Does Rochester perhaps refer to Dryden's not infrequent half-lines?

But he departs sharply from Horace's praise of Lucilius. The Latin master "rubbed the city down with much salt" (i.e. satirized it), while Dryden "justly pleased the town" (i.e., wrote in such a way that he deserved to please it) . Considering the contempt for the town expressed by both Horace and Rochester throughout their poems, this praise of Dryden is indeed equivocal, if not damningly faint.

Horace's next paragraph (ll. 5–19) is imitated in Rochester's lines 8–36. Granting this one virtue, Rochester (Horace) cannot allow Dryden (Lucilius) all others, for on those grounds — pleasing an audience — even Crowne (Laberius) is a good poet. Now Rochester again diverges from Horace in order to sharpen the satire against Dryden. Horace says simply, "Hence it is not enough to make your hearer grin with laughter — though even in that there is some merit." Rochester changes the terms:

> 'Tis therefore not enough when your false sense
> Hits the false judgment of an audience
> Of clapping fools, assembling a vast crowd
> Till the thronged playhouse crack with the dull load;
> Though ev'n that talent merits in some sort
> That can divert the rabble and the Court.
> [ll. 12–17]

As Rochester warms to his theme — Dryden's appeal to popular taste — he elaborates and alters Horace's qualificaton: Lucilius made hearers laugh; Dryden makes foolish hearers laugh. And when Horace turns back from blame to praise — a movement characteristic of the whole satire ("though even in that there is some merit") — Rochester's equivalent contains a loaded phrase ("divert the rabble and the Court").

Other alterations of the original Latin enable Rochester to pay special tribute to witty contemporaries. Fundanius, "who can charm us with the chitchat of comedies," becomes

Shadwell and Wycherley, who alone of modern wits have "touched on true comedy." Here, Rochester elaborates on Horace's casual remark, adding nine extra lines of judicious and individualized praise:

> Shadwell's unfinished works do yet impart
> Great proofs of force of nature, none of art:
> With just, bold strokes he dashes here and there,
> Showing great mastery, with little care,
> And scorns to varnish his good touches o'er
>
> . . . .
>
> But Wycherley earns hard whate'er he gains:
> He wants no judgment, nor he spares no pains.
> He frequently excels, and at the least
> Makes fewer faults than any of the best.
>
> [ll. 44–48, 50–53]

Pollio, who "sings of kings' exploits," and Varius, who "surpassing all in spirit . . . moulds the valorous epic," are conflated in the figure of Waller,

> by nature for the bays designed,
> With force and fire and fancy unconfined,
> In panegyrics does excel mankind.
> He best can turn, enforce, and soften things
> To praise great conqu'rors, or to flatter Kings.
>
> [ll. 54–58]

Omitting the equivalent of "the valorous epic" perhaps signifies Rochester's recognition that he lives in an unheroic age, an age without a living epic poet (Milton, who would have been out of place in this company anyway, having died a year earlier).[22] The departure signifies also his willingness to alter Horace in order to make a truly English poem, and to make (for example) a subtle joke at the expense of Wal-

22. Note that Rochester limits himself to living poets.

ler who had written panegyrics on both the usurper Cromwell and the restored Charles.

Rochester's fellow rakes likewise receive generous (though
not unmerited) compliments. While Horace mocks "the fop
Hermogenes" for never having read the old masters, Rochester softens the sense and wittily compliments his friend
Etherege — "refined Etherege copies not at all, / But is himself a sheer original" [23] (ll. 32–33). When Horace praises Virgil's pastorals for their "simplicity and charm" (*molle atque
facetum*), Rochester, pastoral being a decadent form, substitutes the well-known tribute to the "gentle art" and "charm"
of Sedley's songs (ll. 61–70). The praise of Dorset (ll. 59–60)
and the subsequent blame-and-praise of Dryden (ll. 71–80)
derive from the following in Horace: "This satire, which
Varro of the Atax and some others had vainly tried, was
what I could write with more success, though falling short
of the inventor; nor would I dare to wrest from him the
crown that clings to his brow with so much glory." For
pointed satires Horace prefers himself over Varro, but
grants that he, in turn, is exceeded by Lucilius. Rochester
takes away from Dryden to give to Dorset; it is Dorset who
is honored for pointed satire, Dryden who "in vain tried"
to write like Dorset (and Sedley). As a result, when Rochester says of Dryden,

> But, to be just, 'twill to his praise be found
> His excellencies more than faults abound;
> Nor dare I from his sacred temples tear
> That laurel which he best deserves to wear,
>
> [ll. 77–80]

the praise seems a mere formality, the credit due an acknowledged master in order to prevent Rochester's case from
being thrown out of court altogether. Lucilius is praised

23. Meaning probably that Etherege did not imitate the great
dramatists of the former age, and that he was "original," or eccentric
in his behavior.

for satire, Dryden for unspecified "excellencies." [24] By contrast, such praise seems mere lip service. Dorset, on the other hand, receives spontaneous praise which, according to Horace's plan and to Rochester's own achievement in writing satire, should have gone to the poet himself. In this light the praise of Dorset is hardly the "invidious panegyric" of a self-sufficient man. [25]

Lines 81–97 follow Horace's lines 50–64, but once again Rochester alters his model in order to turn the screw of the satire on Dryden. Horace asks what forbids him "to raise the question whether it was his own genius [i.e., Lucilius's] or whether it was the harsh nature of his theme that denied him verses more finished and easier in their flow" (ll. 57–59). Rochester leaves Dryden no such escape:

> And may not I have leave impartially
> To search and censure Dryden's works, and try
> If those gross faults his choice pen does commit
> Proceed from want of judgment, or of wit;
> Or if his lumpish fancy does refuse
> Spirit and grace to his loose, slattern muse?
> [ll. 87–92]

Guided by a stronger animus against Dryden than Horace displays against Lucilius, Rochester also omits the praise of his subject's geniality and wit and of works "more polished than the crowd of older poets" (ll. 64–67).

Like Horace, Rochester closes with scorn of popular taste and a catalogue of good critics:

> 'tis enough for me
> If Sedley, Shadwell, Shepherd, Wycherley,
> Godolphin, Butler, Buckhurst, Buckingham,

24. Dryden in 1675 had not yet written any satire.
25. See above, p. 248. Did Dryden perhaps object not because of any alleged insult to Dorset but because he knew that the alteration of Horace had the result of shifting praise from himself to Dorset?

And some few more, whom I omit to name,
Approve my sense: I count their censure fame.
[ll. 120–124] [26]

Rochester's imitation, then, delights by the ingenuity of the parallels and in the significance of the departures, guided as they are by the single principle of sharpening the satire on the older master, so as to produce a tribute much more equivocal than Horace gave Lucilius. But the poem is more than personal satire, for the attack on Dryden is based in turn on another principle — that the poet should scorn common fame and write for the discerning few, should "Scorn all applause the vile rout can bestow, / And be content to please those few who know" (ll. 102–103). In his early work, Dryden, as he himself came to admit and regret, did lower himself to appeal to popular taste,[27] thereby arousing Rochester's contempt, and in part occasioning a response significant not only as an addition to the storehouse of Augustan satirical forms, but also as one of the few poems in which Rochester faces the world with assurance. He looks out on a rabble of hacks and critics, confident of his own powers, surrounded by a few like-minded friends, protected by lofty contempt. It is a position he was rarely able to maintain.

Rochester and Pope

Pope is at once the major Augustan poet most "influenced" — in the traditional sense — by Rochester,[28] and least like him in overall effect. The influence is chiefly stylistic; Pope appears to have built on the work of Rochester (and many others) in developing several satiric techniques. But

26. "Censure" here means "judgment, opinion" (in a neutral sense).
27. See his repentance for his "Dalilahs of the Theatre," Watson, *Of Dramatic Poesy*, (n. 3 above), 1:276.
28. Rochester had surprisingly little influence on two late seventeenth-century satirists, Oldham and Robert Gould.

with such techniques he constructed a body of satire far different in tone and stance from that of his Restoration predecessor.

Pope began his career by imitating Rochester. He owned and annotated a copy of his *Poems* (1696).[29] Like Rochester, he admired and imitated Waller and Cowley, and went on, at the age of thirteen, to imitate "Upon Nothing" in his own "On Silence" (c. 1702), a rather light and ineffectual piece of juvenilia. In later years he occasionally borrowed from Rochester.[30] Lines added to Wycherley's "On Dulness" draw on "Artemisia to Chloe."[31] The *Dunciad* and *Essay on Man* several times echo the "Satyr Against Mankind."[32] Pope also seems to have appreciated Rochester's daring and extravagant wit. He altered the scurrilous portrait of Rochester in Mulgrave's "Essay Upon Satyr" by omitting most of the abuse (e.g., Rochester is a false wit and malicious coward) and mitigating some of the lurid Satanic detail. Though Rochester still emerges lewd and ill-natured, his "sprightly wit" and shining grace are honored.[33] The alteration seems to reflect Pope's own view of the man. Although he told Spence that "Lord Rochester was of a very bad turn of mind, as well as debauched," and as a proud professional no doubt looked down on the aristocratic versifier, Pope nonetheless insisted that Rochester "had much more deli-

29. Now in the Berg Collection, New York Public Library.

30. Vieth points out an early borrowing from the "Epistolary Essay" in the "Prologue Design'd for Mr. Durfy's Last Play" (1713), "Pope and Rochester: An Unnoticed Borrowing," *N & Q*, 211 (1966), 457–458. Pope also seems to have remembered the "Epistolary Essay," ll. 12–13, in his adaptation of Donne's fourth satire (ll. 9–10).

31. Cf. "On Dulness," ll. 1–4, 11–12, and "Artemisia to Chloe," ll. 40–43; "Upon Nothing," ll. 50–51.

32. The Twickenham editors point out *Dunciad* (1729) 1:112–114, and "Satyr," ll. 18–19; *Essay on Man* 3:163–164, and "Satyr," ll. 129–130; *Essay on Man* 4:211–214, and "Artemisia to Chloe," l. 214; but not *Dunciad* (1743) 4:641–642, and "Satyr," l. 17.

33. The alterations appear in Pope's edition of the *Works* of Mulgrave (John Sheffield, later the Duke of Buckinghamshire).

cacy and more knowledge [than Oldham]," and seems to
have felt "kindly" toward his libertine predecessor.[34]

Although he makes no note of it, Pope probably recognized Rochester's achievement in three satiric strategies that
he himself adapted and mastered in his various kinds of
character sketches. In the first of these strategies, conven-
tionalized into genre as the lampoon, the poet emphasizes
the subject's physical appearance, deploys insulting epithets,
and refuses to deal with the subject's feelings or point of
view, preferring rather to remain on the outside.[35] Sporus
belongs in this tradition:

> This painted child of Dirt that stinks and stings
> . . . .
> Whose buzz the Witty and the Fair Annoys,
> Yet Wit ne'er tastes and Beauty ne'er enjoys.
> . . . .
> Half froth, half venom, spits himself abroad,
> In Puns, or Politicks, or Tales, or Lyes
> . . . .
> His Wit all see-saw between that and this,
> Now high, now low, now Master up, now Miss,
> And he himself one vile antithesis.
> Amphibious Thing! that acting either Part,
> The trifling Head, or the corrupted Heart!
> Fop at the Toilet, Flatt'rer at the Board,
> Now trips a Lady, and now struts a Lord
> . . . .

34. Joseph Spence, *Observations, Anecdotes, and Characters of Books
and Men*, ed. James Osborn, 2 vols. (Oxford, 1966), 1:201–202. "By
"delicacy," as by sprightliness, Pope probably meant the qualities of
Horace's finely honed, laughing satire. Pope later said that "Rochester
has neither so much delicacy nor exactness as Dorset, the best of all
those writers." *Ibid.*, 1:202.

35. See Benjamin Boyce, *The Character Sketch in Pope's Poems*
(Chapel Hill, 1962), pp. 80–85.

Beauty that shocks you, Parts that none will trust,
Wit that can creep, and Pride that licks the dust.
["Epistle to Arbuthnot," ll. 310–312,
320–321, 323–329, 332–333]

Compare with this sketch Rochester's attack on "My Lord All-Pride":

Bursting with pride, the loathed impostume swells;
Prick him, he sheds his venom straight, and smells.
But 'tis so lewd a scribbler, that he writes
With as much force to nature as he fights

. . . .

. . . his brain's so weak
That his starved fancy is compelled to rake
Among the excrements of others' wit
To make a stinking meal of what they shit

. . . .

With stinking breath, and every loathsome mark,
The Punchinello sets up for a spark.
[ll. 1–4, 7–10, 17–18]

Some details are similar: both poets use imagery of toads and excrement, attack physical ugliness and weak wit, and condemn the paradox or antithesis of their victims. The difference lies in the large design, between Rochester's relatively crude and merely personal attack and Pope's sophistication: he cools and refines his malice, reducing the blunt physicality of Rochester's attack, and generalizing Sporus into "Fortune's Worshipper" and "Fashion's Fool."

A second kind of character sketch that Rochester practiced (perhaps even introduced) and Pope mastered is the brief dramatic scene in which a fool exposes himself through his conversation and gestures. Rachel Trickett has rightly compared Rochester's gawky, swearing wooer in "Tunbridge Wells" —

> The would-be wit, whose business was to woo,
> With hat removed and solemn scrape of shoe
> Advanceth bowing, then genteelly shrugs,
> And ruffled foretop into order tugs.
>
> . . . .
>
> He, puzzled, bites his nail, both to display
> The sparkling ring, and think what next to say,
> And thus breaks forth afresh: "Madam, egad!
>
> . . . .
>
> God damn me, madam, I'm the son of a whore
> If in my life I saw the like before!"
> ["Tunbridge Wells," ll. 88–91, 102–104, 108–109]

— to Pope's Sir Plume. Pope "compresses his dialogue, description, and gesture to even narrower limits": [36]

> (Sir Plume, of Amber Snuff-box justly vain,
> And the nice Conduct of a clouded Cane)
> With earnest Eyes, and round, unthinking Face,
> He first the Snuff-box open'd, then the Case,
> And thus broke out — "My Lord, why, what the Devil?
> Z——ds! damn the Lock! 'fore Gad, you must be civil!
> Plague on't! 'tis past a Jest — nay prithee, Pox!
> Give her the Hair" — he spoke, and rapp'd his Box.
> [*Rape of the Lock*, 4:123–130]

Although Sir Plume is a different kind of fool — a mannered, fashionable, swearing fop out of the world of the *Tatler* and *Spectator* — from Rochester's clumsier would-be wit, he is smoked in the same manner.

The most important of three characterizing techniques that Pope seems to have found in Rochester (and elsewhere) is the analysis of personality through a brief account of the subject's rise and fall in the world. Pope must have been impressed with the harrowing story of Corinna in "Arte-

36.*The Honest Muse: A Study in Augustan Verse* (London, 1967), p. 170.

misia to Chloe," who "had run / Through all the several
ways of being undone." For a time she lives off men, admired for the "early beauties" of her youth. But Corinna
dotes on a man of wit, is scorned, and forsaken; now a
memento mori,

> Diseased, decayed, to take up half a crown
> Must mortgage her long scarf and manteau gown.
> Poor creature! who, unheard of as a fly,
> In some dark hole must all the winter lie,
> And want and dirt endure a whole half year
> That for one month she tawdry may appear.
>   [ll. 203-208]

Compare Pope's early character of Macer (c. 1715), in which
a young poet's early success and subsequent failure are
likened to the parabolic career of a young girl turned whore:

> So some coarse Country Wench, almost decay'd,
> Trudges to Town, and first turns Chambermaid;
> Aukward and supple, each Devoir to pay,
> She flatters her good Lady twice a Day;
> Thought wond'rous honest, tho' of mean Degree,
> And strangely lik'd for her Simplicity:
>   In a translated Suit, then tries the Town,
> With borrow'd Pins, and Patches not her own;
> But just endur'd the Winter she began,
> And in four months, a batter'd Harridan,
> Now nothing's left, but wither'd, pale, and shrunk
> To bawd for others, and go Shares with Punk.
>   [ll. 15–26]

Pope adopts not only the frame of Rochester's story — the
hopeful beginning, the sordid end — but some illustrative
details as well.

Rochester's booby squire in the same poem, from peda-
gogue and mother just set free, "Comes to town, / Turns
spark, learns to be lewd, and is undone." He is a witless,

country fool used to illustrate the fine lady's thesis that fools repair an undone lady's fortunes. In like manner, Pope uses Sir Balaam, a sober citizen whose life is changed by money, to illustrate his thesis about the various misuses of riches. Both fools, however, trace the same arc. Pope's mode this time is expansive rather than intensive: the sketch covers more than sixty lines. Balaam gains a fortune, remarries, bows at court and grows polite, becomes a cuckold:

> My Lady falls to play; so bad her chance,
> He must repair it; takes a bribe from France;
> The House impeach him; Coningsby harangues;
> The Court forsake him, and Sir Balaam hangs:
> Wife, son, and daughter, Satan, are thy own,
> His wealth, yet dearer, forfeit to the Crown:
> The Devil and the King divide the prize,
> And sad Sir Balaam curses God and dies.
> ["Epistle to Bathurst," ll. 395–402]

Pope's sketch of Sir Balaam, like the similar sketch of "Great Villiers" (ll. 299–314), is more soberly contemplated (by poet and reader) than Rochester's lines on the booby squire. But the biographical technique and the typicality of the story (doubtless true to life) are the same.

Rochester not only showed Pope how parts of his satires might be written, he showed what form a whole satire might take by imitating Horace in a manner that we now call Popean. Pope never imitated Horace's *Satire* 1:10. That he might have composed something very similar to Rochester's version of it is suggested by a comparison between the "Allusion to Horace" and Pope's "Epistle to Augustus" (Horace's *Epistle* 2:1), an imitation very like Rochester's poem. Both poems are paragraph-by-paragraph imitations, with some elaboration and lengthening of Horace's characteristic brevity; both are essays in literary criticism, Rochester discussing the present state of poetry and the uncritical

exaltation of a past master, Pope primarily the latter. Both
Rochester and Pope introduce alterations of their originals
in order to fit the satire more closely to Dryden and George
II. Both poets scorn common fame — the judgment of "the
rabble and the court," the "Taste of the Town . . . the
Court and Nobility" — and insist on being their own men:
Rochester writes for the "few who know," Pope (ironically)
forswears flattery. Pope's satire, however, is more sly and
subtle than Rochester's, his parallels generally more ingenious, and his versification more sophisticated.[37] Indeed, in
matters of style, Pope is everywhere finer, more delicate,
more subtle, than Rochester. In consequence he lacks some
of Rochester's rough energy, a kind of fierceness not com-
patible with finesse.

As a satirist of women (the chief similarity between them),
Pope differs from Rochester not only in style but, more im-
portantly, in attitude. Rochester's central attitude toward
his satiric objects is disgust. Occasionally (as in "Artemisia
to Chloe") he remains a dispassionate spectator and can
even reveal momentary sympathy for his women characters.
But sympathy in Rochester is usually reserved for the rake,
plagued by frustration and failure. In Pope, the range of
feeling is wider. Disgust at female vice and folly is much
more likely to be tempered by admiration and sympathy.

37. Pope told Spence that "Rochester has very bad versification
sometimes" and "instanced this from his tenth satire of Horace, his
full rhymes, etc." Spence, 1:202. The only full rhyme, or *rime riche*, in
Rochester's "Allusion" is obscene / unseen / Queen, and according to
Edward Bysshe, the *rime riche*, usually forbidden in correct versification of the period, was allowed if there was a third (and different)
rhyme. See *The Art of English Poetry* (3rd ed., 1708), p. 21. Pope,
then, may have been referring to the bad versification of an unspecified
kind in the "Allusion" (perhaps to its ten triplets, one per twelve
lines) and to full rhymes in other Rochester poems — there are several
in "Artemisia to Chloe" and "Timon," one each in the "Satyr" and
"Tunbridge Wells." Pope may object to the imperfect rhymes in the
"Allusion" (Rochester is often careless on this point): crowd / load,
least / best, before / more / hour, test / least, Buckingham / name / fame,
circumscribe / tide.

In the second *Moral Essay,* for example, the foolishly ruined lives of self-indulgence, rage, and sterility evoke not only stern judgment but also bewildered compassion for the waste and self-destruction of an Atossa, the "impotence of mind" of a Flavia, or the lonely end of the world's "Veterans." In *Rape of the Lock* likewise Pope does not long allow us a superior smile at Belinda's gay but trivial world. An elegiac current develops strength in the poem, reminding us of the precious fragility of beauty. By the end, the brilliance of wit is softened by a regret, suitably miniaturized, that those fair tresses "shall be laid in dust."

We have been speaking only of the satiric Pope. The celebrative Pope (of *Windsor Forest,* of the epistles to Bathurst and Burlington) is a poet utterly different from Rochester, who celebrates nothing (except Nothing). Pope's two sides are, of course, often found in the same poem. In him, as for Rochester, there exists a gap between actual and ideal. But Pope's ideal is always at least a possibility. It is even realized in a few men and women, like Martha Blount, Bathurst, and Burlington, who stand as pictures of virtue in a fallen world. Even where the gap widens between actual and ideal (as it does increasingly in the later poetry),[38] Pope's despairing response can be distinguished from Rochester's. The latter's despair springs from the belief that the world is controlled by knaves and cheats, and that one has no way to oppose or even to survive but to be a "knave of the first rate." Ideals become irrelevant or even dangerous; even as satirist, one is left without sure bearings. Pope, on the contrary, never loses his bearings, never loses the assurance that he is in the right. Despite the descending curtain of darkness, his values and his satiric stance hold firm. He remains a mighty antipathist, whether the contest is between a retired poet and a prime minister[39] or "the strong antipathy of

38. See Thomas Edwards, *This Dark Estate* (Berkeley, 1963).
39. See Maynard Mack, *The Garden and the City* (Toronto, 1969).

Good to Bad." It is that firm base of assurance that Rochester lacks.

"Upon Nothing"

As I have suggested, the eighteenth century seems to have
been curiously attracted to Rochester's "Upon Nothing." Dr.
Johnson, for example, asserts that "The strongest effort of
his Muse is his poem on Nothing." [40] Johnson does not say
explicitly, as many critics have too quickly assumed, that
"Upon Nothing" is his best poem. "Strongest" probably
meant for Johnson "most vigorous and forceful," with a suggestion of "strong lines" ("Much meaning in few words, . . .
more weight than bulk") .[41] Yet the fact that he devotes a
large part of his brief commentary on Rochester's poetry to
"Upon Nothing" implies that for him this poem was at
least Rochester's most interesting work — and perhaps even
his most successful.

Johnson's judgment was shared by most of Rochester's
eighteenth-century critics, from Addison, who called it "an
admirable poem" upon a "barren subject," to Joseph Warton, who condemned as unworthy to be read all of Rochester
except "Upon Nothing," the "Satyr Against Mankind," and
"An Allusion to Horace." [42] Why the eighteenth century
should have so admired this poem may perhaps be explained
in part by reference to what W. K. Wimsatt has called the
"Augustan mode in English poetry," and to an interest, in

40. *Lives*, 1:129.
41. "Life of Denham," *Lives*, 1:52.
42. *Spectator* 305, ed. Bond, 3:100; *Essay on the Genius and Writings of Pope* (1756) (5th ed., London, 1806), 2:46. Pope's "Upon Silence" imitates Rochester's poem; Swift admired it (see below, n. 80),
as did Elijah Fenton (*Correspondence of Pope*, ed. George Sherburn
[Oxford, 1956], 2:385), Giles Jacob (*An Historical Account of the Lives
and Writings of Our Most Considerable English Poets* [London,
1720], 2:232), William Shenstone (*Letters*, ed. D. Mallam [Minneapolis,
1939], p. 440), and Fielding (*Selected Essays of Fielding*, ed. G. H.
Gerould [New York, 1905], p. 159).

the Augustan age and earlier, in the mock-panegyric. "Up-on Nothing" is in part an ironic poem in praise of an un-worthy subject, an example of a literary form with a long history traceable back through Renaissance paradox and classical rhetoric.[43] In an age of ironical satire, an age that envisioned Dulness as a goddess, Rochester's praise of Noth-ing would have met with a receptive audience. More gen-erally, if the Augustans at their best were, as Wimsatt has called them, "laughing poets of a heightened unreality," [44] what greater unreality might they laugh at than Nothing? Moreover, a number of eighteenth-century poetasters not only resolved like Swift's Modern [45] to write upon Nothing, but actually did so, in the miscellanies and magazines,[46] in the form of ballads, riddles, or short disquisitions.

It is unlikely that many eighteenth-century readers and poets were aware, as Johnson was, that Rochester was not the first to have "chosen this barren topic for the boast of his fertility." [47] Fielding claims in 1743 that, apart from Rochester, "none ever hath dared to write on this subject." [48] Johnson knew that Jean Passerat, "a poet and critic of the sixteenth century in France, had written in Latin on 'Nihil.' "

In fact, Rochester had a series of predecessors, some of whom he possibly knew. The earliest treatments of Nothing of which anything is known are medieval parodic sermons about creation *ex nihilo*. A twelfth-century poem by Wil-

43. See H. K. Miller, "The Paradoxical Encomium: With Special Reference to its Vogue in England, 1600–1800," *Modern Philology*, 53 (1956), 145–178.

44. W. K. Wimsatt, "The Augustan Mode in English Poetry," *ELH*, 20 (1953), 9.

45. *Tale of a Tub*, "Conclusion."

46. *The Athenian Oracle*; *The British Apollo*; *Gentleman's Maga-zine*, and others. For a full bibliography, see Miller, "The Paradoxical Encomium," 173–178.

47. *Lives*, 1:129.

48. *Selected Essays*, p. 159.

liam of Poitier very likely grew from concern with the same question. Rochester's poem demonstrates that this theological paradox still had a powerful appeal to speculative minds [49] in the seventeenth century. Among the many versions of the "praise of Nothing" in the intervening centuries [50] Rochester may have known of Passerat's poem [51] through his reading of the French *libertins* or in the translation by Sir William Cornwallis,[52] and possibly of a poem by Francesco Beccuti, "Capitolo nel quale si lodano le Noncovelle" (c. 1550).[53]

This poem illustrates once again that, more than previous critics and readers have realized, Rochester is a poet whose work — however iconoclastic and strikingly individual — grows out of literary tradition. Whether or not he knew the particular poems of any of his predecessors (and poems on Nothing continued to appear through the seventeenth century),[54] it is certain that he was aware of writing in a tradition. In fact, the poem (as we shall see) probably owes more to Cowley than to the essentially lighthearted comedy of traditional poems (like Beccuti's) on Nothing. What is

49. Despite Rochester's attack, in the "Satyr Against Mankind," on speculative reason, his was a speculative mind. See Burnet, p. 22.

50. (1) Ulrich von Hutten, *Nemo* (1518); (2) Edward Daunce, *The prayse of Nothing* (1585), often attributed erroneously to Sir Edward Dyer; (3) a ballad based on Daunce, "The Praise of Nothing" (c. 1625). For bibliographical details, see Miller, "The Paradoxical Encomium."

51. In *Argumentum ludicorum* (1623), pp. 107, 109.

52. *Essayes or Rather, Encomions* (1616), Sigs. E_3v–E_4v.

53. Pinto has suggested that Rochester may have been shown a poem upon Nothing by someone in the circle of the famous Salvator Rosa, whom Rochester might well have tried to meet. *English Miscellany*, 7 (Rome, 1950), p. 24. Beccuti's poem is quite dissimilar in tone to Rochester's, and shows no parallel in phrasing. *Rime di Francesco Beccuti Detto il Coppetta* (Venice, 1751), pp. 164–168.

54. An epigram (in two variations) by Richard Flecknoe: "To Master W. A., On his Excellent Poem of Nothing, sent with one made of somewhat," *Miscellania, or Poems of All Sorts* (London, 1653), p. 73; "Somewhat to Mr. J. A. [sic] On his excellent Poem of Nothing," *Epigrams of all Sorts* (London, 1670), p. 31. See also Miller, "The Paradoxical Encomium."

particularly interesting about "Upon Nothing," however, is
how Rochester subverted a witty Christian paradox to serve
more skeptical ends than the poem's eighteenth-century
admirers, I suspect, ever imagined.

The poem begins by trying to account for the beginning
of the world:

> Nothing! thou elder brother even to Shade: [55]
> Thou hadst a being ere the world was made,
> And well fixed, art alone of ending not afraid.
>
> Ere Time and Place were, Time and Place were not,
> When primitive Nothing Something straight begot;
> Then all proceeded from the great united What.
>
> Something, the general attribute of all,
> Severed from thee, its sole original,
> Into thy boundless self must undistinguished fall;
>
> Yet Something did thy mighty power command,
> And from thy fruitful Emptiness's hand
> Snatched men, beasts, birds, fire, water, air, and land.
>
> Matter, the wicked'st offspring of thy race,
> By Form assisted, flew from thy embrace,
> And rebel Light obscured thy reverend dusky face.

55. Johnson wonders if Rochester "does not allude to a curious
book *De Umbra*, by Wowerus, which, having told the qualities of
Shade, concludes with a poem, in which are these lines: ". . . Omni-
bus Umbra prior." *Lives*, 1:130.

Wowerus is the classicist Joannes à Wower (1574–1612), author of
Dies Aestiva, sive De umbra paegnion ["A Summer Day, or a sportive
essay about Shade"] (Oxford, 1636), which concludes with a "Hymnus
ad Umbram."

More likely, Rochester may allude to Donne: "This Beginning [of
the world] was, and before it, Nothing. It is elder than darknesse,
which is elder than Light" (*Essays in Divinity*, ed. E. M. Simpson
[Oxford, 1952], p. 19); "Darknesse, Lights elder brother" ("The
Storm," l. 67).

With Form and Matter, Time and Place did join;
Body, thy foe, with these did leagues combine
To spoil thy peaceful realm, and ruin all thy line.

The poem tells not one but as many as three different stories of creation: (1) Nothing begot something, and from their incestuous union all else followed (st. 2); (2) Something was severed or sundered from Nothing, as Eve was sundered from Adam's side, and subsequently severed or "snatched" from Nothing's hand "men, beasts," etc. (sts. 3–4); (3) with terms now shifted from concrete to abstract, from "Something" to "Matter," Matter is born of Nothing but frustrates Nothing's desire for incestuous union, fleeing from its embrace, joining in rebellion against Nothing with Form, Light, Time, and Place (sts. 5–6). Whether Rochester deliberately parodies the double account of man's creation in Genesis (man is born from dust; all men but Adam are born from woman), or whether he has some other purpose in giving a multiple account of creation *ex nihilo* is difficult to say. Although he may simply fail to control his poem, I suspect that he deliberately introduces discrepancies and uncertainties in order to mock the process of explaining origins.

In particular, he mocks the attempts by older poets to describe creation. Cowley's "Hymn to Light" (1663) has creation spring from Chaos:

> First-born of Chaos, who so fair didst come
>   From the old Negro's darksome womb
>   Which when it saw the lovely Child
> The melanchly Mass put on kind looks and smil'd.

Rochester adopts Cowley's generative language (Light born from the womb of Chaos), substitutes Darkness or Shade for Light, and makes Nothing the older brother of Shade, and Light a rebel against Nothing's "reverend dusky face"

(Nothing corresponds to Cowley's Negro). For Cowley's "womb" Rochester has "great united What," a sneer at the Nothing and Something of logicians, and a pun, when the *d* is elided and sounded as *t*, on twat,[56] a bawdy jest at Cowley's expense. In Cowley's *Davideis*, which Rochester more closely recalls, creation springs *ex nihilo*:

> Only [God] spoke, and every thing that Is
> From out the Womb of fertile Nothing rise [sic]
> . . . .
>
> They sung how God spoke out the World's vast Ball,
> From Nothing, and from No where call'd Forth All.
> No Nature yet, or Place for't to possess,
> But an unbottom'd Gulf of Emptiness
> . . . .
>
> An unshap'd kind of Something first appear'd,
> Confessing its new Being . . .
> . . . .
>
> Yet buried in this Matters darksome Womb,
> Lay the rich Seeds of ev'rything to come.[57]

Cowley, of course, is far from "praising" Nothing as primal source, as Rochester professes to do. Elsewhere, however, instead of exalting life over Nothing, he sees little difference between the two. Again Rochester remembers him:

> Oh Life, thou Nothing's younger Brother!
>   So like, that one might take one for the other!
>   What's Some Body, or No Body?
> In all the Cobwebs of the Schoolmens Trade,
> We no such nice Distinction woven see,
>   As 'tis To be, or Not to be.[58]

56. I am indebted to Kristoffer Paulson, "Pun Intended: Rochester's *Upon Nothing*," *English Language Notes*, 9 (1971), 118–121, for this attractive suggestion.
57. *Works*, 11th ed. (London, 1710), 1:303, 318.
58. *Ibid.*, 1:239.

Like Cowley, Rochester mocks the abstractions and distinctions of the Schoolmen, but instead of reducing Life to Nothing (a traditional kind of *contemptus mundi*) Rochester more darkly gives Nothing a life of its own.[59]

Rochester not only substitutes Nothing for God; he mocks the use of terminology drawn from a material, created world to describe an immaterial condition, by solemnly describing general attributes as if they were concrete bodies, and gravely parodying them in "the great united What," a phrase in fact no more nonsensical than "Nothing" or "Something." He had perhaps been reading Sextus Empiricus (in Stanley's *History of Philosophy*, 3rd ed. [London, 1701], pp. 520–522) who argued that notions of "generation and Corruption," of "Place" and "Time" are really unintelligible. Like Rochester, Sextus speaks of Nothing and Something, of Being and "Not-being" (the last used in a positive sense).

The seventh stanza introduces the idea of mortality:

> But turncoat Time assists the foe in vain,
> And bribed by thee, destroys their short-lived reign,
> And to thy hungry womb drives back thy slaves again.

There seems to be an obscure connection between Nothing, in this stanza, and the well-known figures of Error in Spenser and Sin in Milton, or with their common ancestor. Like Sin, Nothing has given incestuous birth to offspring who besiege their parent, until, disturbed by an outside force, they creep back into the womb. Note, too, that Nothing, once masculine (an elder brother, a begetter) is now feminine, perhaps in parody of the Holy Spirit (which in *Paradise Lost* is imagined both as impregnating dove and female

59. Compare the creation piece in Joseph Beaumont's *Psyche* (1648), canto 6, st. 115–117, where "Something" is "son of Nothing." Rochester also seems to parody Du Bartas's *Divine Weeks*: "Before all Time, all Matter, Form, and Place, / God all in all, and all in God it was" (tr. Sylvester, 1605, p. 3).

muse). This stanza also adumbrates a theme that gains importance in the latter part of the poem — treachery and corruption. The great exemplar for human dishonesty is Time itself, a turncoat bribed with the promise of power.

The account of creation and decreation is remarkably sexualized. Sexual union and generation are furthermore acts of violence and mutual hostility, especially in contrast to Cowley's creation pieces (fertile womb, kindly smiling Mother Chaos). Though Something remains an adversary, Mother Nothing continually seeks to re-embrace its hostile offspring, first in (successful) incestuous union, and finally by taking them back, with Time's help, into her "hungry womb." They fall "undistinguished" (i.e., they lose their individuality) into her "boundless self."

"Upon Nothing" and the related translation of Seneca ("After death nothing is") inevitably recall Rochester's poems about sex, especially those where the vagina is imaged as a vast devourer. He follows Seneca closely in speaking of "devouring time" and of death as both womb and grave, "Where things destroyed with things unborn are kept." But he adapts freely in making death a vast lumber room (a storehouse for useless odds and ends) — "Dead, we become the lumber of the world, / And to that mass of matter shall be swept" — like the boundless womb of Nothing into which everything at last flows. Especially in "Upon Nothing," however, re-absorption by a giant womb produces an ambivalent response. On the one hand, only Nothing is not afraid of "ending." Such a death means being eaten, and a loss of identity — an undistinguished blending with the "mass of matter"; on the other, it represents an "end." To be reduced to nothing is "least unsafe and best" (l. 36), for it represents a kind of stability. Nothing is in some respects a maternal comforter providing secure rest within her bosom (l. 35).[60]

60. "The idea of being eaten is not only a source of fear but under certain circumstances may also be a source of oral pleasure. There is

At some level, it seems reasonable to speculate, the poem — like some of the songs — reveals traces of the poet's powerful attachment to his mother.[01]

Beginning with stanza eight, however, the poem changes direction. Having completed his version of creation *ex nihilo* and the return *ad nihilum*, Rochester shifts his ground from the cosmic to the terrestrial:

> Though mysteries are barred from laic eyes,
> And the divine alone with warrant pries
> Into thy bosom, where the truth in private lies.

The laity ("laic eyes") are debarred from theological mysteries; the "divine" or cleric, with a warrant to investigate speculative truths,[62] in fact, says Rochester scornfully, pries into Nothing. Indeed, the divine's investigations, so Rochester implies (pries, bosom, private, lies) are a kind of sexual violation of Nothing, either leering (pry as "peer") or rape (pry as "force"). Stanza nine continues to mock the nothingness of religion:

> Yet this of thee the wise may truly say:
> Thou from the virtuous nothing dost delay,
> And to be part of thee the wicked wisely pray.

not only a longing to incorporate objects, but also a longing to be incorporated by a larger object." Otto Fenichel, *The Psychoanalytic Theory of Neurosis* (New York, 1945), p. 64.

61. "Nothing" is an established euphemism for "country matters" (*Hamlet* 3:2). Psychoanalysts would note that the term signifies the absence or deprivation of a penis, and is thus a sign to the man that the feared castration can really occur. See G. Legman, *Rationale of the Dirty Joke: An Analysis of Sexual Humor* (First Series, New York, 1968), p. 526. Cf. Freud, *Standard Edition of the Complete Psychological Works*, ed. J. Strachey et al. (London, 1953–1966), 11:95, and Fenichel, *Psychoanalytic Theory*, p. 80, on the anxiety caused by the infantile discovery that a woman's penis is "missing."

62. Compare Fanshawe: "a Priest's mind rapt above the Skie / Into th'eternall counsels there can prie" (*The Faithful Shepherd*, 1:4, 785–786).

The sense is difficult. Rochester seems to mock the religious "wise" man who would claim that virtue is its own reward, i.e., it rewards the virtuous without delay, and, in another sense, that God delays until the afterlife the true rewards for virtue and punishments for vice. Rochester says instead, with Seneca, "after death nothing is." Thus Nothing delays nothing (in a negative sense, no reward; in a positive sense, Nothingness itself) [63] for the virtuous. On the other hand, the wicked (who are the truly wise in Rochester's poetic world) wisely pray to be rewarded with nothingness, with oblivion rather than hellfire.

In stanza ten, Rochester continues to sneer at "the wise," the speculative theologians and philosophers:

> Great Negative, how vainly would the wise
> Inquire, define, distinguish, teach, devise,
> Didst thou not stand to point [64] their blind philosophies!

The probable meaning (though not the literal sense) is that the spectacle of Nothing, the end of all philosophy, prevents philosophers from speculating even more wildly than they do. The following two stanzas apply the language of philosophy to affairs of state:

> Is or Is Not, the two great ends of Fate, [65]
> And True or False, the subject of debate,
> That perfect or destroy the vast designs of state —
>
> When they have racked the politician's breast,
> Within thy bosom most securely rest,
> And when reduced to thee, are least unsafe and best.

63. Johnson read only a negative sense, and objected.
64. Point out. The metaphor of a swordsman, standing ready to point, may lie behind the phrase.
65. "The two great ends of fate," being and extinction, perhaps in parody of the "two great ends" for the Christian, salvation and damnation.

A politician must decide if something is or is not true, for example, about another nation, or the effect of a given policy. When the answer to such a question has been found not to matter, or when the difference between "Is" and "Is Not" has been judged to be nothing, then the politician no longer need trouble himself over it — he is safe. Ultimately, the distinction between Is and Is Not, True and False, is imaginary or unreal. Perhaps he means that it is impossible to define what Is and what Is Not, or else not worth the effort.

In the conclusion of the poem Nothing is restored:

> Nothing! who dwellst with fools in grave disguise,
> For whom they reverend shapes and forms devise,
> Lawn sleeves and furs and gowns, when they like thee
> look wise:

The peroration follows in a rush:

> French truth, Dutch prowess, British policy,
> Hibernian learning, Scotch civility,
> Spaniards' dispatch, Danes' wit are mainly seen in thee;

> The great man's gratitude to his best friend,
> Kings' promises, whores' vows — [66] towards thee they bend,
> Flow swiftly into thee, and in thee ever end.

Rochester's satire is a great leveler: grave fools and bishops, the several nations of Europe, great men, kings, and whores — all of their supposed achievement, wisdom, and honesty come to nothing. The conclusion gains some of its power through parodic echoing of the classico-Christian views that the world will end in chaos,[67] and that all matter and spirit

66. Compare Cowley's sarcastic "For Hope": "Thou Captive's Freedom, and thou Sick Man's Health! / Thou Loser's Victory, and thou Beggar's Wealth!" *Works* (1710), 1:124.
67. "The world to chaos shall again return," *The Divine Weeks, The Schisme* (1605), p. 11; "Into this wild abyss, / The womb of na-

derive from one God and will return to him at death.[68] A comparison with Cowley's closing words in the "Hymn to Light" reveals Rochester's parody most clearly:

> But the vast Ocean of unbounded Day
> In th'Empyrean Heaven does stay.
> Thy Rivers, Lakes, and Springs below,
> From thence took first their Rise, thither
> at last must flow.

Rochester's purposes in writing this poem seem to me to have been mixed and misapprehended. He has not written a pure mock-panegyric, in which everything said in praise or in condemnation must be inverted, as Vieth implies he has,[69] and, I suspect, as the eighteenth century read the poem. Neither has he written a poem to say, as one critic has recently put it, that "Nothing is best."[70] The poem does not make fun of God or of Nothingness (as Pinto has claimed it does).[71] Rather he has written, in the opening stanzas, a satire on the idea of the creation *ex nihilo* and on poets and philosophers who try to explain such a process, and in the closing stanzas a bitter attack on a broad spectrum of human pretenses — all of which come to nothing. Put another way, in the first half of the poem Rochester demonstrates wittily that nothing is *something* — endowed with a venerable origin, a creative function, and an epic history. In the second half he presents the corresponding thesis

ture and perhaps her grave," *Paradise Lost* 2:911 (Milton here translates *De Rerum Natura* 5:259).

68. "One almighty is, from whom / All things proceed, and up to him return," *Paradise Lost* 5:469–470; cf. *Georgics* 4:225–226, and Montaigne, "Apologie," *Essayes*, 2:25.

69. "The inverted world of Augustan satire received its most nearly archetypal expression in Rochester's 'Upon Nothing,' an ironic eulogy of an Uncreation opposite to God's original act." *ARP*, p. 106.

70. Anne Righter, "John Wilmot, Earl of Rochester," *Proc. Brit. Acad.*, 53 (1967), 67. She also speaks inaccurately (p. 66) of "the primal rape of Nothingness by Creation."

71. *Enthusiast in Wit*, p. 116.

that what the world values as "something" — the rewards of virtue and faith, the glories of learning and statecraft, the strength of human vows and bonds — is in fact nothing. The two halves of the poem are imperfectly joined; in the middle stanzas, as I have tried to show, the poem changes direction and plan. What does give the poem the unity it has is the continuous current of negative feelings. That current is admirably sustained by Rochester's strong and vigorous triplets, which are given a curious weight and gravity by the alexandrine, producing an effect quite unlike the facetious or frivolous treatments of the theme of Nothing in the eighteenth century. The weight, however, is not that of dignity and order, but of an almost heroic chaos. The triplets, in fact, may provide a prosodic equivalent of the moral and cosmological chaos they prescribe.

By 1675, when the heroic couplet had become the dominant meter for heroic or epic poetry,[72] the triplet was felt to be a violation of couplet order. It was nonetheless used by Dryden and his contemporaries, probably for a variety of reasons — to achieve variation, intensity or emphasis, conclusiveness,[73] and also (no doubt) for convenience. Dryden found triplets (with an alexandrine in the third line) especially useful in his late translations, where, as he says, they enable the translator to "bound the sense" of Latin hexameters and also to lend "majesty" to the verse.[74] Triplets may have also been used, however, to suggest a kind of violated order. In Dryden's earlier couplet poems, triplets often carry suggestions of the low or colloquial (they occur frequently in "MacFlecknoe," "The Medal," and

72. By this date it had probably supplanted the ABAB quatrain, thought to be particularly "heroic" in mid-century poems. The couplet was used in *Davideis* (1656), *Cooper's Hill* (1642, 1655), Waller's "Panegyric on Cromwell" (1655), and, as Dryden remarks in 1672, in almost every heroic play (*Of Dramatic Poesy*, ed. Watson, [n. 3 above] 1:156).

73. See Conrad Balliet, "The History and Rhetoric of the Triplet," *PMLA*, 80 (1965), 528–534.

74. Dedication to the *Aeneis*.

"The Hind and the Panther")[75] or of chaos. In a satire rightly called "heroic," Achitophel's overflowing energy and the threat to order he represents are conveyed in a triplet —

> A fiery soul, which, working out its way,
> Fretted the pygmy body to decay,
> And o'erinformed the tenement of clay

— which literally "o'erinforms" the couplet measure. Later Dryden says of Achitophel,

> To compass this the triple bond he broke,
> The pillars of the public safety shook,
> And fitted Israel for a foreign yoke.

Not all eight triplets in the poem describe disorder, but in three cases [76] broken order (both original order — the tenement of clay, the triple bond — and violation — fretted, broke, shook) seem strongly stressed, as if Dryden felt here that prosody suited sense.

Rochester often uses triplets in his couplet satires, sometimes to lend speed to the flowing tide, often (to be sure) out of carelessness. But in "Upon Nothing" triplets (with alexandrine) seem to be used with particular appropriateness. Perhaps Rochester sensed that the extra rhyme and extra foot suggested to Restoration readers the threat to order that Achitophel and (above all) Nothing might embody. Then, too, having already, in the mock-heroic "Maimed Debauchee," parodied the heroic poem in rhymed quatrains, he here, in a mock-panegyric, may have intended to parody the other heroic measure, the couplet, by continually violating it.

In some satire, negative feelings of blame and a sense of chaos are balanced by positive feelings of implied praise and a sense of order. But "Upon Nothing" allows us to infer

75. See Balliet, "The History and Rhetoric of the Triplet," 530–531.
76. See also ll. 704–706.

nothing about positive standards, projects its gloomy vision on no ground of certainties. If, as Wimsatt has argued ("The Augustan Mode," *ELH*, 20 [1953], p. 9), "The peculiar feat of the Augustan poet was the art of teasing unreality with the redeeming force of wit — of casting upon a welter of unreal materials a light of order and a perspective vision," then this poem is profoundly un-Augustan; it casts no light of order. It is rather, to adapt Hazlitt's fine phrase, a poem of sublime contempt.[77]

Rochester and Swift

"Upon Nothing" displays a Rochester more like Swift than Pope, who rarely makes an unsettling challenge to his reader, but rather tends to establish an alliance of shared moral certainty with him. Swift and Rochester, on the contrary, seek to make a reader unsure of his moral bearings, to keep him off balance by asking provocative questions rather than assuring him of the sharp distinctions between good and evil. The essential continuity between Rochester and Swift — whose intellectual and literary roots in the Restoration have recently been re-emphasized [78] — lies more in satiric temperament than (as with Pope) in technique and style.

The one clear borrowing is a major one: the definition of happiness in the "Digression on Madness" as a "perpetual possession of being well deceived" derives from "Artemisia to Chloe" — "the perfect joy of being well deceived." Swift was interested, too, in Rochester's versification. The famous ending to the "Description of a City Shower" —

77. "[Rochester's] contempt for everything that others respect almost amounts to sublimity. His poem upon Nothing is itself no trifling work." *Lectures on the English Poets and the English Comic Writers*, ed. W. C. Hazlitt (London, 1870), p. 110.

78. See K. Williams, "Restoration Themes in the Major Satires of Swift," *RES*, 10 (1965), 258–271, and I. Ehrenpreis, *Swift: The Man, His Works, and the Age*, vol. 1 (London, 1962).

Sweepings from butcher's stalls, dung, guts and blood,
Drown'd puppies, stinking sprats, all drench'd in mud,
Dead cats and turnip tops come tumbling down the flood.

— owes a clear debt to the triplet with alexandrine in "Upon
Nothing," and especially the tumbling torrent of the
conclusion. Though Swift boasted that by his triplet upon
a ridiculous subject he had banished what he considered a
vicious way of rhyming (the "mere effect of Haste, Idleness,
and Want of Money" in bad versifiers),[79] he probably ex-
cluded Rochester's poem from his contempt, perhaps because he, too, sensed that triplets were an appropriate measure for describing the rush and tumble of chaos, whether
in the cosmos or a city street.[80]

More significant than borrowings, however, are some simi-
latries in technique, tone, satirical target, and temperament.[81] Both satirists, for example, are fascinated and repulsed (more strongly than Pope) by the corrupt or decaying
physicality of the female body. The aging host's wife in
"Timon," the sterile women in "Tunbridge Wells," Chloris
of the pigsty, and the swollen and dirtied women in obscene
lyrics prefigure the women in Swift's dressing-room poems
("The Lady's Dressing Room," "Upon a Beautiful Young
Nymph Going to Bed") and Sheelah in the coarse mock–
"Pastoral Dialogue." The decline of Corinna into tawdry
decay finds an analogue in the fate of Swift's Corinna:

79. *Correspondence*, ed. Ball (London, 1913), 5:162, and the note in
Swift's Poems, ed. H. Williams (2nd ed., Oxford, 1958), 1:139–140.
80. Swift seems to have admired the poem. It is transcribed (in
Swift's hand) into his interleaved copy of Harward's *Almanack* (*Swift's
Poems*, ed. H. Williams, 3:1059). The "Letter from Wharton" speaks of
Rochester's "excellent poem upon Nothing" (*Political Tracts, 1711–
1713*, ed. H. Davis [Oxford, 1951], p. 153).
81. I have been unable to give much substance to Ronald Paulson's
suggestion that Rochester "is much closer to the Swift of the popular
ballads and the Irish satires than to Dryden and Pope (Review of
ARP, Journal of English and Germanic Philology, 63 [1964], 361), although the rollicking coarseness of these poems recalls Rochester's
lighter lampoons and ballad-measure poems.

At twelve, a Wit, and a Coquette;
  Marries for Love, half Whore, half Wife;
Cuckolds, elopes, and runs in debt;
  Turns auth'ress, and is Curll's for life.[82]

and in that of Phyllis and Celia of the progress poems —
Phyllis, who marries the butler, pawns her trinkets, breaks
her marriage vows, gets the pox, and turns landlord's wife
and whore; Celia, whose daily repairs at toilet eventually
fall behind her beauty's relentless decay ("The Progress of
Love," "The Progress of Beauty"). However, whereas Rochester's response to female decay is essentially that of a libertine — disgust at age and determination to enjoy beauty's
youth and cleanliness while they last — Swift's range of response is wider. In the Stella poems and some few others
he balances disgust with wry Platonic flights, and with genuine and loving praise of good women like Biddy Floyd.[83]
When Swift does become obscene, he no more seeks to
titillate than does Rochester. Although Swift's obscenity
sometimes seems to have literary purpose, either as parody
of stale conventions of praise, or as satire against the fashion
of praising women for their physical beauty alone,[84] some of
his bawdiness can be set down as Rabelaisian coarse fun or
as neurotic obsession. With Rochester, whose obscenity is
more copulative than excremental, literary purpose, as we
have seen, seems to count for less than in Swift, delight in
coarseness, and perhaps a neurotic loathing, for more.

Another affinity between Rochester and Swift is the burlesque tone and mode of their poetry. Rochester burlesques
the pastoral, the heroic, and at times the love-lyric modes
and attitudes in a spirit of raucous irreverence. Swift's, too,
is a "burlesque style," degrading and ridiculing what previous poets have elevated and honored: the "love song in the

82. "Corinna," ll. 25–28, *Swift's Poems*, ed. H. Williams, 1:150.
83. *Swift's Poems*, ed. H. Williams, 1:118.
84. Irvin Ehrenpreis, *The Personality of Jonathan Swift* (Cambridge,
Mass., 1958), pp. 29–49.

modern taste," the eclogue, the mythological love poem. One of the effects of Swift's burlesque verse, and of his more bitter satires ("The Legion Club," for example), is to corrode by constant irony that complacency and blind pride in human enterprise which he finds characteristic (and despicable) in the Yahoo species. Rochester's satiric tone, particularly in "Upon Nothing," "Tunbridge Wells," and the "Satyr Against Mankind," is equally acid. He often sounds La Rochefoucauld's cynical note, and the *Maximes*, it is well known, were admired by Swift.

The most corrosive feelings in both Rochester's and Swift's poems take the form of misanthropy, and it is here that most readers will feel their similarity. Rochester's savage denunciations of mankind are equaled, for example, in Swift's "Day of Judgment," where the satirist's contempt of proud Man is transferred to an angry God:

> Offending race of human kind
> By nature, reason, learning, blind;
> You who thro' frailty step'd aside;
> And you who never fell — thro' Pride
> . . . .
> The world's mad business now is o'er,
> And I resent these pranks no more.
> I to such blockheads set my wit!
> I damn such fools! — Go, go, you're bit.

The theriophilic strain in Rochester's "Satyr" likewise reappears in Swift's "Beasts' Confession to the Priest" —

> Creatures of ev'ry kind but ours
> Well comprehend their nat'ral pow'rs;
> While we, whom reason ought to sway,
> Mistake our talents ev'ry day

— in which the satirist concludes with the sardonic admission that now and then "Beasts may degen'rate into Men."

Likewise, in "Tunbridge Wells," which contrasts ridiculous man, priding himself with "noise of reason," and the horse, void of reason and of foppery, yet "wiser" and "happier," Rochester may have had in mind the common logician's examples of rational man and irrational horse, which R. S. Crane has persuasively presented as the tradition of ideas behind the contrast in the Fourth Voyage between Houyhnhnms and Yahoos.[85] The effect of Swiftian and Rochesterian satire is similar but not identical: both attack the complacency of that vain animal who is so proud of being rational. Rochester admits man is a rational creature, yet finds beasts wiser and more "humane." Reason in Rochester only corrupts; his "right reason" is an impossibility. Swift, on the other hand, shows the falsity of the definition *homo est animal rationale* by imagining a truly rational animal. The reason that governs the Houyhnhnms is a more comprehensive faculty than Rochester's libertine governor of appetite. But Swift no less than Rochester shows man as truly incapable of attaining such reason. Both see the wanton treachery of rational man as more savage than the natural hostility of beasts: "When a creature pretending to reason could be capable of such enormities, he dreaded lest the corruption of that faculty might be worse than brutality itself" (*Gulliver's Travels*, 4:5).

The spectacle of mankind provokes in both poets Juvenalian outrage and profound disgust. What Leavis said of Swift's characteristic irony might even better be said of Rochester: "We have, then, in his writings probably the most remarkable expression of negative feelings and attitudes that literature can offer — the spectacle of creative powers (the paradoxical description seems right) exhibited

85. R. S. Crane, "The Houyhnhnms, the Yahoos, and the History of Ideas," *Reason and the Imagination: Studies in the History of Ideas, 1600–1800*, ed. J. A. Mazzeo (New York, 1962), pp. 245–248. Crane shows the horse-man distinction to be a cliché of seventeenth-century elementary logics. At Oxford, Rochester would almost certainly have at least begun a course in logic.

consistently in negation and rejection." [86] Both satirists are better at attacking than proposing an ideal. But here Rochester needs to be carefully distinguished from Swift. The latter satirist, though he sees horrors, is not finally an utter nihilist and cynic.[87] Swift does have "positives." Even those critics who recognize rightly the "subversive" in Swift agree that his moral vision rests "on some great commonplaces of Christian and humanist thought." [88] Although he would have been attracted by Rochester's skepticism and paradoxes he would have condemned his libertinism and disbelief. Swift, for whom free-thinkers are no thinkers at all ("Letter to a Young Gentleman"), remains a believer and an idealist. Although, like Rochester (and like all the Augustans), he is aware of a gap between ideals and actual experience, he retains a belief in an ideal world "beyond material sense." That world may be unattainable, in the same way that the Houyhnhnms are beyond human possibility, but it remains as a utopian "city in the mind," a constant measure of the compromises one must make in order to live in the world.[89] For Swift, in other words, there is at least a relation between "the realms of the actual and of the ideal," [90] whereas for Rochester, any ideal, like generosity or right reason, is not only impossibly remote, but obliterated by the absolute necessity of single-mindedly playing the world's knavish game in order to survive.

86. "The Irony of Swift," *The Common Pursuit* (Peregrine edition, 1962), p. 86.

87. Swift scholars will recognize my debt to John Traugott and C. J. Rawson, whose several essays on Swift have largely shaped my view of him. I do not pretend to offer a complete picture of Swift, only a sketch. My chief interest is in illuminating by contrast Rochester's peculiar pessimism.

88. C. J. Rawson, "The Character of Swift's Satire," in *Focus: Swift*, ed. Rawson (London, 1971), p. 22.

89. John Traugott, "A Voyage to Nowhere with Thomas More and Jonathan Swift," *Swift: A Collection of Critical Essays*, ed. E. Tuveson (Englewood Cliffs, 1964), p. 160.

90. *Ibid.*, p. 169.

Swift differs from Rochester not only in his idealism, but in his pragmatism as well. He keeps one eye on an absolute realm and the other on the daily business of living. He is perfectly willing to arrange necessary compromises and rig up *ad hoc* arrangements,[91] and implicitly to recommend decent men — like Munodi and Don Pedro in *Gulliver* — as the best that man can reasonably hope to be. Rochester has no sense of getting on with the business of life. He is far more like Gulliver in the stable than like the Swift who smilingly edges away from his alienated and incapacitated misanthrope. Through his libertine satirists Rochester can only flee in disgust from foolish man, or fly in reaction from "right reason" to knavery; he can imagine no middle ground.

Swift is then less intellectually dispiriting than Rochester; the effect of his satire is also more positively invigorating. He evokes in us both disgust and delight. The bleakness of his moral vision is in part lightened by the fantastic fertility of imagination,[92] the inventiveness, the suppleness, the inexhaustibly witty mind playing with the inexhaustible vagaries of a mad world. Rochester, by contrast, evokes much disgust but little delight. The pleasure in reading him is rarely unmixed with a rueful wince. The relentless energy and forcefulness of the "Satyr Against Mankind" and "Upon Nothing" are neither ebullient nor inspiriting. We can admire and to some degree share the witty mastery of their unblinking perception and expression of the world's baseness. But one has a sense not of zany fertility but of a severely focused power. The result (in the reader) is certainly not inert despair (else why would Rochester continue to be read?) but an actively unsettled mind.

91. Emphasized throughout Rawson's "The Character of Swift's Satire."

92. A point made in Traugott's essay on "A Tale of a Tub," in *Focus: Swift*, ed. C. J. Rawson, pp. 114–115.

Rochester and Restoration Drama

After looking ahead into the eighteenth century, it is appropriate, at the close, to return Rochester to his Restoration context, in part to re-emphasize that no poetic talent, even one so individual as Rochester's, exists in a vacuum. His achievement is seen most clearly when considered in relation to the works of the age. His natural affinities, in fact, are not with the satirists Butler, Marvell, and Dryden, but with the comic playwrights, especially Etherege and Wycherley.

Some aspects of Rochester's relations with Restoration drama have already been suggested. His activities as patron of dramatists, as critic of the drama, and as contributor of epilogues are well known from standard biographies. So, too, is the inspiration he provided for the dramatists. Contemporaries believed that Etherege's Dorimant, perhaps the most famous of the stage rakes, was modeled on Rochester.[93] Less known is that in Lee's *Princess of Cleve* (1680), Rochester, as the recently dead "Count Rosidore," is remembered by the play's rake, Nemours, as "the Spirit of Wit," [94] and taken by him as a model. It is possible that the witty and cynical Nemours is meant by Lee to embody the darker side of Rochester's character, as Rosidore embodies the brighter. By calling Nemours "the Rising Star" [95] he perhaps puns on both "Rosidore" and "Rochester." Nemours himself quotes the words of "Rosidore in the Urn" on "lovely extreams," "the Spirit of Wit lying in the extravagance of pleasure," and "Fury" that leads one to defy death.[96]

93. See *Critical Works of John Dennis*, ed. E. N. Hooker (Baltimore, 1943), 2:248.

94. Act II, sc. 1 in *The Works of Nathaniel Lee*, ed. T. B. Stroup and A. L. Cooke, 2 vols. (New Brunswick, 1955), 2:162.

95. Act III, sc. 2 in *ibid.*, 2:192.

96. Act III, sc. 1 in *ibid.*, 1:188. Nemours may have in mind "Upon Nothing" and "After death nothing is" when he says of Rosidore: "I saw the mighty thing a nothing made, and swept to that cold Den,

Also well known is Rochester's deep personal interest in impersonation (best exemplified in the famous Alexander Bendo incident). I have also sought to show his interest in a related theatrical practice, self-projection, not so much a disguise as a calculated extension of self into the series of libertines in his satires. That Rochester had a deep interest in and knowledge of stage acting is suggested by the old story that he transformed Elizabeth Barry from a girl with neither beauty nor talent into one of the greatest actresses of the period.

It is perhaps not so surprising, then, that Rochester tried his hand at playwriting — both heroic drama (the unfinished adaptation of Fletcher's *Valentinian*[97], and the scene from Howard's *Conquest of China*) and prose comedy (the fragmentary scene set in "Mr. Daynty's Chamber"). It is surprising, perhaps, that he was attracted as a dramatist more to heroic drama than to comedy. Perhaps he wanted to show he was capable of matching Dryden on his own terms. As J. H. Wilson has shown,[98] he remodeled Fletcher's play to incorporate contemporary heroic sentiment. For the chaste heroine, Lucina, Rochester added a pastoral idyll (3:2), for Maximus the hero and Valentinian the villain he added fine speeches of heroic rant (5:5).

Perhaps Rochester was drawn to Fletcher's play because, as Wilson has also suggested,[99] he saw some resemblance between the lecherous Valentinian and Charles II, between

where Kings lye crumbled just like other men." II, 1 in *ibid.*, 2:162. In *Nero*, IV, 3, Lee translates the same passage from Seneca (*ibid.*, 1:56).

97. The adaptation was done some time during Rochester's last years. Wolseley says Rochester intended to alter and correct the play more completely (preface to *Valentinian*, in Spingarn, 3:1). He altered the beginning and ending of Fletcher's play, omitted three scenes from the middle of the play and virtually all of Fletcher's Act 5, and added two new scenes of his own.

98. "Rochester's *Valentinian* and Heroic Sentiment," *ELH*, 4 (1937), 265–273.

99. "Satiric Elements in Rochester's *Valentinian*," *PQ*, 16 (1937), 41–48.

the Emperor's philosophical-minded favorite, Maximus,
and himself. The alterations in Valentinian's character may
have been made to increase the resemblance. Charles's famous leniency, for example, may be reflected in Maximus's
description of the Emperor in Act 1:

> Yet even his errors have their good effects,
> For the same gentle temper which inclines
> His mind to softness, does his heart defend
> From savage thoughts of cruelty and blood,
> Which through the streets of Rome in streams did flow
> From hearts of senators under the reigns
> Of our severer warlike emperors!
> While under this scarcely one criminal
> Meets the hard sentence of the dooming law,
> And the whole world dissolv'd into a peace,
> Owes its security to this man's pleasures.
> [Hayward, *Collected Works*, p. 167]

He may have felt the heroic play offered a suitable medium
for his imagination's visions of chaos and violence.

> In what fantastic new world have I been?
> What horrors past? What threat'ning visions seen?
> Wrapt as I lay in my amazing trance,
> The host of heav'n and hell did round me dance.
> . . . .
> Misshapen monsters round in measures went
> Horrid in form with gestures insolent;
> Grinning through goatish beards with half clos'd eyes,
> They look'd me in the face, frighted to rise!
> In vain I did attempt, methought no ground
> Was to support my sinking footsteps found.
> In clammy fogs like one half choak'd I lay,
> Crying for help my voice was snatch'd away.
> [3:3, pp. 192–193]

Compare with these lines the translation of Seneca and the horror in the lines on the ignis fatuus. With the translation from Lucretius and "Upon Nothing," compare Maximus's challenge to the heavens:

> Supreme first causes! you, whence all things flow,
> Whose infiniteness does each little fill,
>
> . . . .
>
> Had your eternal minds been bent to good,
> Could humane happiness have prov'd so lame?
> Rapine, Revenge, Injustice, thirst of Blood,
> Grief, Anguish, Horror, Want, Despair and Shame,
> Had never found a Being nor a Name.
>
> 'Tis therefore less impiety to say,
> Evil with you has Coeternity,
> Than blindly taking it the other way,
> That merciful and of election free,
> You did create the mischiefs you foresee.
>
> [4:3, p. 215]

Far less known, however, than Rochester's activity as patron, critic, model, or dramatist, is the pervasive relation between his poems, both satires and lyrics, and contemporary plays. As H. M. Richmond has shown, during the period there was a close connection between the love lyric and the drama.[100] Dorimant often has the words of Waller on his lips; Millamant, like Timon's wife in Rochester's poem, praises "natural, easy Suckling." As Wycherley's Sparkish says, all men write songs: "Everybody does it. 'Tis even as common with lovers, as playing with fans; and you can no more help rhyming to your Phyllis, than drinking to your Phyllis" (*The Country Wife*, 3:2).

Just as Rochester as song writer may have inspired the dramatists, so his satires seem to have been inspired by

100. *The School of Love* (Princeton, 1964), pp. 264–273.

some stage traditions, and share with stage comedies some settings, type characters, and assumptions. Rochester's satires often etablish a dramatic situation in a specific setting. Even the "Satyr Against Mankind," as I have suggested, seems to call forth a scene in the streets of London. "The Maimed Debauchee" implies a tavern setting, common in the comedies. "Artemisia to Chloe" takes place largely in a ladies' drawing room, a common stage setting and situation, as in *The Country Wife* (2:1), or *The Way of the World*, where ladies gather to sit in judgment on jealous men and the reputations of women. The same poem makes use of the standard opposition between lively, sophisticated town and simple, quiet country which informs much stage comedy — *The Country Wife* and *The Man of Mode*, for example — and forms the basis of a minor genre, the letter between correspondents in town and country. Two other satires, "St. James's Park" and "Tunbridge Wells," seem to grow out of stage traditions.

In at least two stage comedies written just prior to "St. James's Park," part of the action unfolds in the Park, and in the nearby Mall and Mulberry Garden, a public garden adorned with shrubberies, walks, and arbors, and frequented by fashionable courtiers and citizens alike. The wide variety of social activities conducted there is suggested in Sedley's *The Mulberry Garden* (1668), where Wildish and Modish hunt beauties only to find citizens picnicking, and settle for a bottle of Rhenish. Night, however, apparently fulfilled the expectations of wits like Wildish, for in Wycherley's *Love in a Wood: or St. James's Park* (1671) the Park is several times the scene of a midnight sexual chase. Either by stage convention or as a reflection of the truth, the Park had evidently become a place for hunting women, whether in the course of drinking or of sobering up. Eager women, of course, like Rochester's Corinna, knew of the Park's reputation as well. Wycherley's Lady Flippant, a husband-hungry widow, tries to lure first Sir Simon Addleplot, a coxcomb, and then Dapperwit, a young brisk (2:1). Returning to the Park at night "on purpose to be chased," she finds "not so much as a satyr" will accost her: "No Burgundy man or drunken scourer will reel my way. The rag-women, and cinder-women, have better luck than I" (5:2). It is on this stage tradition, and probably on the truth it reflects, that Rochester's satire draws.[101]

"Tunbridge Wells," likewise, shows affinities with the contemporary watering-place play. Rochester, it is true, had very likely been to Tunbridge Wells, or a similar spa, for treatment of his varied illnesses. The poem shows a knowledge of the topography of the area. With personal experiences, however, he seems to have combined descriptions of watering-places in stage comedy. Shadwell's *Epsom Wells,* the first English watering-place comedy, very popular with the Court, was printed in February 1673/74, some three or four months before "Tunbridge Wells" was written. Rochester's poem shows his familiarity with Shadwell's play, a gay comedy with the usual Restoration mixture of men and ladies of wit, cuckolded citizens, a discontented old country justice, a husband-hunter, and two cowardly bullies. The last are named Cuff and Kick, and appear as brawny blades in "Tunbridge Wells." Like Shadwell's play, Rochester's poem begins with a reference to heavy drinking the night before. But the differences between the two pieces are

101. In a number of plays written after his poem, scenes take place in St. James's Park: *The Mall: or the Modish Lovers* (1674) by "J. D."; *The Man of Mode* (1675–1676), 3:3; Otway's *Friendship in Fashion* (1678), 1:1, and *The Soldier's Fortune* (1679–1680); Congreve's *The Old Bachelor* (1692–1693), 4:4 and 5, and *The Way of the World* (1700), 2:1; and an anonymous play, *St. James's Park* (1733).

The stage tradition gave birth, apparently, to a minor satiric tradition of poems about St. James's Park, of which Rochester's poem is the earliest exemplar. *St. James's Park: A Satyr*, attributed to [?]Browne, appeared in 1708. The speaker, definitely not a libertine, surveys the conventional kinds of fops, rakes, cits, footmen, and apes of the nobility to be found in the Park, contrasting them with the good, honest, modest, and graceful men and women whom he names.

greater than the similarities; where Shadwell's play is a light comedy about cuckoldry and marriage, Rochester's has moved beyond gay libertinism to bitterness and harsh scorn.[102]

His satires share type characters as well as settings with the comic stage. Both have their full share of fools, fops, knaves, decaying lustful ladies; the poems of Butler, Marvell, and Dryden, however, with political or religious targets, usually do not. Rochester's Maimed Debauchee was probably a familiar figure in many early comedies, as Shadwell complains in the preface to the *Royal Shepherdess* (1669): "I find, it pleases most to see Vice encouraged, by bringing the characters of debauched People upon the Stage, and making them pass for fine Gentlemen who openly profess Swearing, Drinking, Whoring, breaking Windows, beating Constables, etc."It is almost as if Rochester perversely wrote his poem to Shadwell's order, stimulated afresh, perhaps, by the remark in *The Country Wife* (published in 1675, the year of "The Maimed Debauchee," but acted earlier) that "an old maimed general, when unfit for action, is fittest for counsel" (3:2).

The woman of fashion, likewise, figures in Rochester's poems and on the stage. "Artemisia to Chloe" follows the Restoration fashion of mocking those who ape the mode. Two of the best stage comedies of the 1670s, Dryden's *Marriage à la Mode* (1672) and Etherege's *The Man of Mode* (1675), satirize, in their subplots, the type who obsessively affects the latest (French) fashion in dress and speech — Melantha in Dryden's play and Sir Fopling Flutter in Etherege's. Vieth has pointed out that Rochester's fine lady resembles Melantha — "both women are hyperconscious of social norms, loquacious, and fond of affected French terms

102. Several watering-place comedies followed Rochester's poem: *Tunbridge-Wells: or, A Day's Courtship* (c. 1676–1678), attributed to Thomas Rawlins; *Wexford Wells* (1721), by Concannon; *Richmond Wells* (1722), by John Williams.

as well as the expression 'Let me die' "[103] — and elsewhere has noted that both Etherege and Rochester suggest that the true fop is a product of art, not nature.[104]

Satire on fashion-conscious country ladies (always a year behind the town) also links Rochester, Dryden, and Etherege. Rochester's fine lady asks "who are the men most worn of late," relating that fools were in fashion when she was married (ll. 101–107). In *Marriage à la Mode* country ladies are said to "live this year upon last year's knowledge" (3:1). And in *The Man of Mode* Welsh ladies visiting London ask Bellinda "a thousand questions of the modest intrigues of the town, and I have told 'em almost as many things for news that hardly were so when their gowns were in fashion."

Two other conventional figures, the libertine rake and the railer, seem to evoke in Rochester's poems and contemporary plays a more complex response. Dorimant's cruel and imperious disposal of Loveit in *The Man of Mode* resembles the almost exactly contemporaneous disposal of Ephelia by Bajazet in the "Heroical Epistle."

> We are not masters of our own affections; our
> inclinations daily alter. Now we love pleasure,
> and anon we shall dote on business. Human frailty
> will have it so, and who can help it?
>
> .   .   .   .
>
> Constancy at my years? 'Tis not a virtue in season;
> you might as well expect the fruit the autumn ripens
> i' the spring.
>
> .   .   .   .
>
> What we swear at such a time may be a certain proof
> of a present passion, but to say truth, in love there
> is no security to be given for the future.
>
> [Act 2]

103. *Complete Poems*, p. 106n.
104. "Etherege's 'Man of Mode' and Rochester's 'Artemisia to Chloe,' " *N & Q*, 203 (1958), 473–474.

The conventional libertine arguments, wittily advanced by Bajazet and Dorimant, make us feel both discomfort (at the brutality and pain) and delight (in the performance, the rake following his "type").

The Restoration railer derives, probably, from malcontents like Malevole and Vendice, creations (significantly) of writers — Marston and Tourneur — who turned from verse satire to satiric drama after the 1590s. These railers, like Shakespeare's Timon, are foul-mouthed and vindictive, yet speak bitter truth. After the Restoration, interest in railers was perhaps reinvigorated by Molière's *Misanthrope* (1666), but it seems to have taken several years before English dramatists did more than laugh at them. In Shadwell's *The Sullen Lovers* (1668) two young misanthropes are mercilessly mocked; in Wycherley's *Gentleman Dancing Master* (1672), Shadwell's *The Virtuoso* (1676), and Etherege's *The Man of Mode* (1676), those who rail against "the deprav'd appetite of this vicious Age," Mrs. Caution, Snarl, and Lady Woodvil, are clearly meant to be ill-natured old fools, either privately vicious or unable to enjoy the pleasure they therefore condemn. Railing in Restoration comedy up to about 1676 (the date of Rochester's "Satyr") exhibits an excess of feeling and therefore becomes suspect. In that year, however, the appearance of Wycherley's *The Plain Dealer* marks a turning point, of sorts, in attitude.[105] Adapted from the *Misanthrope*, this play presents a protagonist, Manly, who like Alceste is seen on the one hand as credulous and self-deceived, though morosely vain of his perspicuity, and on the other as a bluntly honest man plagued by knaves and fools. The significance of Wycherley's play for Rochester's poems, particularly the "Satyr," is not so much that it makes railing attractive in literature as that it signals among Resoration readers and audiences a deeper interest in the am-

105. As Anne Righter has argued in "William Wycherley," *Restoration Theatre*, ed. J. R. Brown and B. Harris (New York, 1967), pp. 71–92.

bivalent figure of the railer, which Rochester was able to feed.

The interest in railing grew in drama and satire alike. Shadwell's adaptation of Shakespeare's *Timon* appeared in 1678. Other playwrights, following in Wycherley's footsteps, found further use for railers,[106] or railed at the age themselves, as Lee does in the prologue to *The Princess of Cleve* (1680):

> since that Law and Treachery came in,
> And open Honesty was made a Sin,
> Men wait for Men as Dogs for Foxes prey,
> And Women wait the closing of the day.
> There's scarce a man that ventures to be good,
> For Truth by Knaves was never understood.
> [ll. 7–12]

Rochester too, as we have seen, rails at the universal corruption of the age in letter and satire alike. But the railers in his poems — the "Satyr," "Timon," and "Tunbridge Wells" — are viewed with some ambivalence. Perhaps as railing became first acceptable and then fashionable (and therefore a prime target for mockery) in life and on stage, so in Rochester's poems the railer satirizes ridiculous humanity only to become himself the object of satire.

In some less specific ways, too, Rochester's satires ask to be considered together with Restoration comedies. Many common assumptions (if not explicit themes) seem to underlie them. The wit's disgust at the female practice of taking fools for lovers unites Dorimant's withering scorn at Loveit's alleged dalliance with Sir Fopling Flutter — "To be publicly so transported with the vain follies of that notorious fop, to me is an infamy below the sin of prostitution with another man" (*The Man of Mode*, 5:2) and Loveit's defense of

106. See, for example, the attacks on the general profligacy of the times in *The Country Wife* (1675) and Otway's *The Atheist* (1683), 1:1.

morophilia — with "St. James's Park" and "Artemisia to Chloe."[107] The hatred of fools for poets and wits is another common assumption. Compare the "Satyr" —

> Women and men of wit are dangerous tools,
> And ever fatal to admiring fools
>
> . . . .
>
> And therefore what they fear at heart, they hate

— with the wouldwit Sparkish in *The Country Wife*, who hates poets, finds fault, and thinks himself wittier than they (3:2), or with the prologue to *The Plain Dealer*, where fine gentlemen are said to hate poets, like friends to whom they are in debt, like dupes who laugh "to see undone / Those pushing gamesters whom they live upon." Indeed the image cluster of bubbles and cheats (often associated with wits and whores) is a recurrent metaphor both in Rochester and in comic writers (especially Etherege and Wycherley) for the deceptions and exploitations men practice on each other.[108] Compare the "Satyr" —

> Mankind's dishonest; if you think it fair
> Amongst known cheats to play upon the square,
> You'll be undone.

— with Freeman in *The Plain Dealer*: "Telling truth is a quality as prejudicial to a man that would thrive in the world, as square play to a cheat, or true love to a whore!" (1:1), or with Dorimant's cynical advice to Loveit: "You have an indifferent stock of reputation left yet. Lose it all like a frank gamester on the square; 'twill then be time

107. See Vieth, "Etherege's 'Man of Mode,'" *N & Q*, 203 (1958), 473–474. In *The Country Wife*, 5:3, Alithea, once a devotee, now denounces the practice of marrying fools.

108. In the prologue to *The Way of the World*, "Poets are bubbles, by the town drawn in, / Suffered at first some trifling stakes to win. / But what unequal hazards do they run! / Each time they write they venture all they've won."

enough to turn rook and cheat it up again on a good substantial bubble" (*The Man of Mode*, 5:1). Dorimant, in effect, admits that the frank (or honest) people lose, that only cheats (like Rochester's Corinna) win.[109]

In style and structure, too, Rochester's satires, both for their "talky" couplets (especially in "Artemisia to Chloe") and their episodic quality (especially "Tunbridge Wells") have affinities with comic drama. A number of his satires — "The Maimed Debauchee," "Timon," "St. James's Park," "Artemisia to Chloe" — might be narrative versions of a scene from a possible play.

Finally, Rochester's satires and Restoration drama seem to share what has been called "the paradoxical ethic of the Restoration," a "sentimental nostalgia for the heroic" imposed on "an obsessive commitment to naturalism," [110] the former typically expressing itself in panegyric (like Rochester's earliest extant poem) [111] and heroic drama (like *Valentinian*), the latter in stage comedy and satire. But satire and stage comedy themselves seem to express that paradoxical ethic. In the poems, an ideal of conduct seems, as I have argued, placed within a real and "worldly" context, where it is made to appear remote and unrealizable. The same dichotomy and sense of inappropriateness characterizes some of the best stage comedies.

As is well known, for instance, the stage rake (Dorimant, Horner, Freeman) stands often in contrast to his young, well-bred friend (Bellair, Harcourt, Manly). The former is often

109. Compare Shadwell's *Epsom Wells*, 2:1:
Woodly.   "But there are some left that can love upon the square."
Carolina.   "A woman may be undone upon the square, as well as a
          gamester, if she ventures too much."
(*Complete Works of Shadwell*, ed. Montague Summers [London, 1926],
2:123).

110. John Traugott, "The Rake's Progress from Court to Comedy,"
Studies in English Literature, 6 (1966), 396.

111. The panegyric on the restored Charles, "Virtue's triumphant
shrine."

witty, cynical, without principles, and a philanderer; the latter not quite so witty, sincere, principled, and bent on honorable marriage. Our response to both figures is somewhat ambivalent. By the standards of naturalism and of his hypocritical society, the rake is attractive. By the same standards the foil seems without fire or force.[112] Yet, by the foil's plain-dealing principles the rake seems vicious. At play's end the foil often marries a virtuous young lady (Emilia, Alithea, Fidelia) while the rake escapes unpunished (Horner, Freeman) or promises to reform (Dorimant). The rake's reform must have struck contemporary audiences, as it does ours, as an unconvincing attempt to force a resolution of the two contrasting ideals in favor of principles and marriage. Where the rake escapes, the virtuous pair do not strike the audience as the focus of the play's moral scheme, or of the world the play realizes. In either case, the ideal which the comic dramatists seem to advance at play's end seems simply out of place in the world which the plays themselves have so richly presented. This presence of an "ideal" within a "realistic" situation, found by one recent critic to be true of all great Restoration comedies, has been labeled a symptom of approaching sentimentalism.[113] On the contrary, I would say that such an unbridgeable gap between actual and ideal is central to Restoration comedy, as it is to Rochester's satires. While the comic dramatists find this gap to be cause for fairly good-natured ironic laughter, Rochester typically responds to it with darker mockery and disgust. Even in Wycherley, the harshest of the dramatists and the most like a satirist, the plays remain comedies. Manners provide a social link between rake and honest virgin; Alithea and Horner remain friends. The virtuous couple brings some pressure to bear on the rake, but not enough to destroy

112. Manly's case is somewhat different: he is forceful to the point of moroseness, while Freeman is elegantly courteous.

113. Norman Holland, *The First Modern Comedies* (Cambridge, 1959) p. 85.

him. He holds our attention; we continue to delight in his energy and vitality. Though in Rochester the rake commands our interest and sympathy, he is finally a failure. Not so in the drama, where the rake remains triumphant, discomfited perhaps like Horner, but never daunted.

Rochester and Dryden

Although Rochester's closest affinities in the Restoration are to the comic dramatists, no account of his achievement would be complete without comparison with the major writer of his age. Such comparison, furthermore, may serve as a conclusion, by giving a clear idea of Rochester's limits and by showing how Dryden and Rochester, between them, variously reflect the different aspects of their age.

Between a professional middle-class poet and an aristocratic court wit, an Anglican turned Catholic and a libertine freethinker, we expect to find the kind of rivalry and hostility evinced in their well-known quarrel. But if we step back for a moment, differences recede and we can see some similarities. These similarities are not a matter of mutual influence between the two leading poets of the 1670's so much as a result of their common environment. Dryden borrows only insignificantly from his aristocratic rival,[114] but, more generally, shares with Rochester a skeptical, inquiring temper. Dryden's *Religio Laici* (1682) is not influenced by Rochester's "Satyr Against Mankind," but it does spring from the same climate of thought:

> Dim, as the borrow'd beams of moon and stars
> To lonely, weary, wand'ring travelers
> Is Reason to the Soul: and as on high,
> Those rolling fires discover but the sky

114. Compare Dryden's tr. of *De Rerum Natura*, 4:28, with the "Satyr Against Mankind," l. 87; "Absalom and Achitophel," l. 229, with "My Lord All-Pride," l. 2.

Not light us here; so Reason's glimmering ray
Was lent, not to assure our doubtful way,
But guide us upward to a better day.
And as those nightly tapers disappear
When day's bright lord ascends our hemisphere;
So pale grows Reason at Religion's sight;
So dies, and so dissolves in supernatural light.

[ll. 1–11]

Dryden, with other writers and other purposes in mind,[115] both extends and implicitly answers Rochester's attack on reason. For both poets, reason is dim and glimmering. Rochester would not follow its light; Dryden on the other hand would follow it, not like Rochester's stumbler, to find his own "doubtful way," but to be guided upward to another light. As in Rochester's poem, the light of reason disappears or dies; but in Dryden it leaves man not in natural darkness but in the presence of "supernatural light." Dryden counters not only Rochester's metaphor, but also a traditional way of describing the effect of the glaring light of reason on wonders or mysteries (compare Rochester's "For wonder by clear knowledge is destroyed"). For Dryden, the cold light of reason does not dissolve the supernatural; on the contrary, it is itself dissolved.

The difference between these two great passages on the weakness of reason is reflected in the greater difference between the poems. Doubting pure speculative reason, Rochester concentrates his gaze within the empirical limits of man's world. He has a weak sense of the infinite or the eternal, and no idea how to reach out to them. For Dryden, too, finite reason cannot reach infinity; but through faith and revelation, he gains a vision of cosmic order which in-

115. Compare *Aeneid* 6:268–272. Philip Harth (*Contexts of Dryden's Thought* [Chicago, 1968]) compares Richard Burthogge's *Causa Dei* (1675). Harth argues, furthermore (p. 31), against Bredvold, that Dryden's "skepticism is a confident affirmation of the powers of human reason."

cludes man and is partially comprehensible to him. Unlike Rochester, Dryden is not bound within the empirical world.

Yet when Dryden restricts his gaze to the world of empirical experience, he can make one of his characters sound uncannily like Rochester. Compare the underlying metaphor in the "Satyr Against Mankind" and "Artemisia to Chloe" — that man is plagued by cheats and sharps — with the celebrated "complaint of life" in *Aureng-Zebe*:

> When I consider life, 'tis all a cheat;
> Yet, fooled with hope, men favour the deceit;
> Trust on, and think to-morrow will repay:
> To-morrow's falser than the former day;
> Lies worse, and, while it says, we shall be blest
> With some new joys, cuts off what we possest.
> Strange cozenage! None would live past years again,
> Yet all hope pleasure in what yet remain;
> And, from the dregs of life, think to receive,
> What the first sprightly running could not give.
> I'm tired with waiting for this chemic gold,
> Which fools us young, and beggars us when old.
>   [4:1]

In Dryden as in Rochester, men contribute to their own betrayal: they "favour the deceit." Rochester, characteristically not so grave as Dryden is here, shares with him the sense of cozenage and unrewarded living.

Heroic drama, as we have seen, is also a part of Rochester's sensibility. But it is not, except in a fragmentary way, part of his literary achievement, as it is part of Dryden's. Rochester, furthermore, felt much more strongly the "committment to naturalism" and Dryden the "nostalgia for the heroic." On the other hand, it has been held that Dryden did not take heroic drama with complete seriousness. Nell Gwyn's famous epilogue to *Tyrannic Love* suggests that dramatist, actor, and audience all maintained a sense of the ludicrous disparity between stage heroism and court manners.

It has been argued, furthermore, that Dryden used the ideas of power and grandeur chiefly "as a playground for his powers of wit and rhetoric," and that the theme of heroism "also stimulated another side of his nature — his satirical and skeptical spirit." [116] The similarities between Rochester and Dryden, some of them inevitable, some of them surprising, are finally less significant than the differences. A review of those differences will indicate, I think, how Dryden and Rochester between them affirm the salient characteristics of the Restoration and will suggest that, however much both poets spoke to the men of the early eighteenth century, they are chiefly the reflections and reflectors of their own age.

Dryden reflects the heroic impulses of the age, and Rochester the anti-heroic. For Dryden, to write an epic is a life-long goal, an ambition partly satisfied no doubt by his translation of the *Aeneid*. Rochester, to whatever degree he shares the age's "nostalgia for the heroic," more truly mirrors the age's impulse toward travesty, burlesque, and mockery of the heroic and panegyric modes.

To come at the differences from another angle, Dryden's couplet (perhaps because he thought of satire as a species of heroic poetry) [117] is sonorous and noble, the epic strain, learned probably from Virgil and Juvenal,[118] Rochester's is rough and vigorous, clear and lively without Dryden's smoothness and refinement, a conversational strain. Dryden know how to join "The varying verse, the full-resounding line, / The long majestic march, and energy divine" ("Epis-

116. D. W. Jefferson, "The Significance of Dryden's Heroic Plays," *Restoration Drama: Modern Essays in Criticism*, ed. J. Loftis (New York, 1966), pp. 165, 176–177.

117. *Of Dramatic Poesy*, ed. Watson (n. 3 above), 2:149.

118. "Give me leave . . . to say that Virgil could have written sharper satires than either Horace or Juvenal. . . . Juvenal was the greater poet [than Horace], I mean in satire." *Ibid.*, 2:131. Dryden, of course, translated the *Aeneid* and the declamatory satires of Juvenal, while Rochester translated the more conversational Horace.

tle to Augustus" [ll. 267–269]), how to choose "the flowing and the sonorous words, to vary the pauses and adjust the accents, to diversify the cadence, and yet preserve the smoothness of his metre." [119] More careless and hasty, more negligent of correctness than even Dryden,[120] Rochester probably derived his couplet from the conversation of witty gentlemen at Court and in prose comedy.

Stylistically, we can find difference within apparent similarity. Rochester's satires tend to end abruptly, to change direction stylistically or thematically, to fall into set pieces (often of explicitly moral content). "Absalom and Achitophel" and "MacFlecknoe" display the same characteristics, but the set pieces in the one take the form of character sketches (a traditional epic device) and the abrupt ending is a satisfying structural equivalent for the sudden revelation of David's royal power. In the other, the shifts in style are appropriate to mock-heroic, and the abrupt end a witty descent into bathos or a symbolic violation of the ceremony of coronation. But in Rochester, such stylistic discontinuities seem to be a structural equivalent of Rochester's own sense of the discontinuity of experience — the discontinuity between what is desired and what is offered (the disproportion of things), between experienced life and a projected ideal felt to be unrealizable.

Shifting the angle of vision once again, Dryden is a public and political poet, Rochester a poet of narrow private experience. Dryden continually engages in political and religious controversy, Rochester typically scorns public issues.[121] Dryden, for all his skeptical and inquiring temper,

119. Johnson, *Lives*, 1:260.

120. Many of Rochester's triplets, hemistiches, and near-rhymes are probably the result of carelessness. He averages one triplet per twenty lines, Dryden one per thirty-nine lines (in the late translations, one per twenty). Balliet, "The History and Rhetoric of the Triplet," *PMLA*, 80, 533–534.

121. "They who would be great in our little Government, seem as ridiculous to me as School-boys, who with much endeavour, and some

is finally a poet of certainties, or in search of certainties. His great poems ultimately deal with the need for authority in literature, religion, and politics. Rochester stands for those impulses in his time that question or undermine authority, in literature, religion, epistemology, and ethics. More than Dryden, he is in tune with the age's interest in Hobbes, in Epicurus, in Pyrrhonic skepticism, and in the radical empiricism of the *Leviathan* and Locke's *Essay*. With all this Dryden is familiar, but he continually reaffirms an essentially classico-Christian orthodoxy. Rochester, cut loose from orthodoxy, flies to extremes. Typically, Dryden succeeds in projecting an ideal. Rochester, in "Tunbridge Wells," "Upon Nothing," and many of the shorter satirical pieces, projects rejection and negation; in others, the "Satyr Against Mankind," the "Heroical Epistle," "Artemisia to Chloe," and some of the love songs, he envisions an ideal which proves to be unrealizable in a world of cheats and knaves. Despite this sense of failure, Rochester often longs, like Dryden, for some kind of certainty, "some farther prospect of felicity and glory" [122] — in love, in friendship, in sense experience, in religion — but his poetry always conveys a sense that certainty is impossible.

Sociologically viewed, Dryden represents the middle class and the professional writer of the age, Rochester the aristocrat and the amateur poet. Dryden wrote under the conditions of professionalism, and fell, on the one hand, into flattery of his patrons, and on the other, into pandering to the taste of his audience. Rochester, for his part, wrote under the conditions of aristocratic amateurism, allowing himself only occasional fits of study and writing between bouts of debauchery and intrigue. At best half-educated, Rochester can have known far less of "man in his general nature" than Dryden, whose scholastic education, wide-ranging

danger, climb a Crab-tree, venturing their Necks for Fruit which solid Piggs would disdain if they were not starving." *Letters*, p. 41.

122. Hayward, p. 288.

mind, and habits of comprehensive speculation were praised by Johnson.[123] As a consequence of imperfect education and narrow experience, Rochester's poems deal with much less of human experience than Dryden's. On the other hand, they deal far more acutely with libertine aristocratic experience, with the pains of sexual love, and with the tendencies (shared by many now as then) toward skepticism and savage scorn. As a man, Rochester, especially when drunk, was guilty of the vices of his class, cruelty and ill-temper, and a flagrant disregard for any who stood in the way of his pleasure. As a poet, he could afford to be contemptuous of the rabble, caring to please only himself and his friends. The greatness of Rochester, however, is that he was able to transcend the limitations of polite learning, class, and literary amateurism. Perhaps because he was more philosophically minded than his fellow court wits, perhaps because he developed the fortunate habit of withdrawing into the country for intervals of reflection and study, perhaps because he, more than most, was able to redirect a rake's passionate energy and vigor into poetry, he surpassed all noble poets of the age, and all professionals except Dryden, to make a major contribution to our literature.

123. *Lives*, 2:214.

❧ Appendix

Additions to Vieth's "Checklist of Rochester Studies, 1925–1967" (see Complete Poems, pp. lii–lxix)

Berlind, Bruce P. "Studies in Rochester and his Circle." Ph.D. dissertation, Johns Hopkins, 1957.
Some outdated work on Rochester's text and canon. Two chapters of criticism.

Davies, Paul C. "Rochester: Augustan and Explorer," *Durham University Journal*, 30 (1969), 59–64.
Supports Vieth against Erskine-Hill.

————. "Rochester and Boileau: A Reconsideration," *Comparative Literature*, 21 (1969), 348–355.
Restates the case for Boileau's influence on the "Satyr."

————. "Who Wrote 'In Defence of Satyr'?" *Etudes anglaises*, 23 (1970), 410–414.
Attributes the poem to Rochester.

Farley-Hills, David, ed. *Rochester: The Critical Heritage*. London, 1972.
A useful collection of critical comment, 1672–1903.

Field, P. J. C. "Dryden and Rochester," *N & Q*, 215 (July 1970), 259–260.
Notes similarity between "Satyr" and opening of "Religio Laici."

Hayman, John. "An Image of the Sultan in Waller's 'Of Love' and 'A Very Heroical Epistle in Answer to Ephelia,'" *N & Q*, 213 (1968), 380–381.
Note on an echo of Waller.

Knight, Charles A. "The Paradox of Reason: Argument in Rochester's 'Satyr against Mankind,'" *Modern Language Review*, 65 (1970), 254–260.
Contends that the poem argues "playfully" for hedonism.

Love, Harold. "Rochester and the Traditions of Satire," in *Restoration Literature: Critical Approaches*, ed. H. Love (London, 1972), 145–176.
Distinguishes between lampoon and Horatian elements in "Tunbridge Wells," "Timon," "Artemisia to Chloe."

Paulson, Kristoffer F. "A Subject of Debate: A Revaluation of the Major Satires of John Wilmot, 2nd Earl of Rochester." Unpublished Ph.D. dissertation, University of California, Davis, 1968. *Dissertation Abstracts*, 29 (1969), 2223A.
Close readings of four poems, arguing unconvincingly for "persona" interpretations.

―――. "Pun Intended: Rochester's *Upon Nothing*," *English Language Notes*, 9 (1971), 118–121.
Claims that "what" / "twat" pun helps establish exuberant tone.

―――. "The Reverend Edward Stillingfleet and the 'Epilogue' to Rochester's *A Satyr Against Reason and Mankind*," *PQ*, 50 (1971), 657–663.
Argues the "Epilogue" is a response to Stillingfleet's sermon attack on the "Satyr."

Pinto, Vivian de Sola. "'The History of Insipids': Rochester, Freke, and Marvell," *Modern Language Review*, 65 (1970), 11–15.
Suggests Rochester authorship.

Quaintance, Richard E. "Passion and Reason in Restoration Love Poetry." Unpublished Ph.D. dissertation, Yale, 1962.
Erotic traditions in seventeenth-century French literature as background to Rochester and others.

Righter, Anne. "John Wilmot, Earl of Rochester," *Proc. Brit. Acad.*, 53 (1967), 47–70.
Rochester's role-playing in life and poems. Rochester and Byron.

Rochester. *Sodom or the Quintessence of Debauchery.* Regent House, North Hollywood, 1966.
Paperback edition (based on existing manuscripts and texts) of a play falsely attributed to Rochester.

Selden, R. "Rochester, Lee, and Juvenal," *N & Q*, 217 (1972), 27.
Allusion to Juvenal in "Allusion to Horace."

Thorpe, Peter. "The Non-Structure of Augustan Verse," *Papers on Language and Literature*, 5 (1969), 235–251.
Some remarks on the "non-structure" of the "Satyr."

Vieth, David M. "Toward an Anti-Aristotelian Poetic: Rochester's *Satyr Against Mankind* and *Artemisia to Chloe*, with Notes on Swift's *Tale of a Tub* and *Gulliver's Travels*," *Language and Style*, 5 (1972), 123–145.
Offers theory to account for thematic discontinuities in Rochester.

Weinbrot, Howard D. "The Swelling Volume: The Apocalyptic Satire of Rochester's *Letter from Artemisia in the Town to Chloe in the Country*," *Studies in the Literary Imagination*, vol. 5, no. 2 (October 1972), 19–38.
Reads poem as the progressive moral degeneration of Artemisia.

Index

Abraham, Karl: on premature ejaculation, 121n, 123n, 125n, 126n; on alcoholism, 127n

Addison, Joseph: praises "Upon Nothing," 266

alcoholism: drunkenness in poems, 26, 41, 52, 54–55; Rochester's, 80, 114, 125–127

antirationalism, 146, 160, 163, 174. *See* Quaintance; skepticism

Aubrey, John: *Brief Lives*, 1n

"Augustan": Rochester not "Augustan," 5, 77, 245

Barry, Elizabeth, 288; Rochester's letters to, 18, 76, 238n

Belleau, Remy: "Impuissance," 93, 95–96, 98, 99

Berman, Ronald: critic of Rochester's poems, 32n, 108n, 235n

Boileau, Nicholas, 173–175; Rochester imitates *Satire 3* in "Timon," 36–41, 250; *Satire 8* and "Satyr Against Mankind," 156, 157, 165, 166n, 172n, 198, 203–205, 211, 215, 234; *Satire 4*, 232n, 238n; Boileau's imitations, 250–251

Boswell, James: echoes Rochester, 248; challenges Rochester's critical opinion, 248n

Boyle, Robert: *Excellence of Theology*, 183n

Brooks, H. F.: on the imitation, 249–251

Buckhurst. *See* Dorset

Buckingham, George Villiers, Duke of, 3, 68, 69n

Bunyan, John, 3, 193, 219

Burnet, Gilbert: Rochester's conversations with, 6–12, 18; as biographer of Rochester, 13, 181

Butler, Samuel, 71, 211n, 250n; compared to Rochester, 11, 225n, 231n, 240n, 293; poems cited as analogues to Rochester's, 108n, 145n, 180, 211n, 212–213, 216n, 221; influence on Rochester, 180

Calvin, John: *Institutes of the Christian Religion*, 214

Cambridge Platonists: Restoration rationalists, 183, 183n, 186, 186n; anti-Hobbists, 187–188; Rochester mocks, 211, 226–227

Carew, Thomas: Rochester compared to, 105, 106

castration, 123–126, 128

La Chambre, Marin Cureau de: as theriophilist, 165n, 166n, 202

Chanet, Pierre, 166n, 202

Charles II, 13, 22, 28, 39, 242n, 288–289; father-figure for Rochester, 121n

Charleton, Walter: *Epicurus' Morals*, 15, 170n, 183n

Charron, Pierre: *Of Wisdom*, 15, 72n, 163–170, 176

Congreve, William, 297n; on ignis fatuus, 213n

Cornelius Agrippa, 161

Cowley, Abraham: Rochester admires, 3, 156; Rochester parodies, 5, 89n, 268, 270, 271, 273, 277; Cowley on reason, 185–186; Cowley and ignis fatuus, 212n; Cowley's imitations, 249, 250; Pope imitates, 258; Rochester echoes, 276n

Crocker, S. F.: critic of Rochester, 158

Cudworth, Ralph, 3, 183n, 186

Culverwell, Nathanael, 186; *A Discourse of the Light of Nature*, 188

Cyrano de Bergerac: *Histoire des Oiseaux*, 175

Cyrenaics, 171

Davenant, Sir William, 3, 144n; Rochester parodies, 48–49; on ignis fatuus, 213; "Faith and Reason," 217

Davies, Paul C.: critic of Rochester, 5n, 157n, 307

DeHenault, Jean, 173, 174

Denham, Sir John, 3, 166n, 249

Des Barreaux, Jacques Vallée, 15, 158, 174, 176–179

Descartes, René: possible source for Rochester, 218n

Don Juan, 112n; Don Juan figures, 55–56, 153; Shadwell's Don John, 55–56; Don Juanism, 118–122

Dorset, Charles Sackville, Earl of, formerly Lord Buckhurst, 3, 88; friendly lampoon on Rochester, 52, 80; Buckhurst-Etherege epistles, 83; as ironist, 104; Rochester praises, 247, 248, 255, 256

Dryden, John: compared to Rochester, 1, 2, 220n, 300–306; Rochester parodies, 49–51, 62; on satire, 199; attacks Rochester, 247–248, 248n; Rochester satirizes in "An Allusion to Horace," 252–257; triplets, 278–279

— works cited: *Aureng-Zebe*, 62, 63n, 302; "Macflecknoe," 64, 65; "To Dr. Charleton," 185; "Religio Laici," 220n, 300–302; *Marriage à la Mode*, 293–294

Ecclesiastes, 160, 178n

ejaculatio praecox, 120, 123, 125n, 126, 127. *See* "The Imperfect Enjoyment"; impotence

energy: quality of Rochester's poems, 5, 197, 207, 245

Epicurus: Epicureanism, 15, 19n, 62–63, 168–171, 191, 305. *See* sensationalism

Epsom incident, 51, 125

Erasmus: *Praise of Folly*, 200

Erskine-Hill, Howard: critic of Rochester, 5n, 69n

Etherege, Sir George, 3; "Ephelia to Bajazet" and the "Heroical Epistle," 59; poet, 83, 93, 93n, 94, 108n; "To a Lady, asking him how long he would love her" and "All my past life," 112–113; compared to Rochester, 287; *The Man of Mode,* 289–299 *passim;* Rochester praises, 255

Fanshawe, Sir Richard: Rochester echoes *Il Pastor Fido,* 241n, 274n
Fenichel, Otto: *Psychoanalytic Theory of Neurosis,* 118, 121n, 126n, 274n; *Collected Papers,* 124n
Ferenczi, Sandor, 121n
Fielding, Henry: on "Upon Nothing," 267
Fitzherbert, Thomas, 214
Fletcher, John, 288–290
Forget, Pierre, 71
Freud, Sigmund: works cited, 113, 115n, 118–122 *passim,* 125, 128n, 274n
Fujimura, Thomas: critic of Rochester, 157, 172n, 198

Gelli, G.-B.: *Circe,* 165, 166, 167, 205n
Glanvill, Joseph, 183n
Goodman, Godfrey, 161, 162
Gould, Robert: *Satire on Man,* 181n; little influenced by Rochester, 257n

Hazlitt, William: praises "Upon Nothing," 280
hedonism, 170. *See* Epicurus
heterodoxy, 173. *See* paradox; sensationalism; skepticism; theriophily
Hobbes, Thomas, 20, 63n, 140n; Rochester and, 15, 156, 157, 181, 305; minor works, 49, 169n, 171n, 173n; *Leviathan* and "Satyr Against Mankind," 168–173 *passim,* 184, 232n; opposed by Cambridge Platonists, 188
homosexuality: in poems, 53, 81n, 122, 123; Rochester's, 80, 122–123, 127n
Horace: *Satire* 1:9 and "Timon,"

36; *Satire* 1:10 and "An Allusion to Horace," 247–257, 263
hypochondria: Rochester's, 126, 126n

impotence: as subject in poems, 48, 52–53, 91–100, 109, 114–121, 154–155; Rochester's, 123–129. *See* "The Imperfect Enjoyment"; ejaculatio praecox
Ingelo, Nathaniel, 188, 190, 231n; *Bentivolio and Urania,* 188–192, 210

Johnson, Samuel, 81; *Life of Rochester,* 8, 14n, 156, 247, 251, 266, 267, 275n
Juvenal: *Satire* 6, 31n, 34n; imitated in Restoration, 40, 250, 251; *Satire* 15, 166n

La Luzerne, Antoine Baraby de, 173, 174, 175
La Rochefoucauld, 71, 145; *Maximes* a model for Rochester, 16, 53, 158, 179–180, 236, 283
Lee, Nathaniel, 3; *Princess of Cleve,* 61n, 108n, 287, 296; *Nero,* 63n
libertinage, 173–180 *passim. See* Des Barreaux; Regnier
Lucretius, 9n, 51n, 139, 191–192. *See* Epicurus
Luttrell, Narcissus, 58, 58n

Main, C. F.: critic of Rochester, 24n, 172n, 189, 199
Malloch, A. E.: on paradox, 201–203
Marañón, Gregorio, 118n, 122n
Marvell, Andrew, 287; admired Rochester's satire, 1
Menander, 159
Miller, H. K.: on paradoxical encomium, 200–202, 267n
Milton, John, 203; *Paradise Lost,* 166n, 212, 215, 215n, 272, 277n;

Milton omitted from "An Allusion to Horace," 254

misanthropy: in poems, 40, 283; traditional self-abasement, 158–182, 243; in Rochester and Swift, 283–284. See "Tunbridge Wells"; *chapters 4 and 5 passim*

Montaigne, 64, 67n, 87, 94, 174n, 215n; possible influence on Rochester, 9n, 15, 156, 157, 158, 181, 213, 217; *Essais* and heterodoxy, 163–168 *passim*

Moore, John: critic of Rochester, 157, 158n, 234

More, Henry, 3, 186, 187

morophilia, 87–88, 120n, 144–145, 296

Mulgrave, John Sheffield, Earl of, later Duke of Buckinghamshire: Rochester's enemy, 3; and Bajazet in the "Heroical Epistle," 57, 58, 58n, 60, 66, 67; and M.G. in the "Epistolary Essay," 68, 69n; "Essay on Poetry," 84–85, 100n; "Essay upon Satyr" revised by Pope, 258

obscenity, 4, 40, 81–92, 282

Oldham, John, 134n, 135n; translates Boileau, 180n, 204n; his imitations, 247, 250, 251; little influenced by Rochester, 257n; Pope on, 259

Ovid: *Heroides* and "Heroical Epistle," 59–60; *Amores* and "The Imperfect Enjoyment," 91, 91n, 92–93, 95n, 99; Rochester's Ovidian elegies, 91n, 105n

paradox, 200–204; "Satyr Against Mankind" as paradox, 204–206, 239, 244; "Upon Nothing" as paradoxical encomium, 267–269

Parsons, Robert: biographer of Rochester, 12, 13–14

Pascal: and Rochester, 12, 17, 18–19

Patrick, Simon: *Parable of the Pilgrim*, 188–189, 193–194, 210, 215n

Paulson, Kristoffer: critic of Rochester, 195n, 271n, 308

persona, 24, 57

Petronius: *Satyricon*, 92–93

Pinto, Vivian de Sola: as biographer, ix, 5, 6; as editor, 4, 31; as critic, 57, 61, 110, 217, 268n, 277, 308

Pliny: *Natural History*, 159, 176

Plutarch: *Moralia*, 160, 167n

Pope, Alexander: and Rochester, 1, 3, 220, 244, 247, 257–266; *Peri Bathous*, 73–74; borrows from Rochester, 248, 258; and imitations, 251; Pope and Rochester as satirists of women, 264–265; disapproves of Rochester's versification, 264n; on actual and ideal, 265–266

Prinz, Johannes: critic of Rochester, 57, 68

Purchas, Samuel, 161–162

Quaintance, R. E.: "Passion and Reason in Restoration Love Poetry," 87n, 309; on "The Imperfect Enjoyment," 91–99 *passim*; on "Artemisia to Chloe," 144–147 *passim*

rake: Rochester on the rake's failure, 17–20, 67, 77–78, 300

Randolph, Mary Claire: on satire, 200n

Rank, Otto: on Don Juan, 118n

rationalism, 182–188, 195. See antirationalism

reason: in "Satyr Against Mankind," 211–212, 220–222, 225–228; in "Religio Laici," 300–301. See rationalism

Regnier, Mathurin, 72n; Rochester knew poems of, 15, 174–175; Rochester borrows from, 36, 174; "Impuissance," 93n

Righter, Anne: critic of Rochester, 112n, 277n, 295n, 309

Rochester, John Wilmot, Earl of:
— Rochester the man: longs for security and certainty, 5, 17–20, 140; on actual and ideal worlds, 6, 139–140, 154, 232, 244–245, 285, 298–299, 304, 305; morality, 6–12; religious beliefs, 6–12; conversations with Burnet, 6–12; education and learning, 13–14; fear, 13, 236n; reading, 15–16; letters, 14n, 16–18, 21–23, 76, 126, 127n, 152n; as libertine rake, 15–20, 79–80; on friendship, 19, 22; misanthropist, 21; theatrical, 22–23, 55, 126; Huysmans portrait, 23; interest in impersonation, 24, 288; drunkenness, 80, 114, 125–127; homosexuality, 80, 122–123, 127n; relations with women, 113–114, 121–127, 153; impotence, 123–129; hypochondria, 126; cowardice, 126
— Rochester the poet: an obscure figure, 2–5; delights in paradox, 5, 25, 76; delights in parody, 5, 28, 29, 48–51, 61n, 73, 89n, 96, 101–103, 104, 134n; self-projector, 21–25, 79, 288; delights in shocking, 24, 25, 54, 74, 83, 182, 228; satirizes libertine, 27, 32, 43, 47, 48, 78, 296; self-observer, 56, 80, 128; songwriter, 100–114; candor, 129; versification and couplet style, 130, 136, 208–209, 222–223, 228, 264n, 278–279, 280–282, 298, 303, 304; satirist of women, 264–265, 282–283; drawn to extremes, 286, 287, 305
— Poems (cited by title or first line): "Absent from thee," 109–110, 111, 119; "After death nothing is," 9n, 10, 273, 275, 287n, 290; "Against constancy," 115–116; "All my past life,"

111–113; "An Allusion to Horace," 78, 246–257; and Pope, 263; versification in, 264n; Swift borrows from, 280; and Restoration drama, 292, 293, 296, 298; "Epistolary Essay," 67–76, 78, 122; "Fair Chloris in a pigsty lay," 101–103, 281; "The Fall," 66, 108–109; "Heroical Epistle," 56–67, 78, 122, 294; "The Imperfect Enjoyment," 91–100, 103, 114, 116, 116n, 119, 125, 176; "Insulting beauty you misspend," 106–107; "Love a woman," 90, 123; "The Maimed Debauchee," 47–54, 78, 117, 279, 291; "The Mistress," 107; "The Mock Song," 90; "My Lord All-Pride," 260; "A Pastoral Dialogue between Strephon and Daphne," 60, 103–104; "Phyllis be gentler," 105–106; "Quoth the Duchess of Cleveland," 86–87; "St. James's Park," 25–35, 78, 86–87, 88, 115, 124, 124n, 125, 138n, 142, 235n, 291–292, 296; "Satyr Against Mankind," 1, 6, 8, 9n, 11n, 156–245 *passim*, 250, 286, 295, 297; intellectual and literary background to, 156–196 *passim*; and Boileau's *Satire* 8, 156–157, 203–205; as paradox, 203–206; stylistic eclecticism, 206–224; versification in, 206–209, 222–223, 264n; critical reading of, 197–245 *passim*; "Satyr on Charles II," 29n, 39, 49, 50n, 89, 116, 120; "Signior Dildo," 86, 88, 123; "Song of a Young Lady to her Ancient Lover," 117, 130; "Timon," 35–42, 78, 123, 250, 281; and Regnier, 174; versification, 264n; "To the Postboy," 54–56, 78, 115; "Tunbridge Wells," 26, 42–47, 78, 261; and Swift, 281, 284; and Restoration drama, 292–293, 298; "Upon

Nothing," 9n, 202, 266–280, 286, 287n, 290; and Swift, 281; *Valentinian*, 9n, 288–290; "What vain, unnecessary things are men," 130, 131–132; "When to the King I bid good morrow," 90
Royal Society, 183, 185, 186
Rymer, Thomas: critic of Rochester, 48, 157

Savile, Henry, 3; Rochester's letters to, 16–18, 21–23, 152n, 225n, 241
Sedley, Sir Charles, 3, 61n; his obscenity, 82; as ironist, 104; Rochester praises, 247, 248, 255; *Mulberry Garden*, 291
self-disparagement, 158–162
sensationalism, 168–173. *See* Epicurus
Sextus Empiricus, 15, 162, 272
Shadwell, Thomas, 3, 71n; *Epsom Wells*, 38, 298n; and "Tunbridge Wells," 292–293; *The Libertine*, 55, 231n; Rochester praises, 254; *The Royal Shepherdess*, 293; *The Sullen Lovers*, 295; *The Virtuoso*, 295; *Timon*, 296
Sibbes, Richard, 188–189, 194–196
skepticism: Rochester's, 6–12, 303, 305, 306; philosophical skepticism, 162–164; skeptics attacked by Ingelo, 191; Dryden's, 300–301
Smith, John: Cambridge Platonist, 186; on "purified sense," 226–227, 232n
Sodom; or the Quintessence of Debauchery: not by Rochester, 89n, 309
Spenser, Edmund, 210, 211, 272
Stanley, Thomas: *History of Philosophy*, 15, 162, 168–171 *passim*, 272
Stillingfleet, Edward, 194–195, 195n

Stoicism, 170
Swift, Jonathan, 138n; compared to Rochester, 3, 11, 252, 280–286; borrows from Rochester, 145, 280–281; on actual and ideal, 285–286
Sylvester, Joshua: translator of Du Bartas, 272n, 276n

Tennyson, Alfred, Lord: admires "Satyr Against Mankind," 1
Théophile de Viau, 72n, 158, 173, 175
theriophily, 164–168, 202; in French *libertins*, 173, 175; in "Satyr Against Mankind," 200, 206, 224–225, 233–234, 242–243; in Swift, 283–284
Traugott, John, 20, 285n, 286n
Trickett, Rachel, 261

Underwood, Dale, 5n, 181

Vieth, David M.: editor, ix, 4, 5n; critic, 5, 24n, 42, 54, 57, 61, 68, 70, 73, 139, 277, 309
Voltaire: admires Rochester's poems, 1, 157, 197

Waller, Edmund: Rochester praises, 3, 254; Rochester parodies, 5, 28–30, 49, 234n; Rochester borrows from, 65, 240n; Pope admires and borrows from, 258
Warton, Joseph: praises Rochester, 266
Weinbrot, Howard, 200n, 309
Whichcote, Benjamin, 3, 62n, 186, 187, 188
Wilmot, Anne, Countess of Rochester: Rochester's letters to, 17, 22
Wilson, J. H.: critic, 42n, 68n, 100n, 288
Wolseley, Robert: Preface to *Valentinian*, 84–86
Wood, Anthony, 14n, 15

Wycherley, William, 3; poems, 181n; Rochester praises, 247, 248, 254; Rochester compared to, 287, 299; *The Country Wife,* 180, 290–299 *passim; Love in a Wood,* 291; *The Gentleman Dancing Master,* 295; *The Plain Dealer,* 295–299 *passim*